QuickBASIC™ Made Easy

D1316353

QuickBASIC™
Made Easy

Bob Albrecht,
Wenden Wiegand,
and Dean Brown

Osborne **McGraw-Hill**
Berkeley New York St. Louis San Francisco
Auckland Bogatá Hamburg London Madrid
Mexico City Milan Montreal New Dehli Panama City
Paris São Paulo Singapore Sydney
Tokyo Toronto

Osborne **McGraw-Hill**
2600 Tenth Street
Berkeley, California 94710
U.S.A.

For information on translations and book distributors outside of the
U.S.A., write to Osborne **McGraw-Hill** at the above address.

A complete list of trademarks appears on page 385.

QuickBASIC™ Made Easy

1234567890 DOCDOC 898

ISBN 0-07-881421-9

CONTENTS

Preface ix

About This Book x
QuickBASIC Made Easy Convenience
   Disk xi
QuickBASIC Made Easy Teacher's
   Guide xii
QuickBASIC Made Easy Workbooks xii

1   Getting Started 1

A Byte of BASIC History 2
QuickBASIC 4.5—The Package 4
Making Copies of the QuickBASIC
   Disk Set 6
Making QuickBASIC Work and
   Help Disks 14

2   The QuickBASIC Windows 23

Loading QuickBASIC 24
The QuickBASIC Control Center 25

3   Introduction to Programming 47

Entering a Command in the Immediate
   Window 48
Using the View Window 62

4   **Number Crunching**   **79**

Arithmetic Operators   80
Exponents and Floating Point
    Numbers   86
Numeric Types   90
Numeric Variables   96
Programming with Variables   101

5   **Making Programs More Useful**   **123**

String Variables   124
The DO...LOOP Structure   127
The QuickBASIC Rainbow   146
Making Music   150

6   **Editing and Dynamic Debugging**   **157**

Editing   158
Dynamic Debugging   170

7   **Function Junction**   **183**

Built-in Functions   184
User-defined Functions   193
Some New Control Structures   205

8   **Arrays**   **215**

Array Variables   216
Programming with Arrays   220
Manipulating Arrays   235

9   **Unstructured Sequential Files**   **247**

Types of Data Files   248
Unstructured Sequential Files   250
Some Useful Suggestions About
    File Names   268

10 **Structured Sequential Files**   **271**

Two Ways to Write to a Text File   272
Structured Sequential Files   276
Japanese Words and Phrases   285

11 **Random-Access Files**   **299**

Sequential and Random-Access
    File Storage   300
Create Japanese.Ran, a
    Random-Access File   303
Create Japanese.Ran, Input from
    the Keyboard   309
Scan the Japanese.Ran File   312
PUT or GET Individual Records   314
A Personal Camping Equipment
    Catalog   318
Get Individual Records from
    Camping.Cat   324

12 **FUNCTION and SUB Procedures**   **327**

Accessing Full Menus   328
QuickBASIC Procedures   329

A   **ASCII Codes for the PC**   **357**

B   **QuickBASIC Reserved Words**   **365**

C   **Error Messages**   **369**

Selected Error Messages   370

Index   **387**

PREFACE

About This Book
QuickBASIC Made Easy Convenience Disk
QuickBASIC Made Easy Teacher's Guide
QuickBASIC Made Easy Workbooks

BASIC is the most popular programming language in the world. Today, various versions of BASIC are running on more than 25 million computers. BASIC is such a popular language because it easy to learn and use, yet extremely powerful.

QuickBASIC 4.5 is the newest and best version of BASIC. QuickBASIC is designed for the absolute beginner, as well as for the advanced programmer. Although it is simple to learn and use, it includes some of the most sophisticated programming structures and editing and debugging features available in any programming language.

QuickBASIC's richness is the distillation of almost 25 years of worldwide use of BASIC. Its features facilitate structured programming, making programs more powerful and easier to understand. QuickBASIC combines full editing and debugging capabilities with a state-of-the-art on-line help system. If you do not already know how to use a word processor, you will learn many of the standard word processing editing keys and features while learning to use QuickBASIC (two for the price of one!). In addition, Quick-BASIC's on-line help system is hypertext-based; it provides help when you simply select any word in your program. You can browse through any topic in the help system, or you can access help as needed when you write programs. In very little time a beginner can write simple yet powerful programs.

Learning a general-purpose programming language and applying it to interesting problems is the most effective way of tapping into the power of your computer. QuickBASIC is the best language for learning and teaching this high-level skill.

ABOUT THIS BOOK

If you have had no previous programming experience, this is just the book for you. All instructions required to learn and use QuickBASIC are included as needed in each chapter. The programming concepts and methods you will learn in this book can be transferred easily to other versions of BASIC, as well as to other programming languages like Pascal and C.

The QuickBASIC 4.5 package comes with two user manuals: *Learning to Use Microsoft QuickBASIC* and *Programming in BASIC*. In addition, you can order the *QuickBASIC Language Reference* from Microsoft. This book teaches you how to use QuickBASIC and prepares you to make maximum use of these QuickBASIC manuals.

Not only does *QuickBASIC Made Easy* introduce you to QuickBASIC, it also offers a different point of view and a different approach to learning than can be found in other beginning programming books. It is geared to the person with no previous programming experience and even with very little computer experience.

The text is sprinkled with lots of programming examples that are fun (and even useful). New concepts are introduced within the context of executable programs, and each new program is thoroughly explained.

The book starts out by familiarizing you with the QuickBASIC programming environment. Here you will learn about the View and Immediate windows and how to use the QuickBASIC menus. You begin by giving simple commands in the Immediate window, and then you use these same commands in your first programs. Next you learn how to use QuickBASIC to do some simple arithmetic, first without and then with numeric variables. Examples are drawn from the area of personal finance.

You will then use some of QuickBASIC's elegant control structures to make your programs more useful, more efficient, and more easily understood. If you make mistakes in your programs, you can use QuickBASIC's editing keys and Edit menu to make changes easily. You will also learn to use some of QuickBASIC's debugging features, which help you to find and fix errors in your programs.

There are a number of useful preprogrammed functions in QuickBASIC that make programming quicker and easier. Many of the features you need to write programs quickly are already part of the language. In addition, if you need to perform the same procedure or calculation frequently in a program, you can define your own functions.

Arrays allow you to store and access related information easily and efficiently. You will learn why arrays are so powerful, and how to use them for such tasks as sorting and printing lists of names.

The next three chapters introduce you to three different kinds of data files: unstructured sequential files, structured sequential files, and random-access files. You will learn how to store and retrieve information from each kind of file, and which kind of file is best for different applications.

The book ends with a discussion of modular programming. Here you will be shown how to use FUNCTION and SUB procedures to create modules that can be used in several different programs.

QuickBASIC is an exceptionally rich and powerful programming language. This book introduces you to its possibilities. In addition, the book will help you develop your own skills in formulating problems and in writing elegant programs.

QuickBASIC MADE EASY CONVENIENCE DISK

You may order a disk containing all programs and data files discussed in *QuickBASIC Made Easy*. This disk includes

- All QuickBASIC programs discussed in the book.

- Variations of many of the programs discussed in the book, showing alternative ways to accomplish the programming task. These variations do not appear in the book.

- All data files discussed in the book.

- Variations of data files discussed in the book.

- A bonus: several additional programs you can't live without.

Two sizes of disk are available:

5 1/4-inch disk	$6.00
3 1/2-inch disk	$7.00

QuickBASIC MADE EASY
TEACHER'S GUIDE

QuickBASIC is the ideal computer language for both teachers and students. This loose-leaf teacher's guide includes exercises, solutions, COPY ME instructional material, and other materials to help teachers teach, and students learn, QuickBASIC.

Available April, 1989.

QuickBASIC Made Easy Teacher's Guide: $9.95

QuickBASIC MADE EASY WORKBOOKS

To further assist you in the enjoyable task of learning QuickBASIC, the authors are developing three ongoing series of workbooks for self-instruction. The first workbook in each series will be available in March, 1989.

- *Datafile Programming in QuickBASIC*, Book 1. Supplements and expands on the material in Chapters 9, 10, and 11 of *QuickBASIC Made Easy*. 64 pages. $4.95

- *QuickBASIC Graphics and Sound*, Book 1. A beginner's introduction to QuickBASIC's extensive repertoire of graphics and sound features. 64 pages. $4.95

- *QuickBASIC for Math and Science*, Book 1. This series of workbooks begins where Chapter 4 of *QuickBASIC Made Easy* leaves off. It explores diverse applications in mathematics and science. 64 pages. $4.95

Send your orders to

Different Worlds
2814 19th Street
San Francisco, CA 94110

You may use the order form that follows.

Different Worlds

2814 - 19th Street
San Francisco CA 94110

Name _____

Address _____

_____

City/State _____ ZIP _____

Phone ( ) _____

Send check or money order. Foreign customers send international money order available at post offices and banks.

Item Description	Qty	Price Each	Total Price

SATISFACTION GUARANTEED

Postage & Handling: Add $2.00 for first item and $1.00 for each additional item. To shipping points outside U.S., add $3.00 for first item and $1.00 for each additional item. Shipped via surface mail.

This is solely the offering of the authors. Osborne/McGraw-Hill takes no responsibility for the fulfillment of this offer. Please allow four to six weeks for delivery.

Subtotal	
Calif. residents add appropriate sales tax	
Postage & Handling	
TOTAL ENCLOSED	

1

GETTING STARTED

A Byte of BASIC History
QuickBASIC 4.5—The Package
Making Copies of the QuickBASIC Disk Set
Making QuickBASIC Work and Help Disks

Relax. Make yourself comfortable. To acquaint yourself with QuickBASIC, in this chapter you will

- Learn a little about the history of BASIC, from its birth in 1964 to its present status as the world's most popular computer language

- Be introduced to QuickBASIC 4.5, the newest and best form of BASIC

- Make QuickBASIC work and help disks that you will use throughout this book as you learn to understand, use, and enjoy QuickBASIC

Those of you who are unfamiliar with computers and with the MS-DOS (Microsoft Disk Operating System) commands available to you will learn everything you need to get started in this chapter; those of you who are already somewhat familiar with MS-DOS may wish simply to scan these sections.

A BYTE OF BASIC HISTORY

Dartmouth College made a commitment in 1963 to make all its computers easily available to all students. This meant that the college's large, expensive computers needed to be available to several students at once; in response to this need, the first fully functional time-sharing system was developed. A time-sharing system is one in which the computer partitions time among several users. In addition, if computers were to be accessible to all students, a new language was needed that would enable just about anyone to program and easily control a computer. This language was BASIC.

Dartmouth professors John G. Kemeny and Thomas E. Kurtz developed the original BASIC language as an instructional tool for training novice programmers. Their purpose was to design a language that would be easy to learn, but still useful for any programming task. On May 1, 1964 at 4 A.M., John Kemeny and a student simultaneously entered and ran separate BASIC programs—making use of both the new language and the new time-sharing system. The success of BASIC (Beginner's All-purpose Symbolic Instruction Code) and its widespread use are due to its simplicity, ease of use, and general-purpose computing power.

The original features of BASIC were designed to

- Be general-purpose in nature and thus useful for writing any type of program

- Allow for advanced features to be added later

- Provide for user/computer interaction

- Provide clear and friendly error messages

- Give fast response for small programs

- Require no hardware knowledge

- Shield the user from the computer's operating system

In 1965, BASIC became available outside of Dartmouth, initially by means of time-sharing systems. Its use later spread to less expensive dedicated minicomputers. When microcomputers were introduced to the public in the 1970s as personal computers, the computer moved from the realm of the professional programmer into the domain of the creative amateur. The only higher-level language available for these early personal computers was BASIC. See Table 1-1 for highlights of the early history of BASIC.

In the early days of microcomputing, memory was very expensive and BASIC programs were crunched into the smallest possible space. As a result

Early 1960s   The National Science Foundation approved funding for a project staffed by Kemeny, Kurtz, and a dozen undergraduates to develop a time-sharing system at Dartmouth College. This marked the beginning of personalized, interactive computing.

Kemeny, Kurtz, and students worked with compilers, FORTRAN, ALGOL, and experimental languages, all of which influenced later development of BASIC.

1963   A decision was made at Dartmouth to enable all students to become computer literate. Kemeny and Kurtz, with help from students, began the development of a general-purpose, time-sharing computer system and a new language (BASIC) to introduce beginners to programming and to serve all applications for large and small systems.

1964   Equipment on which the time-sharing system and BASIC were to be developed arrived in February, 1964. The equipment was fully functional by March 1, 1964, when, at 4 A.M., John Kemeny and a student programmer entered and ran separate BASIC programs on the new system. Time-sharing and BASIC were born.

1964-1971   The growth of BASIC in this period predated personal computers. BASIC at Dartmouth made the transition from a language suitable only for small programs to a language suitable for building large application programs.

Two main genealogical lines grew out of the original Dartmouth BASIC. Large-machine BASIC versions were probably direct descendants of GE BASIC, which in turn descended from Dartmouth BASIC. Most small-machine BASIC versions descended from versions that first appeared on the Hewlett-Packard HP-2000 or the Digital Equipment PDP-8. GE BASIC and Dartmouth BASIC were very similar until around 1970; Dartmouth had built its time-sharing systems around GE hardware.

By the end of 1971, Dartmouth BASIC had reached its sixth version and was a huge success.

This history is based on *Back to BASIC*, by J.G. Kemeny and T.E. Kurtz (Reading, Mass.: Addison-Wesley, 1985), which is recommended reading.

TABLE 1-1   Early BASIC History

they were unreadable to anyone not very familiar with the language and the computer in which it operated. You can see remnants of this today in computer magazines that publish programs understandable to the dedicated user, but incomprehensible to most of us.

Fortunately, things have improved. Computers are less expensive and more powerful, memory is larger and much cheaper, and BASIC has become better and better. Now there is QuickBASIC 4.5, the best BASIC yet. It is easy to learn, easy to use, and very capable. You can learn to write programs in QuickBASIC easily, programs that tell the computer to do what you want it to do the way you want it done.

QuickBASIC 4.5—THE PACKAGE

QuickBASIC 4.5 comes in a package containing two manuals and a set of disks containing the many files that give you the power of QuickBASIC. Separate packages are available for users who have computers that use 5 1/4-inch disk drives and for those who have computers with the newer 3 1/2-inch disk drives.

- **Microsoft QuickBASIC 4.5 (catalog # 007-114V450)**   This package contains two manuals and five 5 1/4-inch disks.
- **Microsoft QuickBASIC 4.5 (catalog # 007-095V450)**   This package contains two manuals and three 3 1/2-inch disks.

In the following sections you will learn how to make copies of your QuickBASIC disks; you will also learn how to prepare a QuickBASIC work disk and a QuickBASIC help disk that contain only a few of the files from the original disks that come in the QuickBASIC package.

The QuickBASIC Manuals

The QuickBASIC manuals contain an enormous amount of information. You will appreciate these manuals more and more as your knowledge of Quick-BASIC grows. One of the purposes of this book is to help you read, understand, and enjoy the wealth of information in the manuals and disks included in QuickBASIC 4.5.

Here are brief descriptions of the two QuickBASIC manuals:

- *Learning to Use Microsoft QuickBASIC* explains how to install and use QuickBASIC on your computer. Begin with this book. It tells you how to install QuickBASIC on a hard disk system, and how to instruct QuickBASIC to perform various actions.

- *Programming in BASIC* explains how to use QuickBASIC to perform programming tasks such as creating graphics, managing data files, and building complex programs with subprograms and functions. This book contains many practical programming examples.

The two QuickBASIC manuals were written primarily for people who have previous experience with MS-DOS (Microsoft Disk Operating System) and some version of BASIC. They do not attempt to teach you how to use MS-DOS or how to begin programming in BASIC.

The QuickBASIC Disk Set

Your QuickBASIC 4.5 package contains, in addition to the two manuals already discussed, five 5 1/4-inch disks or three 3 1/2-inch disks. Both disk sets are briefly described in the sections that follow.

THE 5 1/4-INCH DISK SET   If you have a computer that uses 5 1/4-inch disk drives, you should have a QuickBASIC 4.5 package with five 5 1/4-inch disks, as follows:

- **Disk 1 is the Setup and QB Express disk**   It contains the Setup program and some demonstration programs.

- **Disk 2 is the Program disk**   It contains the most important file of all, QB.EXE, and one of the two help files you will need on your Quick-BASIC help disk, QB45QCK.HLP. You will use QB.EXE to create, run, and debug programs.

- **Disk 3 is the Utilities 1 disk**   It contains some QuickBASIC utilities. The files on this disk are intended for advanced users.

- **Disk 4 is the Utilities 2 disk**   It contains additional QuickBASIC utilities, including MOUSE.COM and QB45ENER.HLP. You will need MOUSE.COM if you wish to use a mouse with QuickBASIC. You will need the help file, QB45ENER.HLP, on your QuickBASIC help disk.

- **Disk 5 is the QB Advisor disk**   It contains the QB Advisor, Quick-BASIC's on-line reference/help system. This system provides on-line access to the complete language reference information.

THE 3 1/2-INCH DISK SET   If you have a computer that uses 3 1/2-inch disk drives, you should have a QuickBASIC 4.5 package with three 3 1/2-inch disks, as follows:

- **Disk 1 is the Setup and QB Express disk**   It contains the Setup command and some demonstration programs.

- **Disk 2 is the Program and QB Advisor disk**   It contains the most important file of all, QB.EXE, and one of the two help files you will need on your QuickBASIC help disk, QB45QCK.HLP. You will use QB.EXE to create, run, and debug programs. The QB Advisor is an on-line reference/help system that provides on-line access to the complete language reference information system.

- **Disk 3 is the Utilities disk**   It contains the QuickBASIC utilities, including MOUSE.COM and QB45ENER.HLP. You will need MOUSE.COM if you want to use a mouse with QuickBASIC. QB45ENER.HLP is the second help file you will need on your QuickBASIC help disk.

MAKING COPIES OF THE QuickBASIC DISK SET

Before you do anything else, you should make backup copies of your QuickBASIC disks. A backup copy of a disk is one that can be used as "backup" if something happens to the original. Often, a backup copy is used rather than the original disk, and the original is kept in a safe place to make other copies from if needed. Making a backup copy of any disk involves several steps: write-protecting the original disk; formatting a new disk; labeling the backup disk; and copying from the original disk to the backup disk. To make this process clear, each step is described in detail in this chapter. The steps involved in making copies of your QuickBASIC disk set include

- Write-protecting a disk
- Formatting a disk
- Copying one disk to another

All commands that you will be giving the computer appear in boldface. When entering a command, type exactly what is in boldface and include any spaces, and then press ENTER to instruct the computer to execute the command you have typed.

Throughout this book, it is assumed that your computer system has only one disk drive. The instructions that follow are therefore for a computer with only one disk drive. If you have more than one disk drive, or a hard disk, you may choose to use only one of your drives and follow these instructions as written, or you may modify the instructions in this section for use with more than one drive, as appropriate.

Write-protecting Disks

You should be sure to protect all of your QuickBASIC disks from accidental erasure and over-writing. This is known as write-protecting your disks. To write-protect your disks, follow the appropriate procedure for your disk set, as follows:

- If you have the 5 1/4-inch disk set, protect all five disks by putting an opaque tab (a write-protect tab) over the write-protect notches on each disk. A write-protect notch is shown in Figure 1-1.

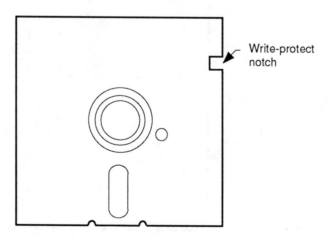

Write-protect notch

FIGURE 1-1   A write-protect notch on a 5 1/4-inch disk

- If you have 3 1/2-inch disks, protect all three disks by sliding the write-protect switch to the "no-write" position on each disk. When this switch covers a small opening, the disk can be written to or erased; when this small opening is uncovered, the disk is protected from erasure and cannot be written to. The write-protect switch is shown in Figure 1-2.

Formatting Disks

Before beginning, make sure that you have your computer's A-prompt (A>) on the screen. This is the signal that the computer has completed a given task and is ready for another command. Also, find enough disks (new, or used disks that can be erased) to make at least one copy of your QuickBASIC disk set. If you have 5 1/4- inch disks, you will need five disks; if you have 3 1/2-inch disks, you will need three disks.

Formatting a backup disk is required if the disk has never been used before; if a disk has not been formatted, the computer cannot write to it or read from it. Formatting a disk prepares a previously unused disk for use by your computer. A used disk can also be formatted—doing so will erase it so be sure that whatever is on it is no longer needed.

Put your MS-DOS disk in the disk drive and close the drive door.

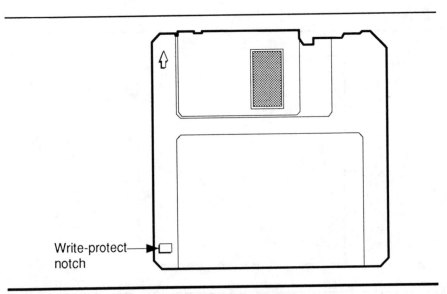

Write-protect notch

FIGURE 1-2   A write-protect notch on a 3 1/2-inch disk

Type:
FORMAT A:
and press ENTER

You will then see this message:

```
Insert new diskette for drive A:
and strike ENTER when ready
```

Take the MS-DOS disk out of the drive, put one of the disks to be formatted in the drive, and press ENTER. The drive's busy light will go on and you should hear the disk drive humming. When the disk has been formatted you will see one of the following two messages.

If you have 5 1/4-inch disks you will see this message:

```
Format complete

362496 bytes total disk space
362496 bytes available on disk

Format another (Y/N)?_
```

If you have 3 1/2-inch disks you will see this message:

```
Format complete

730112 bytes total disk space
730112 bytes available on disk

Format another (Y/N)?_
```

Remove the newly formatted disk from the drive and put a clean, blank label on it. This makes it easy to keep track of which disks have been formatted. To format the next disk, put it in the drive and do the following.

Type:
Y
and press ENTER

Repeat this process until you have formatted all of the disks needed for the backup copy of the QuickBASIC disk set. When the last disk has been formatted and you see this message:

```
Format complete

......bytes total disk space
......bytes available on disk

Format another (Y/N)?_
```

type:
N
and press ENTER

You will then see A> and the blinking cursor.

Labeling Disks

If you have not already done so, put a blank label on each of your formatted disks. There should be one formatted, blank disk for each one in your QuickBASIC disk set. Write on each label a clear description of what each disk will contain, including the information that is on the QuickBASIC disks.

Figure 1-3 shows examples of labels for a backup copy of a 5 1/4-inch QuickBASIC disk set. Figure 1-4 shows examples of labels for a backup copy of a 3 1/2-inch QuickBASIC disk set. Once your disks are properly labeled, you are ready to copy the QuickBASIC disks to them.

Copying Disks

Although your computer has only one disk drive, you can still copy one disk to another. There is only one *physical* disk drive, but to the computer there are two *logical* disk drives. Part of a disk is copied at a time, with the computer keeping track of which disk is in at a given time. The computer will tell you when to swap the original disk for the disk you are copying to.

QuickBASIC 4.5   Setup and
Copy #1   QB Express
Disk 1 of 5

QuickBASIC 4.5   Program Disk
Copy #1
Disk 2 of 5

QuickBASIC 4.5   Utilities 1
Copy #1
Disk 3 of 5

QuickBASIC 4.5   Utilities 2
Copy #1
Disk 4 of 5

QuickBASIC 4.5   QB Advisor
Copy #1
Disk 5 of 5

Figure 1-3   Examples of labels for a backup copy of 5 1/4-inch QuickBASIC disk set

```
+-----------------------------------------------+
|  QuickBASIC 4.5       Setup and               |
|  Copy #1              QB Express               |
|  Disk 1 of 2                                  |
+-----------------------------------------------+
```

```
+-----------------------------------------------+
|  QuickBASIC 4.5       Program and             |
|  Copy #1              QB Advisor               |
|  Disk 2 of 2                                  |
+-----------------------------------------------+
```

```
+-----------------------------------------------+
|  QuickBASIC 4.5       Utilities               |
|  Copy #1                                      |
|  Disk 2 of 2                                  |
+-----------------------------------------------+
```

FIGURE 1-4   Examples of labels for a backup copy of 3 1/2-inch QuickBASIC disk set

Make sure that your MS-DOS disk is in the disk drive and that the drive door is closed; then do the following.

Type:
DISKCOPY A: B:
and press ENTER

You will then see this message:

```
Insert SOURCE diskette in drive A:
Press any key when ready. . .
```

The disk you are copying from is the source disk. The disk you are copying to is the target disk. When this message appears, take the MS-DOS disk out of the drive and put the first QuickBASIC disk, the Setup disk, in the drive. Press any key (ENTER is a good choice) to start copying. You will then see one of the two following messages.

If you have 5 1/4-inch disks you will see this message:

```
Copying 40 tracks
9 Sectors/Track, 2 side(s)
```

If you have 3 1/2-inch disks you will see this message:

```
Copying 80 tracks
9 Sectors/Track, 2 side(s)
```

In a few moments you will see this message:

```
Insert TARGET diskette in drive A:
Press any key when ready. . .
```

Remove the QuickBASIC Setup disk from the drive and put the backup Setup disk in the drive; press any key to start writing to this disk. In a short time you will again see this message:

```
Insert SOURCE diskette in drive A:
Press any key when ready. . .
```

You will be asked to insert the source and target disks alternately until the source disk has been completely copied, when you will see this message:

```
Copy another (Y/N)?_
```

Remove the target disk from the drive.

Type:
Y
and press ENTER

You will see this message:

```
Insert SOURCE diskette in drive A:
Press any key when ready. . .
```

Put the next QuickBASIC disk, the Program disk, in the drive and press any key to start copying. As before, you will be asked to insert the source disk and the target disk alternately until the source disk has been completely copied. When the Program disk has been copied, you will see this message:

```
Copy another (Y/N)?_
```

If you have still other QuickBASIC disks to copy, do the following.

Type:
Y
and press ENTER

Repeat these steps for each QuickBASIC disk you wish to copy, until you have copied the last QuickBASIC disk. Then do the following.

Type:
N
and press ENTER

You will then see A> again.

Put your original QuickBASIC disk set in a safe place away from the computer. These disks should not be used except for making more backup copies. Also, write-protect the backup copies of the QuickBASIC disks that you just made.

Using the QuickBASIC backup disk set that you just made, you will now learn how to make a QuickBASIC master work disk and a QuickBASIC master help disk.

MAKING QuickBASIC WORK AND HELP DISKS

Now that you have made a backup copy of the QuickBASIC disks, you will make at least two copies of the QuickBASIC work and help disks. The work disk contains only one of the files provided on your QuickBASIC disk set; the help disk contains only two files. These are the files that you, the beginner, will need when you begin using and programming in QuickBASIC.

Making the QuickBASIC work and help disks involves several steps: formatting disks; labeling the newly formatted disks; and copying files from the QuickBASIC disk set to the work and help disks. Each step in this process is described next.

Formatting Disks

If you have 5 1/4-inch disk drives you will now need to format four disks: two work disks and two help disks. If you have 3 1/2-inch disk drives you will format two work/help disks.

Put your MS-DOS disk in the disk drive and close the drive door.

Type:
FORMAT A:
and press ENTER

You will then see this message:

```
Insert new diskette for drive A:
and strike ENTER when ready
```

Take the MS-DOS disk out of the drive, put one of the disks to be formatted in the drive, and press ENTER. When this disk has been formatted you will see one of the following two messages.

If you have 5 1/4-inch disks you will see this message:

```
Format complete

362496 bytes total disk space
362496 bytes available on disk

Format another (Y/N)?_
```

If you have 3 1/2-inch disks you will see this message:

```
Format complete

730112 bytes total disk space
730112 bytes available on disk

Format another (Y/N)?_
```

Remove the newly formatted disk from the drive and put a label on it; this makes it easy to distinguish the formatted from the unformatted disks. Insert the next disk to be formatted in the drive.

Type:
Y
and press ENTER

This disk will now be formatted. Repeat this process until you have formatted all the disks you need. When the last disk has been formatted and you see this message:

```
Format complete

. . . . . .bytes total disk space
. . . . . .bytes available on disk

Format another (Y/N)?_
```

type:
N
and press ENTER

You will then see A>. You should now label the disks you just formatted.

Labeling Disks

If you have 5 1/4-inch disks, label four formatted disks as shown in Figure 1-5. Notice that two of these disks are master disks. These should be put away in a safe place after you finish making them; use them only to make more regular work disks.

If you have 3 1/2-inch disks, label two formatted disks as shown in Figure 1-6. One of these disks is the master work/help disk. After you finish making this disk, it should be put away and used only to make backup copies.

Copying Files from One Disk to Another

There are three files that you will be copying from your QuickBASIC disk set to the QuickBASIC master disks: QB.EXE, QB45QCK.HLP, and

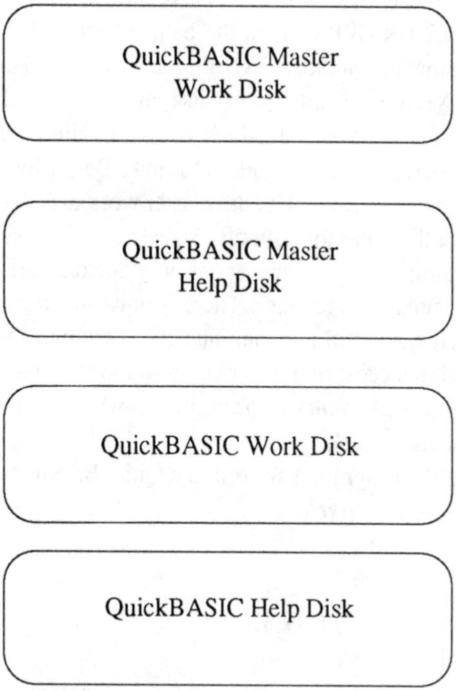

QuickBASIC Master
Work Disk

QuickBASIC Master
Help Disk

QuickBASIC Work Disk

QuickBASIC Help Disk

FIGURE 1-5   Examples of labels for 5 1/4-inch QuickBASIC work and help disks

QuickBASIC Master
Work/Help Disk

QuickBASIC Work/Help
Disk

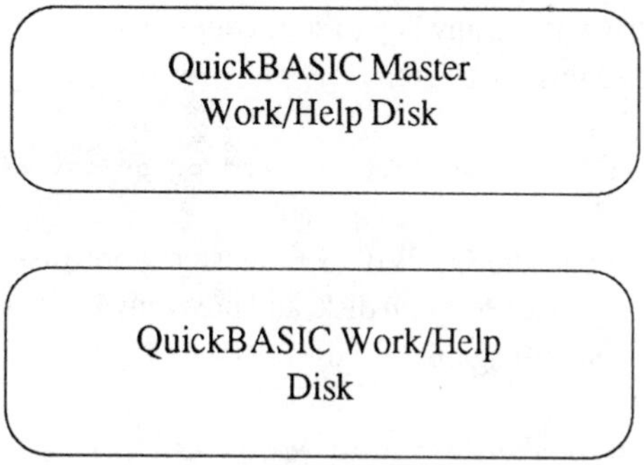

FIGURE 1-6   Examples of labels for 3 1/2-inch QuickBASIC work and help disks

QB45ENER.HLP. QB.EXE is the QuickBASIC file; QB45QCK.HLP and QB45ENER.HLP contain the help information that you might need when operating in QuickBASIC. If you have 5 1/4-inch disks, you will copy QB.EXE to the master work disk, and the two HLP files to the master help disk. If you have 3 1/2-inch disks, all three files will be copied to the QuickBASIC master work/help disk. Begin by copying the QB.EXE file from the Program disk to the master work disk. The instructions to copy this file are the same for both disk sizes.

Although your computer has only one disk drive, you can still copy a file from one disk to another. There is only one *physical* disk drive, but, as you learned earlier, to the computer there are two *logical* disk drives. A file is copied in pieces: first, it is read from the source disk, and then it is written to the target disk. You will be prompted when it is time to swap the source disk for the target disk.

Put the Program disk from the QuickBASIC backup set in the disk drive and close the drive door.

Type:
COPY A:QB.EXE B:
and press ENTER

In a few moments, you will see this message:

```
Insert diskette for drive B: and press any key when ready
```

A: is the logical drive that contains the source disk; B: is the logical drive that contains the target disk. Remove the QuickBASIC Program disk (the source disk), and put the QuickBASIC master work disk (the target disk) in the drive. Press any key to start copying to the work disk. In a short time you will see this message:

```
Insert disk for drive A: and press any key when ready
```

Remove the QuickBASIC master work disk from the drive, insert the QuickBASIC Program disk, and press any key to continue copying. In a short time you will again see this message:

```
Insert diskette for drive B: and press any key when ready
```

You will be asked alternately to insert the disk for Drive B: (the target disk), and to insert the disk for Drive A: (the source disk). When the file copying is complete, you will see this message:

```
1 file(s) copied

Insert disk for drive A: and press any key when ready
```

Put the QuickBASIC Program disk back in the drive and press any key; you will then see A>.

If you have 5 1/4-inch disks, the next two files will be copied to the QuickBASIC master help disk. If you have 3 1/2-inch disks, these files will be copied to the same disk you just copied to, the QuickBASIC master work/help disk. Make sure that the QuickBASIC Program disk is in the drive.

Type:
COPY A:QB45QCK.HLP B:
and press ENTER

In a short while, you will see this message:

```
Insert diskette for drive B: and press any key when ready
```

The disk for Drive B is the target disk, the disk for Drive A is the source disk. If you have 5 1/4-inch disks, insert the QuickBASIC master help disk in the drive and press any key to start copying to it. If you have 3 1/2-inch disks, insert the QuickBASIC master work/help disk and press any key to begin copying to it. In a little while you will see this message:

```
Insert disk for drive A: and press any key when ready
```

Remove the master help disk from the drive, and insert the QuickBASIC Program disk, and press any key to continue copying. You will soon see this message:

```
Insert diskette for drive B: and press any key when ready
```

You will be asked to insert the disk for Drive B (the target disk), then to insert the disk for Drive A (the source disk) alternately. When the file has been copied, you will see the following message.

```
1 file(s) copied
```

```
Insert disk for drive A: and press any key when ready
```

Put the QuickBASIC Program disk back in the drive and press any key; you will then see A>.

The third file to copy, QB45ENER.HLP, is on the fourth QuickBASIC disk, the Utilities 2 disk, if you have a 5 1/4-inch set. It is on the third QuickBASIC disk, the Utilities disk, in the 3 1/2-inch set. Locate the correct QuickBASIC disk and put it in the disk drive.

Type:
COPY A:QB45ENER.HLP B:
and press ENTER

You will then see this message:

```
Insert diskette for drive B: and press any key when ready
```

Take the QuickBASIC disk out of the drive and put the master help disk in the drive. Press any key to start copying to the help disk. As before, you will be prompted alternately to insert the disk for Drive B (the target disk), then the disk for Drive A (the source disk). When the file has been copied, you will see this message:

```
1 file(s) copied
```

```
Insert disk for drive A: and press any key when ready
```

Put the QuickBASIC disk back in the drive and press any key; you will then see A>.

Remove the QuickBASIC disk from the drive. Depending on your disk size, you have now made a master work disk and a master help disk (5 1/4-inch disks), or you have made a master work/help disk (3 1/2-inch disks). Write the names of the files that you just copied to the disks on their labels. Examples of labels for your 5 1/4-inch master work and help disks are shown in Figure 1-7. An example of a label for your 3 1/2-inch master work/help disk is shown in Figure 1-8.

Write-protect your QuickBASIC master work and help disks and put them in a safe place. You should only use them to make new work and help disks.

Follow the preceding instructions for copying files to copy QB.EXE, QB45QCK.HLP, and QB45ENER.HLP to the QuickBASIC work disk and

```
QuickBASIC Master
Work Disk
Contains: QB.EXE
```

```
QuickBASIC Master
Help Disk
Contains: QB45QCK.HLP,
QB45ENER.HLP
```

FIGURE 1-7   Examples of labels for 5 1/4-inch QuickBASIC master work and help disks

disk (5 1/4-inch disks) or to the QuickBASIC work/help disk (3 1/2-inch disks), which you have already formatted. When all three files have been copied to the work and help disks, be sure to add these names to the disk labels.

As you use this book, you will be using the QuickBASIC work and help

```
QuickBASIC Master Work/Help
Disk
Contains: QB.EXE
QB45QCK.HLP, QB45ENER.HLP
```

FIGURE 1-8   Example of labels for 3 1/2-inch QuickBASIC master work/help disk

disks that you have just made. Keep the work disk in a convenient place where you can easily find it. Now you are ready to explore QuickBASIC and its window environment in the next chapter.

BASIC was designed in the early 1960s at Dartmouth College as the first powerful, easy-to-use programming language. It has since become the most popular computer language in the world; about 500,000 high school and college students enroll in BASIC classes each year.

QuickBASIC 4.5 is the newest and best version of the BASIC language. In just a short time, you will be writing QuickBASIC programs that allow you to tell your computer what you want it to do. This book will teach you how. The first thing to do once you open the QuickBASIC package is to write-protect all the disks. This will prevent accidental erasure or over-writing. Next, make a backup copy of all the QuickBASIC disks, labeling each one appropriately. Put the original QuickBASIC disks away; use them *only* to make copies.

Make a QuickBASIC master work disk and a QuickBASIC master help disk (5 1/4-inch disks) or a QuickBASIC master work/help disk (3 1/2-inch disks). Also, make at least one copy of the master disks. This requires first formatting the new disks, and then copying QB.EXE, QB45QCK.HLP, and QB45ENER.HLP to the appropriate number of disks. Carefully label each disk. Write-protect the master disks and put them away also. Use them *only* to make copies.

2

THE QuickBASIC WINDOWS

Loading QuickBASIC
The QuickBASIC Control Center

In this chapter you will explore the QuickBASIC windows and menus. You will learn how to "select" a menu and what each menu looks like. You will also learn how to use the ESC, ALT, and arrow keys to move around in QuickBASIC, as well as how to select an item from a menu. In doing so, you will explore the help available to you in QuickBASIC. In particular, you will

- Learn how to load QuickBASIC

- Learn how to access each menu in the menu bar

- Learn how to highlight and select an option from a menu

- Learn how to use the ESC, ALT, DOWN ARROW, UP ARROW, LEFT ARROW, and RIGHT ARROW keys to move the cursor from one menu to another, and from one option to another

- Learn how to use the TAB key to activate options in a dialog box

- Learn how to use the PGDN and PGUP keys to display several screens in a dialog box

- Explore the Help menu options
- Learn how to exit from QuickBASIC

LOADING QuickBASIC

Begin by using one of the QuickBASIC work disks you made while reading Chapter 1, "Getting Started." If you have not yet made any work disks, do so now; refer to Chapter 1 for details on how to make them. Insert your MS-DOS disk in Drive A and turn the computer on. In a few moments, the computer will display information similar to this:

```
Current date is Tue  1-01-1980
Enter new date (mm-dd-yy):_
```

Notice that a small line is blinking after the colon (:). This is the *cursor*. The cursor tells you that the computer is waiting to receive some instruction from you. After you type an instruction, the computer will do nothing until you press the ENTER key. Pressing ENTER tells the computer to go ahead and do what you just told it to do.

Enter the current date by typing the number of the month (**1** to **12**), a hyphen (**-**), the day of the month (**1** to **31**), a hyphen (**-**), and the last two digits of the year. Here is an example:

```
Current date is Tue  1-01-1980
Enter new date (mm-dd-yy): 3-21-88
```

After typing the date, press ENTER. You will next see the following (or a similar) message:

```
Current time is  0:00:51:37
Enter new time:  _
```

The computer has a 24-hour clock, so enter the time by typing the hour (**0** to **23**), a colon (**:**), the minutes (**0** to **59**), and, if you wish, another colon (**:**) and the seconds (**0** to **59**). For example:

```
Current time is  0:00:51:37
Enter new time:  8:23
```

After typing the time, press ENTER. You will see the disk drive designation (A), the prompt (>), and the blinking cursor, as shown here:

```
A>_
```

The screen on your computer should now be similar to the screen shown here:

```
Current date is Tue  1-01-1980
Enter new date (mm-dd-yy): 3-21-88
Current time is  0:00:51:37
Enter new time:  8:23

Microsoft(R) MS-DOS(R)  Version 3.20
(C)Copyright Microsoft Corp.  1981-1986

A>_
```

Of course, the date and time will be the date and time that you entered; other information on the screen may also differ from that shown. This is the MS-DOS opening screen. Note the disk drive designation (A), the MS-DOS prompt (>), and the blinking cursor that follows.

Remember: Whenever you see the blinking cursor (_), you know the computer is waiting for you to give it an instruction.

In this book, it is assumed that you will use only Drive A. Of course, if you have installed QuickBASIC on your hard disk, you may prefer to work in Drive C. In that case, just think of references to Drive A in this book as references to Drive C.

This book refers only to Drive A for the following reasons:

- Some of you may have a system with only 320K memory (minimum required to use QuickBASIC) and a single disk drive.

- Using only Drive A simplifies your learning task.

THE QuickBASIC CONTROL CENTER

Now it is time to begin using QuickBASIC. To do so, remove the MS-DOS disk from the drive and insert the QuickBASIC work disk. Then at the A-prompt, (shown as A>), do the following.

Type:
qb
and press ENTER

You may also type **QB** or **Qb** or **qB**. However, if you type **bq** or **QV** or **Wb**, you will get a response from the computer similar to this:

```
A>bq
Bad command or file name

A>_
```

If that happens, just try again.

Type:
qb
and press ENTER

The prompt and your command on the screen will look like this:

```
A>qb
```

The light on Drive A will come on and the disk will spin as the computer loads the necessary QuickBASIC files. When the disk stops spinning and the light goes out, you will see QuickBASIC's opening screen, as shown in Figure 2-1. In the middle of the screen is the Welcome *dialog box.* A dialog box appears automatically when a given option is chosen. It may contain instructions, information, or choices for you to make before proceeding. After completing this chapter, you will know how to explore any dialog box; you should then explore the QuickBASIC Survival Guide. Right now, however, clear this dialog box by pressing ESC, as suggested in the bottom line of the box.

Press:
ESC

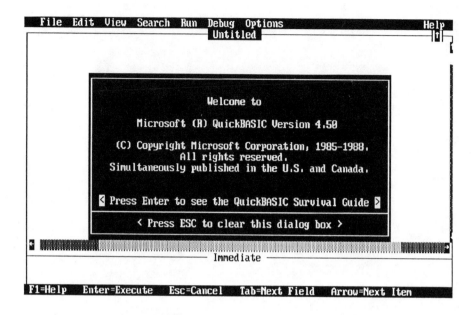

FIGURE 2-1   The QuickBASIC opening screen

When you press ESC, the Welcome dialog box disappears; the screen that you see now is the QuickBASIC *Control Center,* shown in Figure 2-2. The Control Center is the base from which you can enter the many options available in QuickBASIC. You can usually return here by pressing ESC, as you just did. Press ESC again.

Press:
ESC

Did you see anything happen when you pressed ESC? Since you were already in the QuickBASIC Control Center, you should only have seen the screen flicker a little; if you had not been in QuickBASIC Control, ESC would have taken you back to that screen almost instantly.

Remember: To return to the QuickBASIC Control Center, press ESC. Now let your eyes roam about the screen. Notice the following things:

• The screen has two windows.

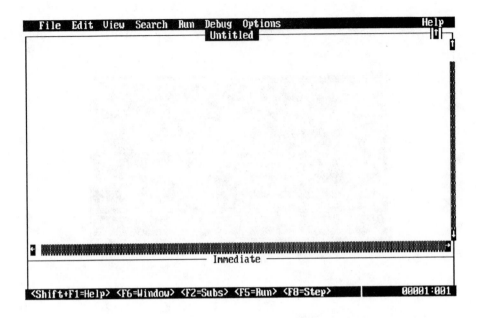

FIGURE 2-2   The QuickBASIC Control Center

- The larger, upper window is the *View window*. At the top of this window, near the center of the screen, is the *title bar,* which now reads "Untitled."

- Near the bottom of the screen is a much smaller window, which is long and narrow. This is the *Immediate window.* The word "Immediate" appears in the top center part of this window.

- Across the top of the screen is the *menu bar*. Within it are the names of other windows and menus you will soon see.

- The line across the bottom of the screen is the *status bar*. When you activate a menu or dialog box, or leave this screen, this line changes. It usually contains a description of where you are, what a given menu option will do, or how to get help.

```
<Shift+F1=Help> <F6=Window> <F2=Subs> <F5=Run> <F8=Step>          00001:001
```

Browsing the Menu Bar

QuickBASIC is like a well-designed shopping center with many stores, arcades, and other interesting places where you can browse, shop, play, create, design, contemplate, or do whatever else you want to do with a computer.

Begin by highlighting the names in the menu bar. To do so, press the ALT key.

Press:
ALT

Notice that the word "File" in the menu bar is now highlighted. Notice also that the status bar at the bottom of the screen has changed, as you can see in Figure 2-3.

Compare Figure 2-2 with Figure 2-3. Note the word "File" in the menu bar and the status bar in the two figures. Press ALT again and the screen in Figure 2-2 reappears. Pressing ALT once more returns you to the screen in Figure 2-3, with File in the menu bar highlighted. Press ESC; the highlight is turned off and you're back again in QuickBASIC Control. Practice using ALT and ESC to highlight and turn off the highlighting in the menu bar. When you are ready to move on, you will learn how to move the highlight back and forth across the menu bar, highlighting each word or menu option in turn.

If File is not now highlighted, press ALT so that the menu bar appears as in Figure 2-3. Watch the menu bar and move the highlight to the right by pressing the RIGHT ARROW key. The Edit option is now highlighted, as shown here.

Press RIGHT ARROW again; View is now highlighted.

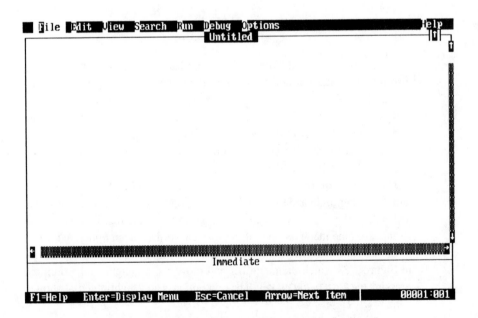

FIGURE 2-3   The menu bar with File highlighted

Press RIGHT ARROW again; the next option, Search, is now highlighted.

Press RIGHT ARROW again; the next option, Run, is now highlighted.

Press RIGHT ARROW again; the next option, Debug, is now highlighted.

Press RIGHT ARROW again; the next option, Options, is now highlighted.

Press RIGHT ARROW again; the last option, Help is now highlighted.

Press RIGHT ARROW one more time; since the last menu bar option, Help, is highlighted, the highlight moves back to the first option, File.

As you've just seen, pressing RIGHT ARROW moves the highlight one word to the right. You can also use LEFT ARROW to move the highlight to the left one word at a time across the menu bar. If the highlight is already at the far left with File highlighted, pressing LEFT ARROW will move the highlight to Help at the far right of the menu bar. Practice highlighting each option in the menu bar by pressing LEFT ARROW and RIGHT ARROW.

No matter which option in the menu bar is highlighted, you can press ESC to return to the QuickBASIC Control Center with nothing in the menu bar highlighted. You can also use ALT to turn off the highlight in the menu bar. Practice using ALT, ESC, RIGHT ARROW, and LEFT ARROW to turn on and off the options in the menu bar.

If you are using a mouse with QuickBASIC, the mouse pointer first appears near the center of the View window. Menus and dialog boxes may be selected by moving the mouse pointer to the appropriate option, then clicking the mouse button.

Browsing the Menus

The words in the menu bar are names of menus. Each menu contains a list of options you can choose from to tell the computer what to do. You can browse the menus as easily as you browsed the menu bar, looking at each menu briefly.

First, press ESC just to make sure you are in the QuickBASIC Control Center with nothing highlighted. The menu bar should look like this:

Now press ALT to highlight File. When the File option in the menu bar is highlighted, press ENTER to select the File menu. The File menu appears in the View window, below its name in the menu bar, as shown in Figure 2-4.

The File menu has five choices. The first choice (New Program) is now highlighted. For now, just look; you will learn how to use the File menu in

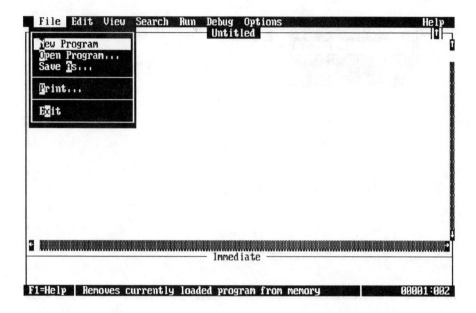

FIGURE 2-4   The File menu in the View window

Chapter 3, "Introduction to Programming." Press ESC to clear the File menu and return to the QuickBASIC Control Center.

Remember: When File is highlighted in the menu bar, press ENTER to select the File menu. Press ESC to return to the QuickBASIC Control Center; the File menu disappears.

The File menu is one of eight menus you can select by moving the high-light across the menu bar. The easiest way to browse all of the menus is to first select the File menu (press ALT, and then press ENTER), then press RIGHT ARROW to display the other menus in the menu bar. Each time you press RIGHT ARROW you will see the next menu. As you browse the menus, just look. Remember, you can press ESC at any time to return to QuickBASIC Control (Figure 2-2).

Begin browsing. Press ESC to make sure you are in QuickBASIC Control. Press ALT, and then ENTER to select the File menu, shown previously in Figure 2-4. Press RIGHT ARROW. The File menu disappears and the Edit menu pops into view, as shown in Figure 2-5. The Edit menu has three choices. The first choice (Cut) is now highlighted. You will learn how to use the Edit menu in Chapter 6, "Editing and Dynamic Debugging."

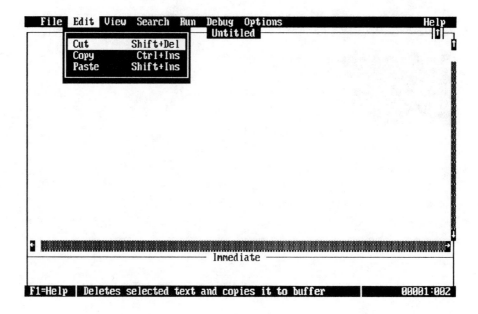

FIGURE 2-5   The Edit menu in the View window

Press RIGHT ARROW again. The Edit menu disappears and the View menu drops down, as shown in Figure 2-6. The View menu has three choices. The first choice (SUBs...) is highlighted. You will learn how to use the View menu in Chapter 12, "FUNCTIONS and SUB Procedures."

Don't do it now, but remember that you can press ESC anytime to return to the QuickBASIC Control Center. Instead of doing that, press RIGHT ARROW again. The menu bar highlight moves to Search and the Search menu appears as shown in Figure 2-7. The Search menu has two choices. The first choice (Find...) is highlighted.

The next menu, the Run menu, is one of the most frequently used. You will use it to run the programs you write. Press RIGHT ARROW to see the Run menu, shown in Figure 2-8. The Run menu has four choices. The first choice (Start) is highlighted. You will learn how to use the Run menu in Chapter 3, "Introduction to Programming."

Press RIGHT ARROW to inspect briefly the Debug and Options menus, shown in Figures 2-9 and 2-10. You will learn how to use the Debug menu in Chapter 6, "Editing and Dynamic Debugging." You will learn how to use the Options menu in Chapter 12, "FUNCTIONS and SUB Procedures."

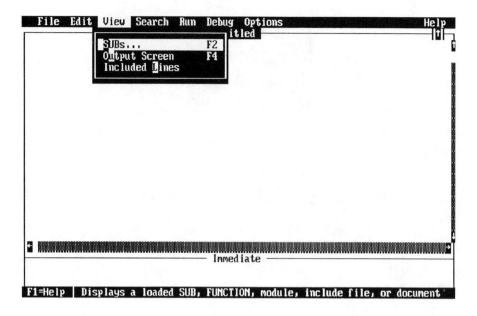

FIGURE 2-6   The View menu in the View window

FIGURE 2-7   The Search menu in the View window

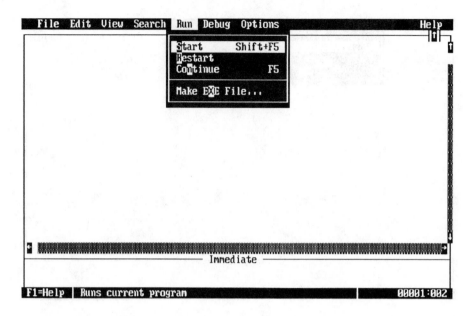

FIGURE 2-8   The Run menu in the View window

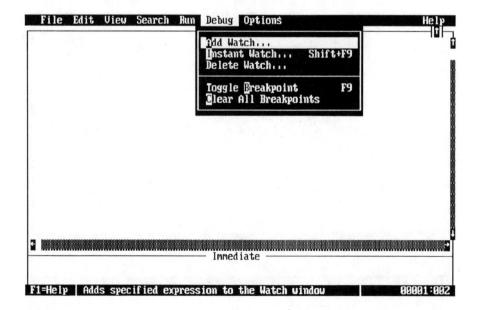

FIGURE 2-9   The Debug menu in the View window

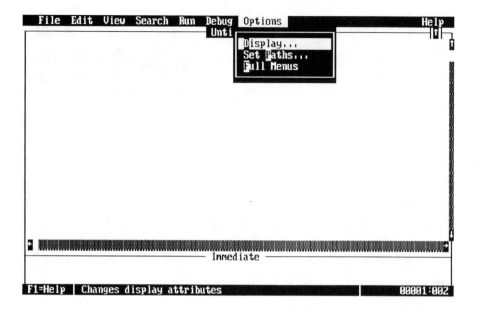

FIGURE 2-10   The Options menu in the View window

The next menu, the Help menu, will be particularly useful to you, as a beginner. Press RIGHT ARROW now to see the Help menu, as shown in Figure 2-11.

You will soon examine the Help menu in more detail. But first, press RIGHT ARROW. This returns you to the first option in the menu bar and you see the File menu again, previously shown in Figure 2-4.

Go through each option in the menu bar and back to the beginning one more time by pressing RIGHT ARROW or LEFT ARROW. When you have finished browsing the menus, press ESC to return to QuickBASIC Control.

Here is a shortcut for accessing any menu directly from QuickBASIC Control, rather than selecting that menu from the menu bar:

- To go directly to the File menu, press ALT, and then press F. Press ESC to return to QuickBASIC Control.

- To go directly to the Edit menu, press ALT, and then press E. Press ESC to return to QuickBASIC Control.

FIGURE 2-11   The Help menu in the View window

- To go directly to the View menu, press ALT, and then press V. Press ESC to return to QuickBASIC Control.

- To go directly to the Search menu, press ALT, and then press S. Press ESC to return to QuickBASIC Control.

- To go directly to the Run menu, press ALT, and then press R. Press ESC to return to QuickBASIC Control.

- To go directly to the Debug menu, press ALT, and then press D. Press ESC to return to QuickBASIC Control.

- To go directly to the Options menu, press ALT, and then press O. Press ESC to return to QuickBASIC Control.

- To go directly to the Help menu, press ALT, and then press H. Press ESC to return to QuickBASIC Control.

In other words, you can go from the QuickBASIC Control Center directly to any menu in the menu bar by pressing ALT, and then pressing the first

Desired Menu	Press
File menu	ALT + F
Edit menu	ALT + E
View menu	ALT + V
Search menu	ALT + S
Run menu	ALT + R
Debug menu	ALT + D
Options menu	ALT + O
Help menu	ALT + H

TABLE 2-1 Shortcut Keys for Accessing Menus

letter of the name of the desired menu. This information is summarized in Table 2-1.

In this table, the phrase "ALT + F " means "Press the ALT key, and then press the F key." (Do not press the PLUS key.) To access any menu, press the keys as shown in the table.

The Help Menu

Having quickly browsed each menu, you are ready to learn how to use and explore each one further. The Help menu is a good place to start.

Are you now at the QuickBASIC Control Center? If not, press ESC. Then access the Help menu by pressing ALT, and then pressing H. You will see the Help menu, shown previously in Figure 2-11. The Help menu has four choices: Index, Contents, Topic:, and Help on Help. The top choice (Index) is highlighted. Whenever you see a menu item highlighted, you know it is *active*, ready to be selected and used. Please read the description of Index displayed in the status bar.

THE HELP MENU: INDEX   The Index option on the Help menu provides information about any of a long list of keywords. To select Index from

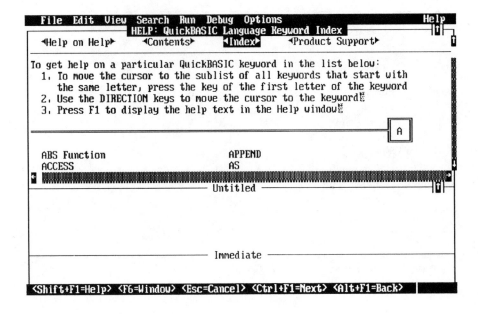

FIGURE 2-12   The Help menu: Index dialog box

the Help menu, press ENTER when this option is highlighted. You will see the first screen of the Help Index, shown in Figure 2-12.

The top line in the Help Index dialog box contains the options Help on Help, Contents, Index, and Product Support. The first three options also appear as options on the Help menu itself; they provide a way to move from a given Help topic without first returning to QuickBASIC Control and selecting that option from the Help menu. The highlighted option is the active option. Notice that the third option, Index, is now highlighted, because you selected it from the Help menu. Do not do this now, but you can use the TAB key to activate the other options.

Study the Help Index dialog box. It explains how to access any of the keywords listed in the index. To get help on a particular keyword, type the first letter of the word you would like help on, then press DOWN ARROW until the cursor is on the word you are interested in. You can also get help on a keyword by pressing TAB until the cursor is on the appropriate keyword. When the cursor is on the correct keyword, press ENTER to see the help text on that keyword. Press ESC to exit when you are ready to return to Quick-BASIC Control.

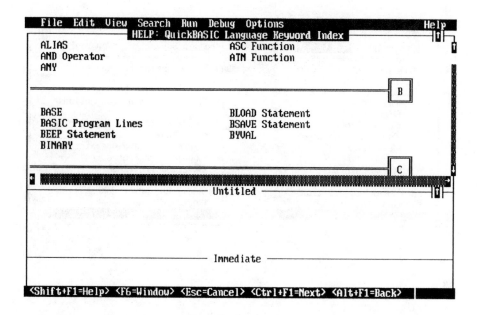

FIGURE 2-13   The Help menu: Index dialog box, second screen

You can also browse the list of index keywords by pressing the PGDN key to display the next screen and the PGUP key to display the previous screen of keywords. Figure 2-13 shows the second screen of index keywords. Use UP ARROW and DOWN ARROW to move to the word you want help on in a given screen, and then press ENTER to select that word. Press ESC when you have finished browsing to return to QuickBASIC Control.

THE HELP MENU: CONTENTS   The Contents option on the Help menu contains a list of the topics that you can get help on. Access the Help menu, then select Contents to display the Help Contents dialog box, shown in Figure 2-14.

Notice that the top line of the dialog box contains the options Help on Help, Contents, Index, Product Support, and Copyright. Again, the first three options also appear as options on the Help menu itself. Product Support and Copyright, as the names imply, contain information on the product support available from Microsoft, and on the copyright restrictions that apply to your use of QuickBASIC. The highlighted option, Contents, is the active option,

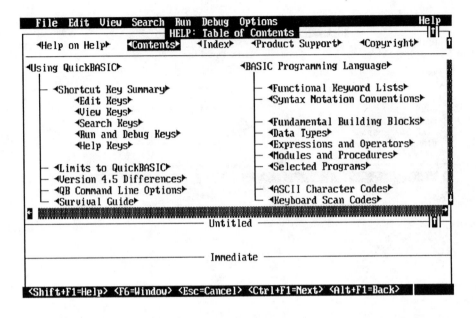

FIGURE 2-14   The Help menu: Contents dialog box

since it was selected from the Help menu. Do not do so now, but you can use TAB to activate (highlight) the other options.

You can get help on any of the topics included in this table of contents. To do so, press TAB until the topic you wish to explore is highlighted, and then press ENTER. You can also use PGDN and PGUP to display the next screen in the list of topics or to go back to a previous screen. Use DOWN ARROW and UP ARROW to move down or up one line at a time in the dialog box. Press ESC when you have finished exploring the Help Contents dialog box to return to the QuickBASIC Control Center.

THE HELP MENU: TOPIC: The next option on the Help menu (Topic:) provides help on the keyword that your cursor is on in the View window when you select this option. Right now, however, this option is a different color from the other menu options; it is grayed. When a menu option is gray, it cannot be selected. Since there is no keyword in the View window that you could get help on, this option is not available. Press ENTER when this option is highlighted: the computer will make some noise, and the Help menu remains unchanged in the View window.

THE HELP MENU: HELP ON HELP   Help on Help provides information on the different options and features of help available to you. The Help on Help dialog box, shown in Figure 2-15, contains three of the same options available from the Help menu (Help on Help, Contents, and Index), and an option to get help on QuickBASIC product support from Microsoft. You can use TAB to activate these other options—but do not do so now. Instead, press PGDN and PGUP to view the various screens. When you have finished exploring Help on Help, press ESC to return to QuickBASIC Control.

Exiting from QuickBASIC

Exit from QuickBASIC whenever you have finished using it for a while or when you are ready to turn off your computer. To exit from QuickBASIC, first make sure that you are in QuickBASIC Control by pressing ESC. Then access the File menu by pressing ALT, and then pressing F. Notice that the

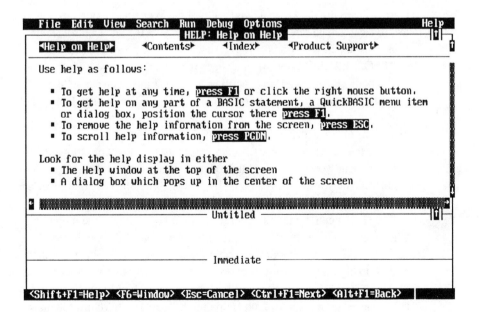

FIGURE 2-15   The Help menu: Help on Help dialog box

access the File menu by pressing ALT, and then pressing F. Notice that the last option on the File menu is Exit. Press DOWN ARROW until Exit is highlighted, then press ENTER. You will return to the A> prompt automatically.

There is another, even simpler way to exit from QuickBASIC. Press ALT + F (the ALT key, and then the F key) to access the File menu. Notice that each option on the File menu has a single letter, usually the first letter, highlighted. Pressing the highlighted letter in a given option selects that option. So, to exit from QuickBASIC, simply press X (upper- or lowercase), and you will return to the A> prompt.

To begin using QuickBASIC, put a QuickBASIC work disk in Drive A and turn on your computer. Enter the current date and time, after which you will see the computer's A-prompt (A>) on the screen. When you have this prompt, load QuickBASIC.

Type:
qb
and press ENTER

Once you are in QuickBASIC you will see the Welcome dialog box; press ESC to clear it. The screen you now see is the QuickBASIC Control Center. From this screen you compose, save, run, and debug programs.

The QuickBASIC Control Center has two windows, the View window and the Immediate window. Above the View window is the menu bar, which contains the options available to you in QuickBASIC. The bottom line is the status bar, which contains information about current menu options or explanations of current choices you may make.

To access a menu, press ALT, then press RIGHT ARROW or LEFT ARROW until the menu you want is highlighted, and then press ENTER to select that menu. You may also access a menu by pressing ALT, then the first letter of the menu name.

The Help menu, on the far right of the menu bar, allows you to get help when you need it on almost any topic or problem you might encounter when using QuickBASIC. Explore the Help menu using DOWN ARROW and UP ARROW to highlight the various options. To select an option from the menu, press ENTER when the option you wish to review is highlighted. Use TAB, PGDN, and PGUP to explore each Help option; press ESC to return to QuickBASIC Control.

To exit from QuickBASIC, access the File menu. To select Exit from this menu, press X (upper- or lowercase), or press DOWN ARROW until Exit is highlighted, and then press ENTER.

3

INTRODUCTION TO PROGRAMMING

Entering a Command in the Immediate Window
Using the View Window

In this chapter, you will begin using some QuickBASIC keywords to tell the computer to do what you want it to do. You will learn how to use the Immediate and View windows, and the File and Run menus. In particular, you will

- Learn how to use QuickBASIC keywords (BEEP, CLS, PRINT, DATE$, TIME$)

- Use the Immediate window to tell the computer to do something immediately after you press ENTER

- Use the View window to write short QuickBASIC programs

- Use the File menu to save the program shown in the View window to the disk in Drive A

- Use the Run menu to run the program in the View window

- Load a previously saved program from disk and display it in the View window

48   **QuickBASIC Made Easy**

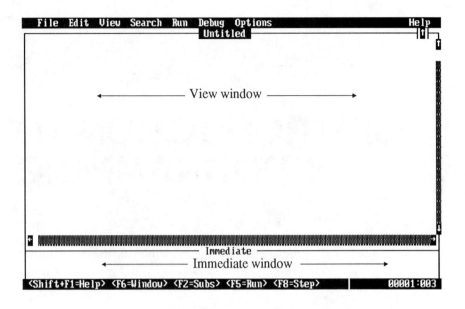

FIGURE 3-1   The QuickBASIC Control Center

Begin in the QuickBASIC Control Center, shown in Figure 3-1. If you do not have this screen on your computer, refer to Chapter 2, "The QuickBASIC Windows," for instructions.

The QuickBASIC Control Center has two windows, the View window and the Immediate window. The View window is used to write and change programs. The Immediate window is used to enter instructions that are executed immediately, as soon as ENTER is pressed. You will first learn how to enter commands in the Immediate window; then you will use these same commands to write a program in the View window, which you can then save and run.

ENTERING A COMMAND IN THE IMMEDIATE WINDOW

Make sure that you are in the QuickBASIC Control Center, with the cursor blinking in the upper left corner of the View window, shown in Figure 3-2. You can move the cursor back and forth between the View window and the

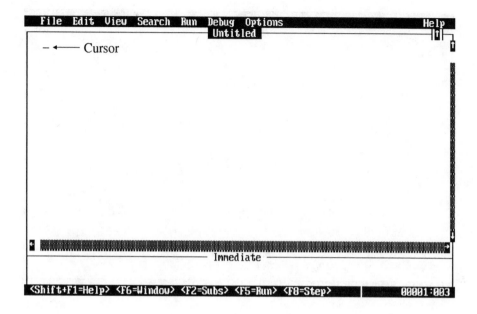

FIGURE 3-2   The QuickBASIC Control Center with the cursor in the View window

Immediate window by pressing F6. Press F6 now. The cursor moves to the Immediate window, shown in Figure 3-3.

Press F6 again. The cursor returns to the View window. Press F6 once more to put the cursor in the Immediate window, shown in Figure 3-3.

Remember: Press F6 to move the cursor from the View window to the Immediate window, and vice versa.

The Beep Command

When the cursor is in the Immediate window, you can type a command and press ENTER. The computer will immediately obey any valid QuickBASIC command. For example, the BEEP keyword is a valid command that tells the computer to make a beeping sound.

Type:
BEEP
and press ENTER

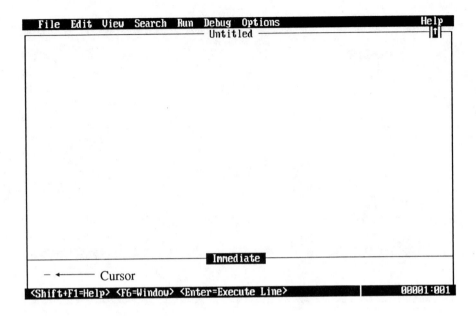

FIGURE 3-3   The cursor in the Immediate window

The computer will beep and the Immediate window will look as shown in Figure 3-4.

RECOVERING FROM MISTAKES   For clarity, all QuickBASIC keywords used in this book are shown in uppercase, but you could also have typed **beep** or **Beep** or even **BeeP**. In QuickBASIC, you can enter commands and instructions in either uppercase or lowercase, whichever you prefer. If you type a command or instruction that QuickBASIC doesn't understand, the Syntax Error dialog box will appear in the middle of the View window. To see this on your computer, spell BEEP incorrectly.

Type:
BOOP
and press ENTER

You should see the Syntax Error dialog box on the screen, as shown in Figure 3-5.

```
┌─────────────────────────── Immediate ───────────────────────────┐
│BEEP                                                              │
│                                                                  │
├─────────────────────────────────────────────────────┬───────────┤
│<Shift+F1=Help> <F6=Window> <Enter=Execute Line>      │ C  00002:001│
└──────────────────────────────────────────────────────────────────┘
```

FIGURE 3-4   The Immediate window after BEEP command

The Syntax Error dialog box has two options: OK and Help. The brackets enclosing the left choice (OK) are highlighted and the cursor is blinking under the letter "O." This tells you that the OK choice is now *active,* ready to be selected. To move to another choice in a dialog box, press TAB. The cursor and the highlighting move to the second choice, Help. That choice is now active. Press TAB again. The cursor and the highlight move back to the first choice, OK. That is now the active choice.

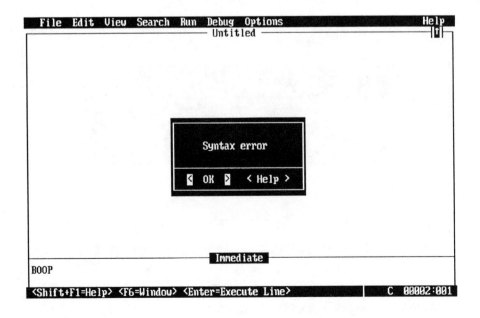

FIGURE 3-5   The Syntax Error dialog box in the View window

Use TAB to make Help the active choice and press ENTER. Pressing ENTER when a given choice is active (highlighted) means you are selecting that option. In this instance, it means that you want to see what help is available on syntax errors.

If you are using 5 1/4-inch disks you will now see the dialog box, shown in Figure 3-6, asking you to insert the disk that contains the file QB45-ENER.HLP. Remove your QuickBASIC work disk from the drive and put the QuickBASIC help disk, which contains the requested file, into the drive; then select Retry. That dialog box disappears, and the Syntax Error dialog box reappears briefly. The Syntax Error dialog box is then replaced by the Help dialog box, shown in Figure 3-7.

If you are using 3 1/2-inch disks, the file QB45ENER.HLP is already on your QuickBASIC work disk, so you will not see this dialog box. Instead, the Syntax Error dialog box is immediately replaced by the Help dialog box, shown in Figure 3-7.

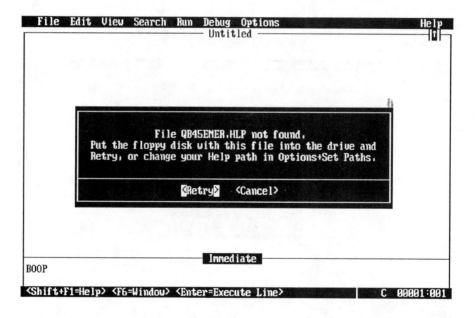

FIGURE 3-6   The Insert QB45ENER.HLP dialog box in the View window

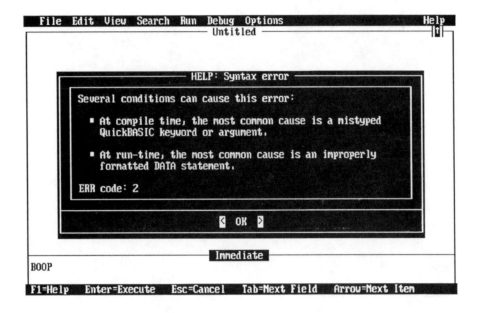

```
 File   Edit   View   Search   Run   Debug   Options                      Help
 ──────────────────────────── Untitled ──────────────────────────────────│↕│
┌─────────────────────────────────────────────────────────────────────────┐
│                                                                           │
│        ┌───────────────── HELP: Syntax error ─────────────────┐          │
│        │                                                        │          │
│        │  Several conditions can cause this error:              │          │
│        │                                                        │          │
│        │   ■ At compile time, the most common cause is a mistyped          │
│        │     QuickBASIC keyword or argument.                    │          │
│        │                                                        │          │
│        │   ■ At run-time, the most common cause is an improperly           │
│        │     formatted DATA statement.                          │          │
│        │                                                        │          │
│        │  ERR code: 2                                           │          │
│        │                                                        │          │
│        └────────────────────────────────────────────────────────┘          │
│        ┌────────────────────────────────────────────────────────┐          │
│        │                    ◄ OK ►                               │          │
│        └────────────────────────────────────────────────────────┘          │
│                                                                           │
│ ────────────────────────────── Immediate ───────────────────────────────  │
│ BOOP                                                                       │
├───────────────────────────────────────────────────────────────────────────┤
│ F1=Help   Enter=Execute   Esc=Cancel   Tab=Next Field   Arrow=Next Item    │
└───────────────────────────────────────────────────────────────────────────┘
```

FIGURE 3-7   The Syntax Error Help dialog box in the View window

The contents of the Help dialog box vary, depending on the particular problem you have. In this case, it contains some information about syntax errors and the most common ways they occur. A *syntax error* occurs when QuickBASIC cannot understand the spelling or structure of an instruction or command, and therefore cannot do what it was instructed to do. When you have finished looking at this dialog box, press ENTER and you will return to the Syntax Error dialog box shown in Figure 3-5.

Remember: Press TAB to move between options in a dialog box. Press ENTER to select the highlighted choice.

You can clear the Syntax Error dialog box by selecting OK. To do so, use TAB to make OK active as in Figure 3-8, then press ENTER. The Syntax Error dialog box will disappear. The cursor will return to the Immediate window and blink on the word the computer doesn't understand, in this case "BOOP," shown in Figure 3-9. If you are using 5 1/4-inch disks, remove the Quick-BASIC help disk from the drive now, and put the QuickBASIC work disk back in the drive.

To change BOOP to BEEP, or to correct any misspelled word, use DEL and BACKSPACE to erase characters, and the arrow keys to move the cursor

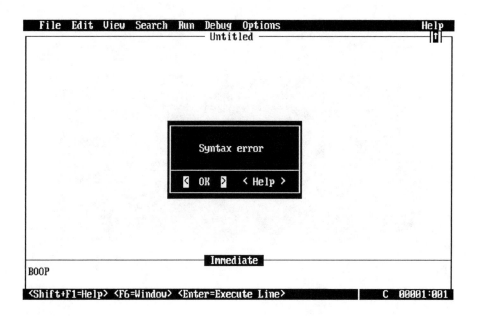

FIGURE 3-8   The Syntax Error dialog box with OK active

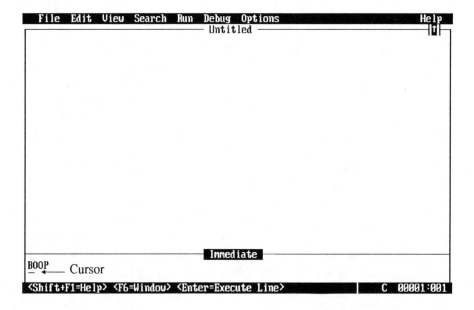

FIGURE 3-9   The cursor blinking on a misspelled word (BOOP)

within a window. The arrow keys move the cursor left, right, up, and down, in the direction of the arrow on the key. BACKSPACE deletes the character to the left of the cursor. Each time you press BACKSPACE, the cursor moves one space to the left and deletes the character in that place. DEL deletes the character at the cursor position. Use DEL, BACKSPACE, and the arrow keys now to change BOOP to BEEP. Then press ENTER and you will hear a beep.

Remember: You can use DEL, BACKSPACE, and the arrow keys to erase characters and move the cursor within a window when correcting mistakes or making changes. Use TAB to move between options in a dialog box.

The CLS Command

Next you will learn how to clear the Output screen. The Output screen is the screen you see when you run a program or give a command that has an effect on what is displayed.

Make sure that you are in the Immediate window. The command to clear the Output screen is CLS.

Type:
CLS
and press ENTER

The QuickBASIC Control screen will disappear and you will see a screen that is blank except for one line at the bottom, which says, "Press any key to continue," shown here:

```
Press any key to continue
```

The CLS command clears any previous text from the Output screen. The QuickBASIC prompt to continue appears whenever QuickBASIC has finished executing a command or program that affects output to the screen. Pressing any key (the SPACEBAR is a good choice) will return you to QuickBASIC Control, with the CLS command and the cursor in the Immediate window as shown in Figure 3-10

Note that only one command is shown in the Immediate window; the BEEP command you entered earlier, for example, is no longer visible. This is because each new command "pushes" the previous command out of the window when ENTER is pressed.

```
┌──────────────────────────────Immediate────────────────────────────────┐
│CLS                                                                     │
│                                                                        │
│<Shift+F1=Help> <F6=Window> <Enter=Execute Line>        │ C  00002:001 │
```

FIGURE 3-10   The Immediate window after CLS command

Printing the Date and Time

When you first turned on your computer, you probably entered the date and time. You can print the current date and time from QuickBASIC, using the PRINT keyword, which is used in commands whenever you want to print something to the screen.

Make sure the cursor is in the Immediate window; if it is not, press F6 to change windows.

Type:
CLS
and press ENTER

This clears the Output screen. Return to QuickBASIC Control by pressing any key (such as the ESC key or the SPACEBAR); then tell the computer to print the date.

Type:
PRINT DATE$
and press ENTER

The screen shown here

```
01-01-1990
```

```
Press any key to continue
```

illustrates the result of this command if the date is January 1, 1990. Of course, if you misspell PRINT or DATE$ you will not see the screen shown here. Instead, you will see the Syntax Error dialog box shown in Figures 3-5 and 3-8. In that event, explore the Help box and then come back to the Immediate window and fix the error.

Press any key to return to QuickBASIC Control from the Output screen. In the Immediate window you will see your last command, as shown in the next illustration.

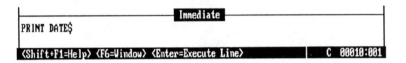

Now tell the computer to print the time of day.

Type:
PRINT TIME$
and press ENTER

The time is printed under the date in the Output screen, as shown here:

```
01-01-1990
08:37:04
```

```
Press any key to continue
```

Since the Output screen was not cleared before printing the time, both the date and time are visible. Return to QuickBASIC Control (press any key) and you again will see your last command in the Immediate window, as follows:

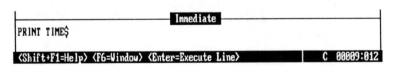

Printing Your Name

So far you have told the computer to beep (BEEP), clear the screen (CLS), print the date (PRINT DATE$), and print the time (PRINT TIME$). In doing so, you have used five QuickBASIC keywords: BEEP, CLS, PRINT, DATE$, and TIME$. Now you will learn how to tell it to print your name.

First, make sure that the cursor is in the Immediate window; then type the keyword **PRINT**, a space, and your name enclosed in quotation marks, and press ENTER. George Firedrake typed this:

PRINT "George Firedrake"

Then he pressed ENTER. The Output screen appeared as shown here:

```
01-01-1990
08:37:04
George Firedrake
```

```
Press any key to continue
```

Type this command yourself now, replacing "George Firedrake" with your name. When you return to the QuickBASIC Control Center, you will see your command to print your name in the Immediate window. George saw this:

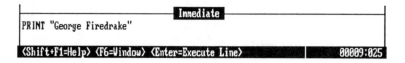

You have now used the PRINT keyword to display the date, the time, and your name. The PRINT keyword can be used to print almost any message, and is thus one of the most used and useful keywords in QuickBASIC. You can use the PRINT keyword to tell the computer to print a message, using these steps:

1. Type the QuickBASIC keyword **PRINT** and a space.

2. Type a quote mark (").

3. Type your name or any desired message.

4. Type another quote mark.

5. Press ENTER.

Setting the Date and Time in the Immediate Window

Just as you can print the date and time from QuickBASIC, you can also use QuickBASIC to set the current date and time. To set the date, first make sure you are in the Immediate window, and then do the following.

Type:
CLS
and press ENTER

This will clear any previous text from the Output screen, so that when the new date is printed, only the date and prompt to continue will be visible. Press any key to return to QuickBASIC Control.

Type:
DATE$ = "1-1-90"
and press ENTER

This command sets the computer's date to 1-1-90, regardless of what the date may have been previously. Now print the date on the screen.

Type:
PRINT DATE$
and press ENTER

The Output screen should now appear as shown here:

```
01-01-1990
```

```
Press any key to continue
```

Press any key to return to the Immediate window. You will now use similar commands to set the time and print it. The following changes the computer's current time to 6:30.

Type:
TIME$ = "6:30"
and press ENTER

Now print the time you set, plus a few seconds, as shown here:

```
01-01-1990
06:38:04
```

```
Press any key to continue
```

Type:
PRINT TIME$
and press ENTER

Press any key to return to QuickBASIC Control, and then print a message appropriate to the date and time.

Type:

PRINT "Good Morning and Happy New Year"

and press ENTER

Now the Output screen contains the new date and time, and whatever message you instructed the computer to display, such as the one shown here:

```
01-01-1990
06:38:04
Good Morning and Happy New Year
```

```
Press any key to continue
```

Return to QuickBASIC Control. You will see your last command and the cursor in the Immediate window, as shown in the next illustration:

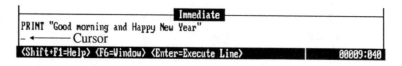

You learned previously how to use DEL, BACKSPACE, and the arrow keys to correct mistakes. You can also use the arrow keys to ask the computer to execute a command again. Using UP ARROW, move the cursor up one line to the first letter of the keyword PRINT, like this:

```
┌──────────────────────────── Immediate ────────────────────────────┐
│PRINT "Good morning and Happy New Year"                             │
│▁                                                                   │
│  ◀─── Cursor                                                       │
│<Shift+F1=Help> <F6=Window> <Enter=Execute Line>          00009:040 │
└────────────────────────────────────────────────────────────────────┘
```

Now press ENTER. The computer will again execute the command to print your message, and you will see the Output screen shown next.

```
01-01-1990
06:38:04
Good Morning and Happy New Year
Good Morning and Happy New Year
```

```
Press any key to continue
```

When ready, return to the QuickBASIC Control Center. Change the date and time several times until you feel comfortable with the steps involved. Practice using the CLS and PRINT keywords to explore further how the Output screen works. Next you will learn how to use the View window to write and run a simple program.

USING THE VIEW WINDOW

The Immediate window is used to enter an instruction that the computer will execute as soon as ENTER is pressed. The View window, however, is used to enter a QuickBASIC program; once entered, such a program can be run or saved for recall and later use.

In writing your program you will use the same keywords (BEEP, CLS, PRINT, DATE$, TIME$) that you used in previous Immediate window commands. However, you will see that they are not executed as soon as you press ENTER. Instead, they are stored in the computer's memory for later execution. After entering a program, you will use the Run menu to run it.

Entering Your First QuickBASIC Program

Begin in the QuickBASIC Control Center with the cursor in its home position in the upper left corner of the View window, as shown in Figure 3-11. If the cursor is in the Immediate window, press F6 to return to the View window; if the cursor is not in its home position, press HOME to send it to the upper left corner of the window.

It is a good idea to begin by telling QuickBASIC that you are going to enter a new program. You will use the New Program option on the File menu to do so. Do the following to display the File menu.

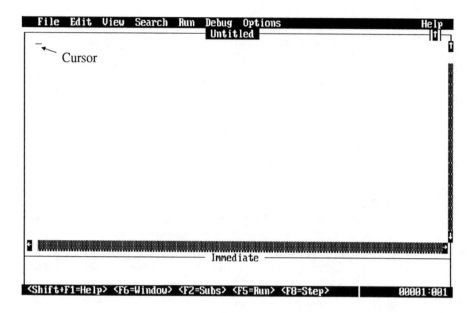

FIGURE 3-11   The cursor in the home position in the View window

Press ALT, and then press F

The File menu is shown in Figure 3-12. Notice that when the File menu is displayed, the New Program choice is highlighted. This means that New Program is the active choice, and you can simply press ENTER to select it. This clears the contents of the View window, allowing you to start a new program, and causes the File menu to disappear. You are now ready to enter your first QuickBASIC program.

Your first QuickBASIC program will clear the Output screen, and then make the computer beep, print the date and time, and print your name or any message you choose. George Firedrake's program is shown here:

```
CLS
BEEP
PRINT DATE$
PRINT TIME$
PRINT "George Firedrake"
```

This program has five lines. Beginning in the upper left corner of the View window, type **CLS** and then press ENTER. Notice that when you press ENTER, the cursor moves down to the next line, but you do not yet see the Output screen. This is because the CLS instruction has not actually been executed; instructions entered in the View window are executed only when you select the appropriate option from the Run menu.

Enter each line in this program, pressing ENTER after you type each line. If you type keywords in lowercase letters (for example, **cls**), QuickBASIC will change them to uppercase letters. This helps you to identify keywords quickly in a program, as you will see when your programs become longer and more complex.

If you make typing errors, you may see the Syntax Error dialog box. QuickBASIC checks your program for obvious errors such as syntax errors as each line is entered. If you do see the Syntax Error dialog box, explore the on-line help and return to the View window to correct any errors. You can use the arrow keys, BACKSPACE, and DEL to make the necessary changes. When finished, your program should appear as shown in Figure 3-13.

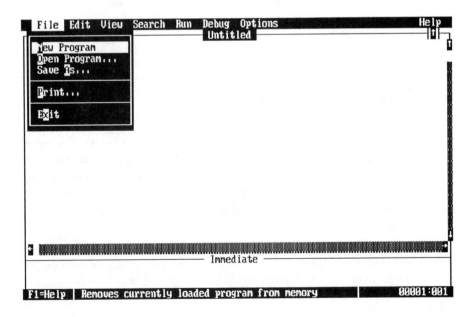

FIGURE 3-12   The File menu with New Program highlighted

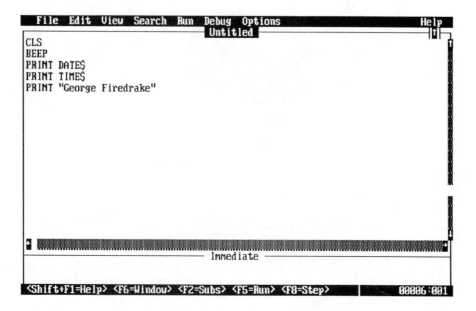

FIGURE 3-13   Your first QuickBASIC program

Your program in the View window is stored in the computer's memory, ready to use. To execute it, you will use the Run menu. To display the Run menu, do the following.

Press ALT + R

The Run menu, with the Start choice highlighted, is shown in Figure 3-14. Don't worry if the menu covers part of your program; it does not affect the program at all. To start running a program from the beginning, select Start by pressing ENTER. You will then see an Output screen similar to the one shown here:

```
01-01-1990
07:22:08
George Firedrake
```

The computer executed each instruction in the program from top (CLS) to bottom (PRINT "George Firedrake"). Press any key to return to Quick-BASIC Control; your program is still in the View window and still in the

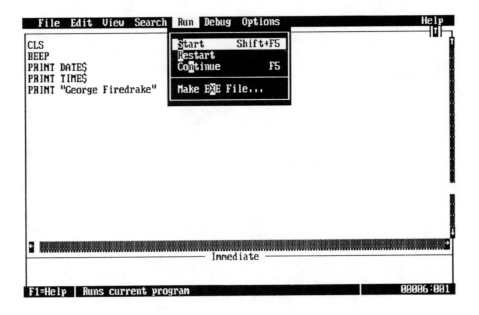

FIGURE 3-14   The Run menu with Start highlighted

computer's memory. Run it again—the Output screen will be the same except for the time, which will be a few seconds later than in the first run.

Saving Your First QuickBASIC Program

You have entered a short QuickBASIC program in the View window and run it. Now you will save your program to the QuickBASIC work disk in Drive A, by using the File menu. To display the File menu, do the following.

Press ALT + F

When the File menu drops down it covers most of your program, but don't worry; the program remains in memory, unaffected by the display of the menu.

The first choice on the File menu, New Program, is highlighted, as previously shown in Figure 3-12. This is not the choice you want, so don't press ENTER. Instead, use DOWN ARROW to move the highlight to Save As, as shown in Figure 3-15. If you overshoot, use UP ARROW to move the highlight back up the options until Save As is again highlighted.

When Save As is highlighted, press ENTER to select it. The File menu will disappear and you will see the Save As dialog box shown in Figure 3-16.

The Save As dialog box contains three smaller boxes labeled File Name, Dirs/Drives, and Format, and three options near the bottom labeled OK, Cancel, and Help. The cursor is blinking in the File Name box, waiting for you to enter a name for your program. The Dirs/Drives box contains the current directory and the disk drives available to save your program on. The Format box allows you to choose how you want to save your program. You can ignore the Dirs/Drives and Format boxes, since in this book you will always be saving onto Drive A in the fast load format. If you would like more information on these options, refer to your QuickBASIC user manuals.

The three options at the bottom of the Save As dialog box are similar to those in the Syntax Error dialog box, which you explored earlier (Figure 3-7). Selecting OK will save the program in the View window with the name entered in the File Name box; selecting Cancel returns you to QuickBASIC

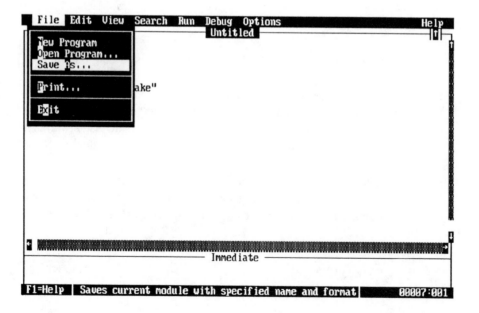

FIGURE 3-15   The View window with the File menu and Save As... highlighted

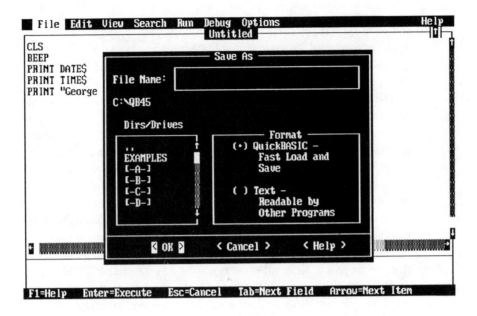

FIGURE 3-16 The Save As dialog box

Control without saving; and selecting Help will display the on-line Help dialog box.

Using TAB to move between options, explore the Save As dialog box, especially the Help option. To select an option, press ENTER when that option is highlighted. When you have finished exploring, make sure that the Save As dialog box is again visible (Figure 3-16), with the cursor in the File Name box.

In order to save a program, you must give it a name, called a *file name*. A file name can have up to eight characters (letters and numbers); the first character must be a letter. Name this program QBME0301.

Type:
QBME0301
and press ENTER

Before you press ENTER, check the file name for accuracy, making sure you typed zeroes, distinguished by a slash rather than the capital letter "O."

Notice that the file name (QBME0301) appears in the File Name box, where the cursor is blinking. The letters "QBME" mean "QuickBASIC Made Easy," the numbers "03" refer to this chapter (Chapter 3), and the numbers "01" tell you it is the first named program in the chapter.

When you press ENTER, the Save As dialog box disappears and the program is written to the disk in Drive A. The program has been saved to Drive A under the file name QBME0301, and its name will appear in the title line at the top of the View window as QBME0301.BAS. ".BAS" is called an extension and indicates that QBME0301 is a BASIC program. The View window with the program and its title are shown in Figure 3-17.

CHECKING THAT YOUR PROGRAM HAS BEEN SAVED Was your program really saved? You can find out what files are on the disk by using the Open Program... choice in the File menu. Press ALT + F (press ALT and then press F) to access the File menu, and then use DOWN ARROW to highlight Open Program..., as shown in Figure 3-18. Press ENTER with Open Program... highlighted to select this option. You will see the Open Program dialog box shown in Figure 3-19.

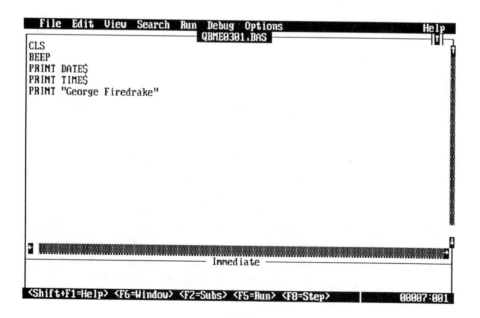

FIGURE 3-17   The program title in the View window after saving

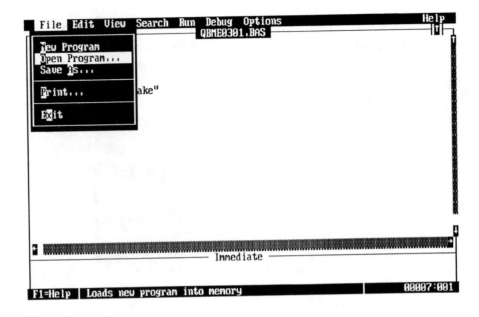

FIGURE 3-18   The File menu with Open Program... highlighted

The Open Program dialog box contains the File Name box, the Files box, and the Dirs/Drives box. As mentioned previously, the Dirs/Drives box lists the available current directory and disk drive, as well as any other available disk drives. You can ignore this box since you will only use Drive A in this book. The File Name box is used to enter the name of a program you wish to open. The Files box contains the names of files stored on your disk. You can see that the the name of your first QuickBASIC program, QBME-0301.BAS, is now listed in the Files box, thus confirming that it really was saved to the disk.

The OK, Cancel, and Help options at the bottom of the dialog box are selected just as those options in the Save As dialog box are. In fact, all dialog box options are selected in the same way: press TAB until your choice is highlighted, and press ENTER to select it. Take a few moments now to explore the options. When you're ready, press ESC to return to the QuickBASIC Control Center, where you will learn how to load a program from disk into Quick-BASIC.

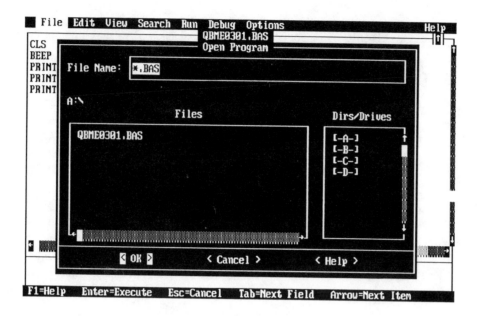

FIGURE 3-19   The Open Program dialog box

Loading a Program from Disk Drive A

You have used the Run menu to execute the program in the View window and saved it on your disk. You will now learn how to load a previously saved program into QuickBASIC so that it can be changed, saved again, or simply run again.

To load QBME0301.BAS from Drive A, use the Open Program... option in the File menu. Go to the File menu (press ALT + F) and use the arrow keys to highlight Open Program...; then press ENTER. You will see the Open Program dialog box shown in Figure 3-19. The cursor is blinking in the File Name box, which contains the name "*.BAS." Ignore it—as soon as you type the first letter of the file name to load, "*.BAS" will disappear.

Type:
QBME0301
and press ENTER

QuickBASIC will automatically add the extension .BAS if you do not include it in the file name. After you press ENTER, the disk in Drive A spins while the program is loaded, the Open Program dialog box disappears, and you are returned to the QuickBASIC Control Center. The View window is cleared, and your program QBME0301.BAS appears (Figure 3-20), as read from the disk.

There is also another way to load a program from disk. Select the Open Program... option from the File menu. When the Open Program dialog box appears, press TAB to move the cursor from the File Name box to the Files box, as shown in Figure 3-21.

The cursor is blinking on the first letter of QBME0301.BAS. Now press DOWN ARROW. The file name QBME0301.BAS will be highlighted and will also appear in the File Name box, as shown in Figure 3-22. Press ENTER when QBME0301.BAS is highlighted; the program will then be loaded and displayed in the View window, as in Figure 3-20. You can also use TAB to move

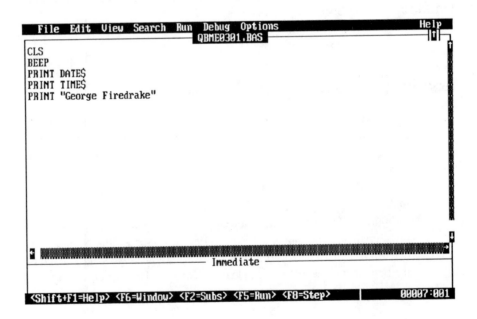

FIGURE 3-20   The View window after loading QBME0301.BAS

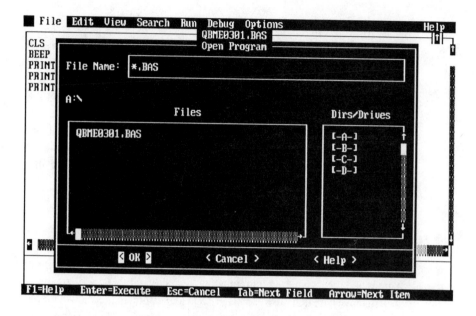

FIGURE 3-21   The Files box activated in the Open Program dialog box

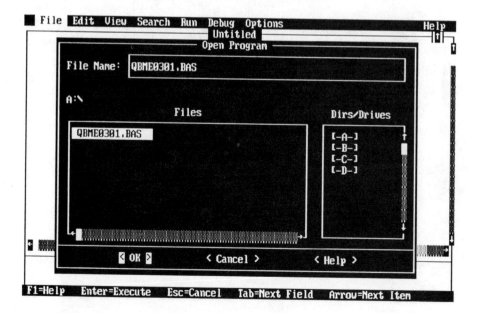

FIGURE 3-22   QBME0301.BAS highlighted in the Files Box

the cursor to the file name in the File Name box, and then press ENTER to load the program.

It is up to you whether to load a program by entering the program name in the File Name box, or to select the highlighted name in the Files box. Whichever way you find easiest and most comfortable is the method you should use—the result is the same.

Remember: You can cancel a program load, or any QuickBASIC dialog box, and return to QuickBASIC Control by pressing ESC. You can also return to QuickBASIC Control by using TAB to highlight the Cancel option and then pressing ENTER.

Saving a Program with a New Name

Once you have saved and loaded a program, you might want to make some changes and then save the program again, possibly with a new file name.

First, make sure that QBME0301.BAS is loaded and in the View window. Next, use DOWN ARROW to move the cursor to the end of the program, one line below the last instruction. Add one more instruction to the program, as in Figure 3-23. Now run your modified program by accessing the Run menu

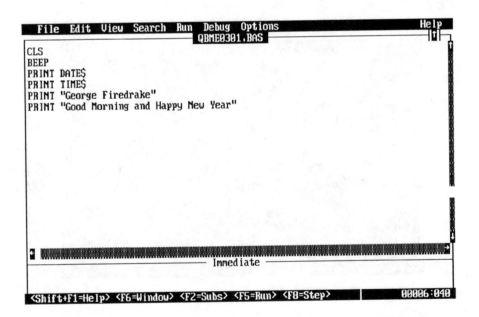

FIGURE 3-23   QBME0301.BAS modified in the View window

(ALT + R), and then pressing ENTER when Start is highlighted. The Output screen should look similar to the one shown here:

```
01-01-1990
10:15:05
George Firedrake
Good Morning and Happy New Year
```

Note that the additional line here is due to the instruction that you just added to the program (Figure 3-23). When you're ready, press any key to return to the QuickBASIC Control Center.

To save your modified program to disk, select the Save As... option from the File menu. The Save As dialog box then appears (Figure 3-24), with the program name already in the File Name box.

To save the program now in memory with the same file name, simply press ENTER. The program already on the disk will be replaced with the program in the View window. Do not do this now. Instead, save the modified program with a new file name, so that both the original program and the modified program are on your disk.

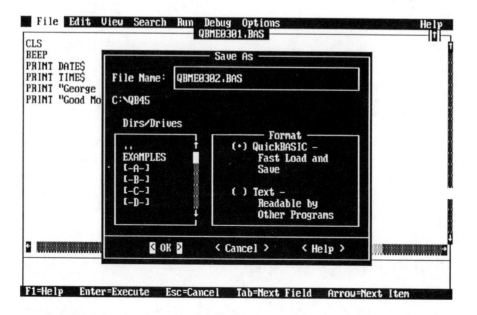

FIGURE 3-24 The Save As dialog box with new program name in the File Name box

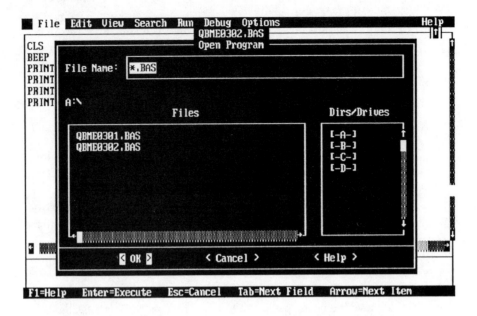

FIGURE 3-25 The Open Program dialog box with two names in the Files box

Type:
QBME0302
and press ENTER

A second file (QBME0302.BAS) is saved to disk and you are then returned
to the QuickBASIC Control Center. To confirm that both files are on your
disk, select Open Program... from the File menu. Both names now appear in
the Files box of this dialog box, as shown in Figure 3-25. Press ESC to clear
the Open Program dialog box and return to the Control Center.

Displaying All Work Disk Files

Sometimes it is useful to see a list of all the files on a disk, not just the
QuickBASIC program files. Especially later, when you begin to work with
data files, you will find this helpful.

If you are using a QuickBASIC work disk in Drive A, it should now contain the following files:

```
QB.EXE                  from the original QuickBASIC disks
QB45QCK.HLP             from the original QuickBASIC disks
QBME0301.BAS            the first program that you saved
QBME0302.BAS            the second program that you saved
```

You can use the Open Program... option in the File menu to verify that these files are on your disk. Select the Open Program... option from the File menu. You will see the Open Program dialog box shown in Figure 3-25, with the cursor in the File Name box.

Type:
.
and press ENTER

When used in a file name, the asterisk (*) stands for any name. So *.* means all files with any first name and any extension. The computer displays the names of all the files on the disk in Drive A in the Files box, as shown in Figure 3-26.

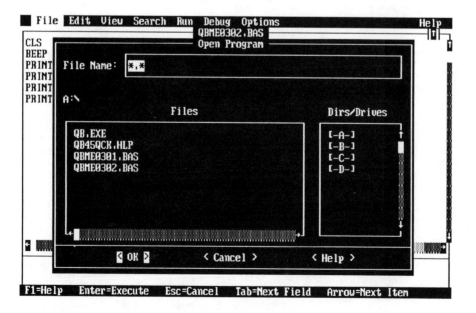

FIGURE 3-26   All file names displayed in the Files box

The QuickBASIC Control Center has two windows: the Immediate window and the View window. The Immediate window is used to enter commands that are executed immediately, as soon as you press ENTER.

The QuickBASIC keywords BEEP, CLS, PRINT, DATE$, and TIME$ can be used in the Immediate window or as part of a program entered in the View window.

A program is entered in the View window starting in the upper left corner. To execute a program in the View window, press ALT, press R to display the Run menu, and select Start. To save a program to disk, access the File menu by pressing ALT + F, and then select Save As.... Type the name of the program in the File Name box and press ENTER to save this program on the disk.

4

NUMBER CRUNCHING

Arithmetic Operators
Exponents and Floating Point Numbers
Numeric Types
Numeric Variables
Programming with Variables

In this chapter, you will learn to do basic arithmetic using QuickBASIC, both in the Immediate window and in a program. You will learn to use the math operators (+ , − , * , /) and the exponent operator (^). You will also learn about the different numeric types in QuickBASIC and numeric variables. Finally, you will learn how to use the INPUT and PRINT USING statements. In particular you will

- Learn how to add, subtract, multiply, and divide in QuickBASIC

- Learn about the exponent operator and how to use it

- Learn about the different numeric types, including integers, long integers, single precision numbers, and double precision numbers

- Learn about floating point notation

- Learn what numerical variables are and how to assign values to them

- Learn how to use the INPUT statement to assign a value to a variable

- Learn how to use the PRINT USING statement to align numbers when printing
- Learn how to print a copy of the program in the View window

Whenever you give the computer an instruction in the Immediate window or enter a new line in a program in the View window, remember to press ENTER when finished typing. Reminders to press ENTER will appear only in the first few pages of this chapter.

ARITHMETIC OPERATORS

You can do basic arithmetic easily using QuickBASIC. From the Immediate window, you can print the sum of two (or more) numbers; using a simple program, you can calculate your checkbook or loan balance. Use $+, -, *$, and $/$ to specify arithmetic operations, as shown in Table 4-1. First you will learn how to use the Immediate window to do simple arithmetic; then you will use the View window to create and run a program to do the same simple arithmetic.

Simple Arithmetic

Make sure you are in QuickBASIC Control, and then press F6 to move the cursor to the Immediate window. Clear the Output screen, as follows:

Operation	Operation Symbol	Example
Addition	+	3 + 4
Subtraction	−	3 − 4
Multiplication	*	3 * 4
Division	/	3 / 4

TABLE 4-1   The Arithmetic Operators

```
Press any key to continue
```

FIGURE 4-1 The Output screen after CLS command

Type:
CLS
and press ENTER

The Output screen is now clear of any previous information and contains only the message "Press any key to continue," as shown in Figure 4-1. Press a key to return to QuickBASIC Control. The CLS command and the cursor are in the Immediate window, as shown in Figure 4-2.

In the Immediate window, you will use the PRINT command and the appropriate arithmetic operator to tell the computer to add, subtract, multiply, and divide numbers and display the result in the Output screen. For example, you can add the numbers 3 and 4 and print the result, as follows.

Type:
PRINT 3 + 4
and press ENTER

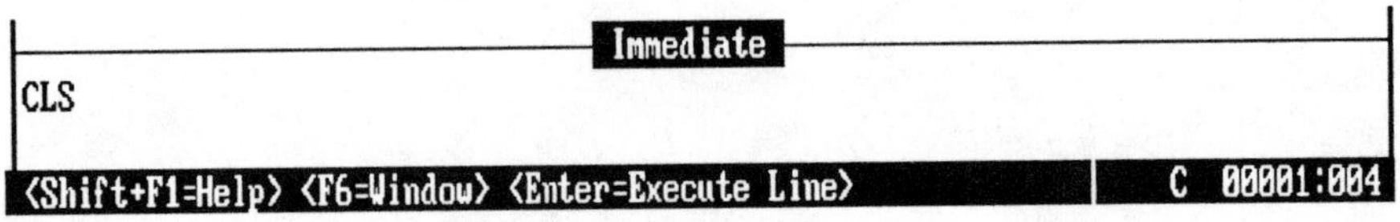

```
┌──────────────────────────────── Immediate ────────────────────────────────┐
│CLS                                                                          │
│                                                                             │
├─────────────────────────────────────────────────────────┬─────────────────┤
│<Shift+F1=Help> <F6=Window> <Enter=Execute Line>          │  C   00001:004  │
```

FIGURE 4-2   CLS command and cursor in the Immediate window

When ENTER is pressed, the computer first adds the numbers (3 + 4), and then prints the result in the Output screen, as shown here:

```
7
```

```
Press any key to continue
```

Return to QuickBASIC Control and subtract, multiply, and divide two numbers. To subtract two numbers, do the following.

Type:
PRINT 3 – 4
and press ENTER

To multiply two numbers, do the following.

Type:
PRINT 3 ∗ 4
and press ENTER

To divide two numbers, do the following.

Type:
PRINT 3 / 4
and press ENTER

The Output screen should now look like the one here, with the results of all four arithmetic operations on the screen. If you make a mistake, use the opportunity to explore and learn more about the on-line help provided by QuickBASIC.

```
 7
-1
 12
 .75
```

```
Press any key to continue
```

Each of the four instructions you just issued consists of the keyword PRINT followed by a numerical expression ($3 + 4$, $3 - 4$, $3 * 4$, or $3 / 4$). The computer evaluates the numerical expression first (does the arithmetic), and then prints the result, a single number.

Notice how the four numbers shown previously were printed: the negative number (-1) was printed beginning in the far left position, but the positive numbers were printed with a blank space in front. Positive numbers (and zero) are always printed with a leading space, while negative numbers are always printed with a leading minus sign ($-$).

PRINT POSITIONS   Sometimes it is useful to print more than one number at a time, possibly lined up in different columns. You can use the PRINT command to print more than one number. The numerical expressions to be printed can be separated by commas (,) or semicolons (;). The separator (, or ;) controls where the numbers will print within a line. Try the following example.

Type:
PRINT 3 + 4, 3 − 4, 3 ∗ 4, 3 / 4

It prints:
7   −1   12   .75

Commas between numerical expressions in a PRINT statement cause the results to be printed in five standard print positions on the screen. Each standard print position is 14 character spaces wide. The standard print positions therefore begin at columns 1, 15, 29, 43, and 57. The following shows positive and negative numbers in the five standard printing positions.

```
12345678901234567890123456789012345678901234567890123456789012345678901234567890
1              2              3              4              5

-1             -2             -3             -4             -5
```

```
Press any key to continue
```

If a PRINT command contains more than five numerical expressions separated by commas, the computer will print five results on each line, using as many lines as required.

You can print results closer together by using semicolons instead of commas to separate expressions. Try the same PRINT command as before, this time using semicolons as separators rather than commas.

Type:
PRINT 3 + 4; 3 − 4; 3 ∗ 4; 3 / 4

It prints:
7   −1   12   .75

Using semicolons as separators in a PRINT command causes positive numbers (or zero) to be printed as a space, the number, and a space. Negative numbers are printed as a minus sign (−), the number, and a space.

More Simple Arithmetic

Now try the following examples, which illustrate more features of Quick-BASIC arithmetic.

Mariko is 57 inches tall. Convert her height to centimeters.

Type:
PRINT 57 * 2.54

It prints:
144.78

People usually give their height in feet and inches. If you ask Mariko how tall she is, she will probably tell you she is 4 feet, 9 inches tall. Convert Mariko's height to inches.

Type:
PRINT 4 * 12 + 9

It prints:
57

The computer first does the multiplication (4 * 12), and then the addition (+ 9). An expression is evaluated in this order: multiplication and division first, and then addition and subtraction.

Given feet and inches, you can write a single PRINT command to compute Mariko's height in centimeters.

Type:
PRINT (4 * 12 + 9) * 2.54

It prints:
144.78

Before he reached his full stature, King Kong was once 37 feet 8 inches tall. How tall was he in centimeters?

Type:
PRINT (37 ∗ 12 + 8) ∗ 2.54

It prints:
1148.08

Note the use of parentheses. The computer does the arithmetic inside the parentheses first, and then does the rest. Here is another example using parentheses.

At the beginning of a driving trip, the odometer showed 19,832 miles. At the end of the trip it read 20,219 miles. The car used 9.3 gallons of gas. How many miles did the car travel per gallon?

Type:
PRINT (20219 − 19832) / 9.3

It prints:
41.6129

Note that commas were not used in typing the numbers 20219 and 19832. Commas may not be used within a number, although commas (and semicolons) may be used to separate numerical expressions in PRINT commands.

EXPONENTS AND FLOATING POINT NUMBERS

Until now, you have been using the arithmetic operators (+, −,∗, /) to add, subtract, multiply, and divide. Now you will use another operator, the exponent (^), to do some more complex calculations. You will also learn about the different number types that you can use in QuickBASIC.

Exponents

If you are shopping for a microwave oven, you will notice that the size of the oven is always given in cubic feet. To make the arithmetic simple, let's say that you are considering buying a microwave oven that is 8 cubic feet. If the oven is a cube, then it is 2 feet wide, 2 feet long, and 2 feet deep. The number of cubic feet, then, is 2*2*2 (= 8) feet. Another way to write this is 2^3 (you would say it as 2 to the third power, or 2 to the power of 3). 2^3 means that 2 is used as a factor three times: 2*2 = 4; 4*2 = 8.

Whenever you see the exponent operator (^), you know that the number before the exponent (in this example, 2) is to be used as a multiplicative factor as many times as the number after the exponent operator (in this example, 3) indicates.

Exponents can be very useful, especially when dealing with large numbers. Consider another example: computer memory capacities. People say a computer has 256K, 512K, 640K, or more bytes of memory. The term "K" comes from the metric term *kilo,* which means 1000. A kilogram is 1000 grams; a kilometer is 1000 meters. The unit 1K therefore means 1000 bytes. However, 1K bytes actually means 2^10 (or 1024) bytes. The number 2^10 is 2 to the power of 10, or 2*2*2*2*2*2*2*2*2*2. Notice how much easier it is to write 2^10 than 2*2*2*2*2*2*2*2*2*2.

The following examples illustrate the use of the exponent operator to compute the actual number of bytes in 1K, 256K, and 512K bytes.

Type:
PRINT 2 ^ 10

It prints:
1024

1K bytes is actually 1024 bytes of memory, not 1000 bytes!
Next, compute the actual number of bytes in a computer with 256K bytes of memory.

Type:
PRINT 256 * 2 ^ 10

It prints:
262144

Since 1K equals 2^10, 256K equals 256 times 2^10. The exponent expression is calculated first, and then that result is multiplied by 256; 256K bytes of memory is actually 262,144 bytes, not 256,000. Now compute the number of bytes in a computer with 512K bytes of memory.

Type:
PRINT 512 * 2 ^ 10

It prints:
524288

Floating Point Numbers

Computer memories are getting bigger. Memories of one, two, or more megabytes are increasingly common. The term *mega* is also borrowed from the metric system. In metric, it means one million. However, in referring to the size of computer memories or hard disk storage capacity, it means 2^20 (2 to the 20th power, or the 20th power of 2).

How many bytes in a megabyte? Use the computer to find out.

Type:
PRINT 2 ^ 20

It prints:
1048576

One megabyte equals 1,048,576 bytes, not 1,000,000 bytes.
Next, compute the number of bytes in a 20-megabyte hard disk.

Type:
PRINT 20 * 2 ^ 20

It prints:
2.097152E+07

20 megabytes equals 20 times 1 megabyte, so 20 megabytes equals 20 times 2^20. QuickBASIC prints this large number as a floating point number. Read it like this: 2.097152E+07 is 2.097152 times 10^7 (10 to the seventh power). Floating point notation is very similar to scientific notation. This number written in scientific notation is 2.097152×10^7. Floating point notation is simply a shorthand way of expressing very large numbers. A floating point number has two parts: a mantissa and an exponent. The mantissa and exponent are separated by the letter "E" (for exponent), as shown here:

```
2.097152E+07
```
Mantissa E
        Exponent

Consider another example, using a very large number. The population of the Earth is about five billion. Tell the computer to print that large number. Remember, though—do not use commas within the number.

Type:
PRINT 5000000000

It prints:
  5E+09

Five billion (5,000,000,000) equals 5 times 10^9, or 5 followed by nine zeroes.

One trillion can be written as 1 followed by 12 zeroes, or 10^12 (10 to the 12th power). Try it both ways.

Type:
PRINT 1000000000000

It prints:
  1E+12

Type:
PRINT 10 ^ 12

It prints:
  1E+12

The national debt of the United States is about three trillion dollars and the population is about 250 million. You can use floating point numbers to compute the debt for each person, as shown in the following example.

Type:
PRINT 3E12 / 250E6

It prints:
  12000

The debt for each person in this country is $12,000!

Three trillion equals 3 times 10^12. In floating point notation, this is 3E+12. Two hundred fifty million equals 250 times 10^6. In floating point notation, this is 250E+6. Note that you can write three trillion as 3E12 instead of 3E+12. Also, note that 250 million can be written as 250E6 instead of 250E+06 or 2.50E+08; all three ways are acceptable.

NUMERIC TYPES

QuickBASIC has several types of numbers: integers, long integers, single precision numbers, double precision numbers, and floating point numbers. So far, you have used three types: integers, single precision numbers, and floating point numbers, examples of which are shown here.

Integers: 3 −1 12 1024
Single precision numbers: .75 1148.08 262144
Floating point numbers: 2.097152E+07 5E+09 1E+12

Each of QuickBASIC's number types is described in the sections that follow.

Integers

An *integer* is a whole number (that is, a number with no decimal point) in the range −32,768 to +32,767. Two bytes of memory are needed to store each integer. An integer is denoted by a percent sign (%) following the number. A *long integer* is a whole number in the range −2,147,483,648 to +2,147,483,647. Four bytes of memory are needed to store a long integer. A long integer is denoted by a number followed by an ampersand (&).

The following example uses a long integer (20&) to force the computer to compute and print the number of bytes in a 20-megabyte hard disk as an "ordinary number" rather than as a floating point number.

Type:
PRINT 20& * 2 ^ 20

It prints:
20971520

You will now explore integers more thoroughly by doing some integer arithmetic. Make sure that the cursor is in the Immediate window, and do the following.

Type:
PRINT 11 * 11

It prints:
 121

Type:
PRINT 111 * 111

It prints:
 12321

In both of these examples, a short integer is multiplied by a short integer; another short integer is the result. However, if two integers are multiplied and the result is not within the range for short integers (−32,768 to +32,767), an error will occur. In the next example, the correct result (1234321) is too large to be stored as a short integer.

Type:
PRINT 1111 * 1111

The Overflow dialog box appears in the View window, as shown in Figure 4-3. QuickBASIC is telling you that the result of the multiplication is too large to be represented as a short integer. It would "overflow" the space (two bytes) allowed for short integers.

This problem has a simple solution. First press ENTER to clear the dialog box. If one of the numbers being multiplied is a long integer, the result will also be a long integer. So, change one of the numbers to a long integer by adding an ampersand, as follows:

Change to:
PRINT 1111 * 1111&

To do this, move the cursor to the right end of the PRINT command, type an ampersand and press ENTER.

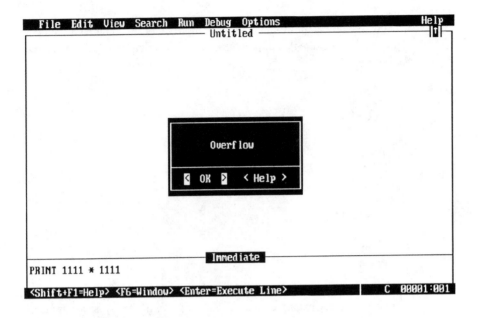

FIGURE 4-3   The Overflow dialog box

Type:
PRINT 1111 * 1111&

It prints:
1234321

Since either number could have been changed to a long integer to correct the overflow, you can also do the following.

Type:
PRINT 1111& * 1111

It prints:
1234321

Note that the result of this multiplication is larger than the range allowed for short integers (–32,768 to +32,767), but is within the range for long integers (–2,147,483,648 to +2,147,483,647).

Try the next two problems in the sequence. Make one of the numbers being multiplied a long integer in each case.

Type:
PRINT 11111 * 11111&

It prints:
123454321

The result (123454321) is within the range for long integers.

Type:
PRINT 111111 * 111111&

The Overflow dialog box is again displayed. The result (12345654321) is too large to be represented as a long integer. There is a simple solution to this problem as well. Before continuing, though, clear the Overflow dialog box by pressing ENTER.

Very large numbers like 12345654321 can be displayed using another number type, double precision numbers. Single and double precision numbers are described in the following section.

Single and Double Precision Numbers

A *single precision number* is a real number of up to seven digits plus a decimal point. A single precision number can have either a whole number (integer) value or a noninteger value in the range – 3.37E+38 to 3.37E+38. A *double precision number* is a real number of up to 16 digits, plus a decimal point. A double precision number can also have an integer or noninteger value; a double precision number is a number in the range –1.67D+308 to 1.67D+308. Both single and double precision numbers are floating point numbers; that is, the decimal point "floats" in its position in the number, depending on the number's value. If the value of a floating point number is too large to be expressed as a simple sequence of digits, it is expressed in floating point notation.

You can identify a number as a single precision number by using an explicit decimal point in the number or by adding an exclamation point (!) to the number. The following examples show single precision number usage.

Type:
PRINT 1111 * 1111.

It prints:
1234321

The second number (1111.) in this example is a single precision number, since the decimal point was explicitly used. The result (1234321) is therefore also a single precision number.

If a single precision number cannot be expressed within seven digits (plus the decimal), it is expressed as a single precision floating point number, as the following example shows.

Type:
PRINT 11111 * 11111.

It prints:
1.234543E+08

Again, since the second number (11111.) includes a decimal point, this number is a single precision number and the result of the multiplication is also a single precision number. The result (123454321) consists of more than seven digits, so it is displayed in floating point notation. To print such large numbers exactly, you can use double precision numbers, which consist of up to 16 digits to the decimal point. To specify a number as a double precision number, append a number symbol (#) to it. Here are some examples using double precision numbers.

Type:
PRINT 11111 * 11111#

It prints:
123454321

One of the two numbers multiplied is a double precision number (11111#), so the result is also a double precision number.

Type:
PRINT 111111 ∗ 111111#

It prints:
12345654321

In this example as well, the result is a double precision number. If you continue this pattern, you will see a double precision floating point number.

Type:
PRINT 111111111 ∗ 111111111#

It prints:
1.234567898765432D+16

A double precision floating point number consists of a mantissa and an exponent separated by the letter "D." The mantissa can have up to 16 digits; the exponent is an integer in the range −308 to +308. Single precision numbers and double precision numbers are actually stored in the computer's memory as floating point numbers. A single precision number uses four bytes of memory space and a double precision number uses eight bytes.

Any number that requires only seven digits of accuracy can be stored as a single precision number, whether that number is large or small. A number that requires 16 digits of accuracy can be stored as a double precision number. A double precision number can be very large, as you have seen, or very small, as in the following example.

The mass of the hydrogen atom is very small; it is about 1.67 times 10 ^ −27 kilograms. Print the mass of the hydrogen atom as both a single precision number and a double precision number. Expressed as a single precision floating point number this is 1.67E−27; as a double precision number it is 1.67D −27. It is, of course, much easier to type 1.67E−27 than to type the following:

.00000000000000000000000000167

Remember: QuickBASIC has four types of numbers. They are summarized here.

- Integers (also called short integers) are whole numbers in the range −32,768 to +32,767. They require two bytes of storage and can be specified by a percent sign (%) following the number.

- Long integers are whole numbers in the range −2,147,483,648 to +2,147,483,647. They require four bytes of storage and are specified by an ampersand (&) following the number.

- Single precision numbers are real numbers (integers or nonintegers) of up to seven digits plus a decimal point in the range −3.37E+38 to 3.37E+38. They require four bytes to store and are specified by an exclamation point (!) following or a decimal point within the number.

- Double precision numbers are real numbers (integers or nonintegers) of up to 16 digits in the range −1.67D+308 to 1.67D+308. They require eight bytes to store and are specified by a number sign (#) following the number.

NUMERIC VARIABLES

The arithmetic that you've just been practicing has been with specific numbers: adding 3 and 4, or multiplying 4 and 12, for example. Usually it is far more useful to print the sum of two numbers without specifying in the command itself the exact numbers to be added or multiplied each time. Numeric variables are used to do this.

A *numeric variable* is a *variable* that represents a number. A variable is identified by a name, but its value at any given time can and does vary. You can think of a variable as similar to a mailbox with the resident's name on it: the contents of the mailbox change every day, but the name on it stays the same. A numeric variable's name, then, is the name on a "number box" in the computer's memory where its value is stored.

A numeric variable is used in much the same way as a number. You can print the value of a variable or add two variables and print the result. You can manipulate a number variable in as many ways as you can a number. Also like a number, a numeric variable is either an integer, a long integer, single precision, or double precision. Since different number types use different amounts of memory (for example, integers use two bytes and double precision numbers use eight bytes), different numeric variable types use different sizes of "number boxes."

A variable is specified by a name. A variable name can be any combination of uppercase and lowercase letters (A to Z, a to z) and digits (0 to 9) up to 40 characters in length. The first character of a variable name must be a letter. A variable name can be followed by a symbol that specifies what kind of number is to be stored in it: % for an integer, & for a long integer, ! for a single precision variable, and # for a double precision variable. If a variable name does not specify with %, &, !, or # what kind of number variable it is, the variable is considered a single precision variable. Here are some sample variable names.

a   x1   pi   Qty   Price   TaxRate
NumberOfShares   PricePerShare

Each of the preceding variables is a single precision variable because none of them contains a symbol specifying a number type. Later you will use integer, long integer, and double precision variables. QuickBASIC does not distinguish between uppercase and lowercase letters; therefore *A* and *a* are the same variable, *X1* and *x1* are the same variable, and *PI* and *pi* are the same. In this book, variable names will appear in lowercase or a mixture of lowercase and uppercase letters. This makes it easy to distinguish variables from keywords (such as PRINT and CLS), which will appear in uppercase letters.

You can assign a value to a variable in much the same way you changed the date and time in Chapter 3, "Introduction to Programming." You can assign a value to a variable in the Immediate window or in a program. First you will assign and print the value of a variable in the Immediate window; later you will write a program that assigns and prints different variable values.

Variable Values

You can use the Immediate window to assign a value to a variable and then print the value of that variable. Go now to the Immediate window, clear the Output screen (type **CLS**), and assign the value 7 to the variable *a*.

Type:
a = 7
(Don't forget to press ENTER.)

The screen flickers a little, indicating that QuickBASIC has reserved a small part of memory (four bytes) as a variable named *a* and assigned the number 7 as the value of *a*. In short, typing **a = 7** tells the computer this: Assign 7 as the value of *a*.

You can use the PRINT command to tell the computer to display the value of a variable on the Output screen.

Type:
PRINT a

It prints:
7

The value of a variable remains the same until you change it. You can verify this by repeating the previous command.

Type:
PRINT a

It prints:
7

The computer has again printed the value of *a*, which is 7.

Now, assign a different number as the value of *a*, then print it. Your new number will replace the old value of *a*.

Type:
a = 1.23

Type:
PRINT a

It prints:
1.23

Assign the value 3.14 to a new variable, *pi,* and print the value of *pi*.

Type:
pi = 3.14

Type:
PRINT pi

It prints:
3.14

Both *pi* and *a* maintain their values until changed. Confirm this by print-ing both variables.

Type:
PRINT pi, a

It prints:
3.14   1.23

In addition to assigning a value to a variable, you can also use variables in computations. For example, you can print the sum of two variables.

Type:
PRINT pi + a

It prints:
4.37

Here is another example of a calculation using a variable: A bicycle has a wheel diameter of 24 inches. How far does the bike travel in one turn of the wheel? The distance is the diameter multiplied by *pi*, calculated like this.

Type:
PRINT pi * 24

It prints:
75.36

The local sales tax rate is 6.0%. Assign this value to the variable *TaxRate*, as follows.

Type:
TaxRate = .06

The variable *TaxRate* is .06 since 6.0% is 6/100, or .06 when stated as a decimal. You can now use *TaxRate* to compute the amount of sales tax for various amounts of money. Here are two examples.

You purchase an item that costs $169. How much sales tax will you pay on this purchase?

Type:
PRINT 169 * TaxRate

It prints:
10.14

You buy a computer game that costs $28.50. How much is the sales tax?

Type:
PRINT 28.50 * TaxRate

It prints:
1.71

If you wish, you can compute the amount of sales tax and assign it to its own variable called, for example, *SalesTax*. Having done so, you can then print the value of *SalesTax*.

Type:
SalesTax = 28.50 * TaxRate

Type:
PRINT SalesTax

It prints:
1.71

Here is another example.

Type:
SalesTax = 225 * TaxRate

Type:
PRINT SalesTax

It prints:
13.5

PROGRAMMING WITH VARIABLES

The computer becomes a much more powerful and useful tool if you create programs that perform calculations using variables rather than specifying the numbers to be added or multiplied in the program itself. The program can then do most of the work automatically. Figure 4-4 shows a program in the View window that uses two variables (*TaxRate* and *SalesTax*) to calculate and print the sales tax on a purchase of $225.

To type this program, return to the View window (press F6), access the File menu (ALT+F), and select New Program. This will erase any old program in memory and clear all variables. It is a good idea to do this before entering any new program.

Type each line in the program, pressing ENTER after each line. Remember, you can enter keywords in lowercase and QuickBASIC will change them to uppercase. Enter the variable names (*TaxRate* and *SalesTax*) exactly as shown in Figure 4-4; QuickBASIC will not change them. Once you have finished typing the program, run it by selecting Start on the Run menu (ALT +R). Notice that the result is the same as when you executed these commands in the Immediate window.

This Sales Tax program would be much more useful if you could enter the sales amount as a variable when the program runs, rather than as a specific assignment within the program itself. There is a way to do this, which is explained in the following section.

The INPUT Keyword

The INPUT keyword takes a value entered during program execution and assigns it to a variable. This variable can then be manipulated within the

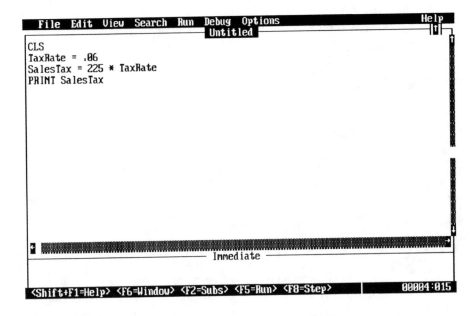

FIGURE 4-4   The Sales Tax program in the View window

program, as can any other variable. The program that follows illustrates the use of the INPUT keyword. Make the necessary changes to the program in Figure 4-4 so your program now looks like this:

```
CLS
TaxRate = .06          (or assign the sales tax rate for
                       your locality)
INPUT SalesAmount
SalesTax = SalesAmount * TaxRate
PRINT SalesTax
```

After you enter the program, the screen should appear as in Figure 4-5.

It is a very good idea to save a program immediately, even before you run it. Use the File menu to save this program with the name QBME0401.BAS. Then, if you lose the program unexpectedly (if the electricity goes out, for example), you can retrieve it from the disk in its original form. Now use the Run menu to run the program. The Output screen is clear, except for a question mark (?) and the blinking cursor in the upper left corner, as shown here:

?_

The computer is executing the INPUT statement (INPUT *SalesAmount*). This statement tells the computer to

- type a question mark

- turn on the cursor

- wait for someone to type a number and press ENTER

When you type a number and press ENTER, the computer assigns the number you typed as the value of *SalesAmount* and goes on to use this amount to calculate and print the amount of sales tax.

Suppose the amount of the sale is $169; enter this amount.

Type:
169

It prints:
10.14

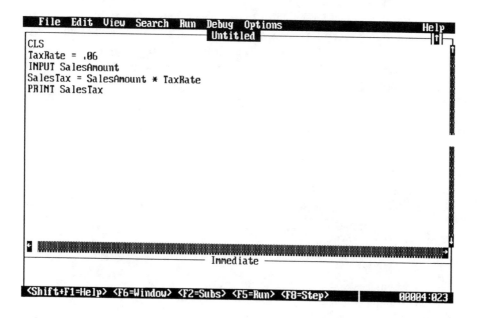

FIGURE 4-5   The Sales Tax program with INPUT command

The computer calculates the sales tax and assigns it as the value of *Sales-Tax,* and then prints the value of *SalesTax* (10.14). Since this is the end of the program, the familiar message "Press any key to continue" appears at the bottom of the screen, as shown here:

```
? 169
 10.14
```

```
Press any key to continue
```

Run the program again and enter a different amount of sale. Try $1, $10, or $100 so you can easily verify that the program is running correctly and producing the right answers. Then examine the program—it works as described in Table 4-2.

The INPUT statement tells the computer to put a question mark on the screen and wait for a number to be entered. This is useful, but it would be much more useful if you could identify what sort of input the computer is waiting for. Again, there is a way to do this. The following program is an improved version of the sales tax program, featuring an "enhanced" INPUT statement.

```
CLS
TaxRate = .06
INPUT "Amount of sale"; SalesAmount
SalesTax = SalesAmount * TaxRate
PRINT SalesTax
```

You can edit the old program to change it to the improved program. Move the cursor under the "S" in *SalesAmount,* as follows:

```
 File  Edit  View  Search  Run  Debug  Options                     Help
                           Untitled
CLS
TaxRate = .06
INPUT SalesAmount
SalesTax = SalesAmount * TaxRate
PRINT SalesTax
        _
```

Type the additional text. Any characters at and to the right of the cursor will move to the right, making room for the new text as you type. The modified INPUT statement should look like this:

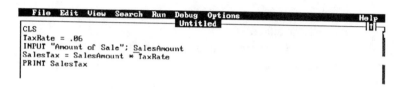

```
 File  Edit  View  Search  Run  Debug  Options                     Help
                           Untitled
CLS
TaxRate = .06
INPUT "Amount of Sale"; SalesAmount
SalesTax = SalesAmount * TaxRate
PRINT SalesTax
```

Program Line	Explanation
CLS	Clear the Output screen
TaxRate = .06	Assign .06 as the value of TaxRate
INPUT SalesAmount	Display a question mark and wait for a number to be entered. This number is then assigned as the value of SalesAmount
SalesTax = SalesAmount * TaxRate	Compute the amount of sales tax and assign it as the value of SalesTax
PRINT SalesTax	Print the value of SalesTax

TABLE 4-2   The Sales Tax Program Explained

Do not press ENTER. If you pressed ENTER the INPUT statement would be broken into two lines, as shown next.

```
 File  Edit  View  Search  Run  Debug  Options                    Help
                            Untitled
CLS
TaxRate = .06
INPUT "Amount of Sale";
SalesAmount
SalesTax = SalesAmount * TaxRate
PRINT SalesTax
```

To correct this, you would press BACKSPACE to bring the two parts of the line back together.

Save the program under the file name QBME0402 and run it. A sample run is shown here:

```
Amount of sale? 345
20.7
```

```
Press any key to continue
```

The statement INPUT "Amount of sale"; *SalesAmount* tells the computer to do the following:

- Print the message "Amount of sale"

- Print a question mark

- Wait for a number to be entered and assign it as the value of *SalesAmount*

Note that the message to be displayed is enclosed in quotation marks and followed by a semicolon.

Now change the program so that it identifies the result as the amount of sales tax. The modified program is shown in the next listing. Be sure to type all punctuation, including quotation marks (") and the semicolon (;) at the end of the first PRINT statement.

```
CLS
TaxRate = .06
INPUT "Amount of sale"; SalesAmount
SalesTax = SalesAmount * TaxRate
PRINT "Amount of sales tax is ";
PRINT SalesTax
```

Save this program under the file name QBME0403 and run it. A sample run is shown here:

```
Amount of sale? 187
Amount of sales tax is  11.22
```

```
Press any key to continue
```

Formatting Commands

The next version of the sales tax program is considerably expanded. It prints the amount of sale entered from the keyboard, the amount of the sales tax, and the total amount of the sale, including sales tax. The TAB function is used to line the numbers up vertically. Blank lines are added to make the program easier to read.

```
CLS
TaxRate = .06

INPUT "Amount of sale"; SalesAmount

SalesTax = SalesAmount * TaxRate
TotalAmount = SalesAmount + SalesTax
PRINT
PRINT "Amount of sale is"; TAB(40);
PRINT SalesAmount

PRINT "Amount of sales tax is"; TAB(40);
PRINT SalesTax

PRINT "Total amount is"; TAB(40);
PRINT TotalAmount
```

Notice several new things in this program.

- The program itself is more readable with blank lines breaking it into separate blocks. These blank lines do not affect the result of the program at all—they are there only for you, the programmer.

- The PRINT keyword on a line by itself causes a blank line to be printed in the Output screen. You can control and improve the appearance of the Output screen by using PRINT instructions appropriately throughout your program.

- The TAB function tells the computer to move the cursor to the column specified in the parentheses, and then to print the number that follows. The TAB function allows you to line up text or numbers.

Save this program with the name QBME0404 and run it. A sample run is shown here:

```
Amount of sale? 200

Amount of sale is                       200
Amount of sales tax is                  12
Total amount is                         212




Press any key to continue
```

THE PRINT USING COMMAND   Although *SalesAmount, SalesTax,* and *TotalAmount* are all printed beginning in the 40th column, the dollar amounts do not line up correctly. To solve this problem, there is a variation of the PRINT command that allows you to line up columns of numbers along the decimal point. The program in Figure 4-6 illustrates this new command. The PRINT USING formatting command allows you to control the positioning of several numbers, and thus line them up along the decimal point.

The following statement tells the computer to print the value of *Sales-Amount* with up to five digits before the decimal point, two digits following the decimal point, rounded if necessary:

PRINT USING "#####.##"; *SalesAmount*

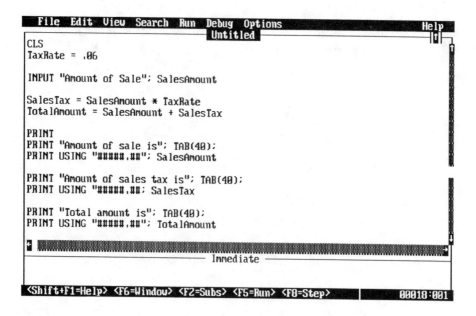

```
 File  Edit  View  Search  Run  Debug  Options                Help
                            Untitled
CLS
TaxRate = .06

INPUT "Amount of Sale"; SalesAmount

SalesTax = SalesAmount * TaxRate
TotalAmount = SalesAmount + SalesTax

PRINT
PRINT "Amount of sale is"; TAB(40);
PRINT USING "#####.##"; SalesAmount

PRINT "Amount of sales tax is"; TAB(40);
PRINT USING "#####.##"; SalesTax

PRINT "Total amount is"; TAB(40);
PRINT USING "#####.##"; TotalAmount

                           Immediate

<Shift+F1=Help> <F6=Window> <F2=Subs> <F5=Run> <F8=Step>        00018:001
```

FIGURE 4-6   The Sales Tax program with PRINT USING formatting

Save this program with the name QBME0405 and run it. Since all three numbers are printed with the same PRINT USING format, they line up along the decimal, as shown in this sample run:

```
Amount of sale? 200

Amount of sale is                     200.00
Amount of sales tax is                 12.00
Total amount is                       212.00
```

```
Press any key to continue
```

The PRINT USING format statement has many variations. Among the most useful of these are printing dollar signs ($) before numbers and automatically putting commas in very large numbers. The following program has been modified to print dollar signs before all amounts and to put commas in large amounts as needed.

```
CLS
TaxRate = .06

INPUT "Amount of sale"; SalesAmount

SalesTax = SalesAmount * TaxRate
TotalAmount = SalesAmount + SalesTax

PRINT
PRINT "Amount of sale is"; TAB(40);
PRINT USING "$$###,###,###.##"; SalesAmount

PRINT "Amount of sales tax is"; TAB(40);
PRINT USING "$$###,###,###.##"; SalesTax

PRINT "Total amount is"; TAB(40);
PRINT USING "$$###,###,###.##"; TotalAmount
```

Modify QBME0405.BAS so that the PRINT USING statements appear as they do in the preceding program. Save the modified program with the name QBME0406 and run it. Enter an amount over $1000 for the sales amount. Notice, as in this sample run,

```
Amount of sale? 3700

Amount of sale is            $3,700.00
Amount of sales tax is         $222.00
Total amount is              $3,922.00




Press any key to continue
```

that the resulting numbers still line up along the decimal point, but now they are preceded by dollar signs and, if the number is large enough, commas appear where they should.

In particular, the format string *$$###,###,###.##* tells the computer to print a number, as follows:

- The double dollar sign ($$) causes a dollar sign to be printed to the left of the number.

- The 12 number signs (#) separated by commas allow up to 12 digits of the number to be printed, with commas inserted every three digits, as needed. If fewer than 12 digits are printed, spaces are printed instead, in this case to the left of the dollar sign.

- The decimal point causes a decimal point to be printed in the number.

- The two number signs to the right of the decimal point cause two digits to be printed to the right of the decimal point in the printed number. If necessary, the number being printed will be rounded to two places.

Program Remarks

It is good practice to put information at the beginning of a program that briefly describes what the program is doing and gives other information such as the date of the last change. The REM (REMark) statement allows you to do this. Any text that follows REM in a program line is ignored when the program is executed. Add some remarks to the sales tax program similar to those in the last, and final (for now), version of the program, shown in the listing that follows. Save the program with the name QBME0407.

```
REM ** QBME0407.BAS **
'    ** 1/1/90 **
'    ** Sales Tax Program **
'    ** Calculates the amount of sales tax and total
'       sales amount **
' QuickBASIC Made Easy, Chapter 4
' Microsoft QuickBASIC 4.5

CLS
TaxRate = .06

INPUT "Amount of sale"; Salesamount

SalesTax = SalesAmount * TaxRate
TotalAmount = SalesAmount + SalesTax

PRINT
PRINT "Amount of sale is"; TAB(40);
PRINT USING "$$###,###,###.##"; SalesAmount

PRINT "Amount of sales tax is"; TAB(40);
PRINT USING "$$###,###,###.##"; SalesTax

PRINT "Total amount is"; TAB(40);
PRINT USING "$$###,###,###.##"; TotalAmount
```

The first seven lines provide information about the program: its name, the date you last changed it, a brief description of what the program is supposed to do, what chapter it appeared in, and what version of QuickBASIC was used. Note the use of the apostrophe (') in the sixth line; the apostrophe can be used as an abbreviation of REM. Any text following ' or REM is ignored when the program is run.

The second line contains the date you last worked on the program. It is a good idea to put this in your programs because it is easy to get old and new versions of a program mixed up. You can tell which of two copies of your program is more current by comparing the dates. You can, of course, add other information to your programs if you wish. Remember, this information is only for you, the programmer. It is ignored by the computer.

Run QBME0407. Notice the Output screen shown here:

```
Amount of sale? 3700

Amount of sale is              $3,700.00
Amount of sales tax is           $222.00
Total amount is                $3,922.00




Press any key to continue
```

Adding the remark lines did not change the execution of the program.

Other Types of Numeric Variables

So far you have used only single precision variables in your programs. They are often sufficient to calculate the value you need. Sometimes, however, it is necessary to deal with very large numbers. When this happens, you will use double precision variables rather than single precision variables to calculate your results.

A STOCK VALUE PROGRAM   If you own or trade stocks, you might find the next program useful. It computes and prints the value of a block of shares of a stock, given the number of shares and the price per share.

```
REM ** QBME0408.BAS **
'    ** 1/1/90 **
'    ** Value of Stocks **
'    ** Calculates the value of stocks **
' QuickBASIC Made Easy, Chapter 4
' Microsoft QuickBASIC 4.5

CLS

INPUT "Number of shares"; NumberOfShares
INPUT "Price per share"; PricePerShare

Value = NumberOfShares * PricePerShare

PRINT
PRINT "The value is ";
PRINT USING "$$#####.##"; Value
```

Save this program under the file name shown in the first line of the program (QBME0408.BAS) and run it. The results of a sample run are shown here:

```
Number of shares? 1200
Price per share? 37.25
The value is $44700.00
```

If you own or trade very large volumes of stocks, QBME0408.BAS may not be able to handle large enough numbers since all of the variables are single precision. Modify QBME0408.BAS so that it uses double precision variables, and will therefore handle numbers of up to 16 digits properly. Save the new program as QBME0409.

```
REM ** QBME0409.BAS **
'    ** 1/1/90 **
'    ** Value of Stocks **
'    ** Calculates the value of stocks using double
'        precision variables **
' QuickBASIC Made Easy, Chapter 4
' Microsoft QuickBASIC 4.5

CLS

INPUT "Number of shares"; NumberOfShares#
INPUT "Price per share "; PricePerShare#

Value# = NumberOfShares# * PricePerShare#

PRINT
```

```
PRINT "The value is ";
PRINT USING "$$############,.##"; Value#
```

Note the format of the PRINT USING statement. The format string $$############,.## is equivalent to the format string $$###,###,###.##, which you used previously. In either case, commas will be printed every three digits, as needed.

A number sign after a variable name defines that variable as a double precision variable. The following are double precision variables:

```
NumberOfShares#
PricePerShare#
Value#
```

A sample run of QBME0409.BAS is shown here:

```
Number of shares? 100000
Price per share? 125

The value is      $12,500,000.00
```

```
Press any key to continue
```

Notice the commas in the result, as well as the large value ($12,500,000.00), which you are now able to calculate.

A FUTURE VALUE—COMPOUND INTEREST PROGRAM   Let's suppose you keep your money in a bank account that pays regular interest, compounded periodically. Here is a program that computes the value of money (principal) invested at a particular interest rate per period, compounded for a given number of periods.

Before looking at the program, examine the following sample runs and think about how you would write the program. The first sample is for $1 invested at 1% interest, compounded for 1 period. This is used to test the program. The answer should be $1.01.

```
Sample run #1:

Principal amount invested ($)? 1
```

```
Interest rate per period (%) ? 1
Number of interest periods   ? 1
At maturity, the value will be              $1.01
```

Now suppose you have a balance of $500 on a credit card that charges 1.5% interest per month and you put off paying it for 12 months.

```
Sample run #2:

Principal amount invested ($)? -500
Interest rate per period (%) ? 1.5
Number of interest periods   ? 12
At maturity, the value will be            -$597.81
```

The "investment" is entered as −500 as a reminder that you owe $500 and that you are therefore paying the interest. The result is −$597.81.

You might find it helpful to write an outline of the program in REM statements first. The next listing shows a possible outline.

```
REM ** QBME0410.BAS **
'    ** 1/1/90 **
'    ** Future Value of Money -- Compound Interest **
'    ** Calculate the future value of an investment,
'       earning interest, for a number of periods **
' QuickBASIC Made Easy, Chapter 4
' Microsoft QuickBASIC 4.5

REM ** Clear the screen **

REM ** Get principal, interest rate, nbr of periods **

REM ** Compute & print future value of investment **
```

Once you have an outline for your program, you can expand it as shown next.

```
REM ** QBME0410.BAS **
'    ** 1/1/90 **
'    ** Future Value of Money -- Compound Interest **
'    ** Calculate the future value of an investment,
'       earning interest, for a number of periods **
' QuickBASIC Made Easy, Chapter 4
' Microsoft QuickBASIC 4.5

REM ** Clear the screen **
CLS
```

```
REM ** Get principal, interest rate, nbr of periods **
INPUT "Principal amount invested ($)"; Principal#
INPUT "Interest rate per period (%) "; InterestRate!
INPUT "Number of interest periods   "; Periods%

REM ** Compute & print future value of investment **
InterestRate! = InterestRate! / 100
FutureValue# = Principal# * (1+InterestRate!) ^ Periods%
PRINT "At maturity, the value will be ";
PRINT USING "$$############,.##"; FutureValue#
```

The program has four blocks. Each block begins with a REM (or ′) statement that tells what the block does. The first block gives the name of the program, the date it was written, a description of the program, where it was first published, and the version of BASIC in which it is written.

The second block clears the screen; if there were any other program setup to do, this block would do that as well.

The third block uses INPUT statements to get values for the three variables used to compute the amount of interest and future value. These three types of variables are used:

- *Principal#* is a double precision variable, useful for handling large values.

- *InterestRate!* is a single precision variable. Since interest rates aren't usually very large, this should be large enough.

- *Periods%* is an integer variable. It is assumed that the number of periods will be an integer in the range −32,768 and +32,767.

The fourth block calculates and prints the future value. The interest rate is first converted to a decimal fraction, then used in the formula to compute the future value. A variation of the program is shown next. It asks for the principal, the yearly interest rate, the number of times per year the interest is compounded, and the number of interest periods.

```
REM ** QBME0411.BAS **
'     ** 1/1/90 **
'     ** Future Value of Money -- Compound Interest **
'     ** Calculate the future value of an investment,the
'        earning interest, for a number of periods **
' QuickBASIC Made Easy, Chapter 4
' Microsoft QuickBASIC 4.5

REM ** Clear the screen **
CLS
```

```
REM ** Get principal, interest rate, nbr of periods **
INPUT "Principal amount invested ($)"; Principal#
INPUT "Interest rate per year (%)    "; InterestRate!
INPUT "Interest periods per year     "; PeriodsPerYear%
INPUT "Number of interest periods    "; Periods%

REM ** Compute & print future value of investment **
PeriodRate! = InterestRate! / PeriodsPerYear% / 100
FutureValue# = Principal# * (1+PeriodRate!) ^ Periods%
PRINT "At maturity, the value will be ";
PRINT USING "$$############,.##"; FutureValue#
```

Here are four sample runs to illustrate the usefulness of this program. Sample run #1 is for an investment of $1000 at 12% per year, compounded annually for one year:

```
Sample run #1:

Principal amount invested ($)? 1000
Interest rate per year (%)    ? 12
Interest periods per year     ? 1
Number of interest periods    ? 1
At maturity, the value will be            $1,120.00
```

Sample run #2 is for an investment of $1000 earning 12% per year, compounded monthly for 12 months:

```
Sample run #2:

Principal amount invested ($)? 1000
Interest rate per year (%)    ? 12
Interest periods per year     ? 12
Number of interest periods    ? 12
At maturity, the value will be            $1,126.83
```

Sample run #3 is for an investment of $1000 at 12% per year compounded weekly for 52 weeks:

```
Sample run #3:

Principal amount invested ($)? 1000
Interest rate per year (%)    ? 12
Interest periods per year     ? 52
Number of interest periods    ? 52
At maturity, the value will be            $1,127.34
```

Sample run #4 is for an investment of $1000 earning 12% per year compounded daily for 365 days:

```
Sample run #4:

Principal amount invested ($)? 1000
Interest rate per year (%)    ? 12
Interest periods per year     ? 365
Number of interest periods    ? 365
At maturity, the value will be              $1,127.47
```

Suppose the interest is compounded hourly, 24 hours a day, for a year. The number of interest periods is 24 * 365 = 8760. If the interest is compounded every minute, that's 525,600 interest periods per year. If compounded every second the result is 31,536,000 periods per year. Since a short integer variable (identified as %) is limited to the range –32,768 to +32,767, modify the program to use long integers for the number of interest periods per year and for the number of interest periods. Save the modified program as QBME0412.BAS. The program should look like this:

```
REM ** QBME0412.BAS **
'    ** 6/7/88 **
'    ** Future Value of Money -- Compound Interest **
'    ** Calculate the future value of an investment,
'        earning interest, for a number of periods **
' QuickBASIC Made Easy, Chapter 4
' Microsoft QuickBASIC 4.5

REM ** Clear the screen **
CLS

REM ** Get principal, interest rate, nbr of periods **
INPUT "Principal amount invested ($)"; Principal#
INPUT "Interest rate per year (%)   "; InterestRate!
INPUT "Interest periods per year    "; PeriodsPerYear&
INPUT "Number of interest periods   "; Periods&

REM ** Compute & print future value of investment **
PeriodRate! = InterestRate! / PeriodsPerYear& / 100
FutureValue# = Principal# * (1+PeriodRate!) ^ Periods&
PRINT "At maturity, the value will be ";
PRINT USING "$$#############,.##"; FutureValue#
```

Run this program, compounding every minute for a year (525,600 interest periods) and compounding every second for a year (31,536,000 interest periods). Note that little is gained by compounding more frequently than daily.

Printing a Program

When you complete a program and have tested it completely, it is usually a good idea to print a copy of it. A printed copy of a program is called a *listing*. You can use listings for backup in case anything happens to your program. You can also use them when you are modifying and enhancing a program—you can make changes on paper, then try them out on the computer.

To print a copy of the program currently in the View window, make sure that your printer is turned on, ready to print, with plenty of paper. Access the File menu (ALT + F), then select Print.... The Print dialog box will appear in the middle of the View window, with the third option, Current Module, active (Figure 4-7). Print the current module by pressing ENTER. When the listing is done, the dialog box is cleared and you are returned to the View window.

Print a copy of each of the programs used in this chapter, noting the differences and similarities between them. Use the Open Program option on the File menu to load each program, then use the Print... option on this menu to print it.

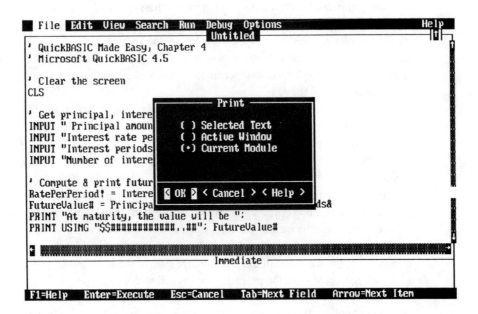

FIGURE 4-7   The Print dialog box

The arithmetic operators (+, −, *, /) and the exponent operator (^) are used to make calculations. You can use the Immediate window or write a program to figure and print your results. Depending on the value of the numbers that you are manipulating, you may use one of the following four number types:

- An *integer,* denoted by a percent sign (%) following the number or variable, is a whole number in the range −32,768 to +32,767.

- A *long integer,* denoted by an ampersand (&) added to the number or variable, is a whole number in the range −2,147,483,648 to +2,147,483,647.

- A *single precision number,* denoted by an exclamation mark (!) added to the number or variable, is a real number of up to seven digits, plus a decimal point. If a number is too large to be represented in seven digits, the number is expressed in floating point notation, rounded to seven digits with an exponent.

- A *double precision number,* denoted by a number sign (#) added to the number or variable, is a real number of up to 16 digits, plus the decimal point. If a number cannot be expressed simply in 16 digits, then it is converted to floating point notation.

A *numeric variable* represents number values that are one of the four number types. A variable is used to represent values that vary. A variable name can be any combination of uppercase and lowercase letters and numbers; the first character of the variable name, however, must be a letter. QuickBASIC makes no distinction between uppercase and lowercase letters in a variable name: *pi* and *PI* are the same.

To make a program more general, the INPUT keyword is used to ask for user input of values during program execution. The INPUT command can be modified to state explicitly what input is expected at a given time.

The PRINT USING statement is used to control the format of numbers when they are displayed. Using this statement, a column of numbers that line up along the decimal can easily be printed. The PRINT USING formatting options include leading dollar signs and comma formatting in large numbers.

Remarks should be included in all programs to make them easier to read and understand. All programs should include a descriptive block at the top, consisting of the file name of the program, the date of the last change, and a brief description of what the program is supposed to do.

Use the Print... option on the File menu to print a copy of the program in the View window. Print a copy of all of the programs used in this chapter and study them, noticing how they are alike and how they differ.

Experiment with the stock value program and the compound interest program to see the effect that different number types make in computing values of small and very large amounts.

5

MAKING PROGRAMS MORE USEFUL

String Variables
The DO...LOOP Structure
The QuickBASIC Rainbow
Making Music

In this chapter you will learn about another kind of variable, a string variable. You will also learn some new ways to control the operation of your programs. You will learn how to make a program that loops, repeating itself automatically, and to control how long these looping programs run. You will also learn how to print the results of a program on your printer. In particular you will

- Learn what string variables are and how to assign values to them

- Learn to use the INPUT statement to assign a value to a string variable

- Learn how to use the string function INKEY$ to store the value of a key when it is pressed

- Learn how to use the DO...LOOP structure to make your programs loop

- Learn how to use the LPRINT statement to print output on your printer

- Learn how to use the IF...THEN conditional construct

- Learn how to use the COLOR keyword to change the color of your screen or the color of your text

- Learn how to use the SOUND keyword to make "music" using your computer

- Learn how to interrupt a running program with CTRL + BREAK

- Learn how to use SCROLL LOCK to "freeze" and "unfreeze" a program that is running

STRING VARIABLES

You learned about numeric variables in Chapter 4, "Number Crunching." There is, however, another kind of variable: the string variable. A *string variable* represents a sequence of characters. A character is any letter (uppercase or lowercase), number, space, or other symbol you can type on the keyboard. Like numeric variables, string variables are used to store information that varies, but unlike numeric variables, they store non-numeric information. They can be used, for example, to store a name and address, date of birth, or telephone number.

A string variable is specified by a name followed by a dollar sign ($). The name can be any combination of letters and numbers, but the first character must be a letter. Here are some examples of string variables:

FirstName$	*Address$*	*DateOfBirth$*
TIME$	*DATE$*	*Description$*

The names of these variables give you some idea of the importance and usefulness of string variables. Note that two of these, *TIME$* and *DATE$,* are already familiar to you. They are string variables; they are also QuickBASIC keywords. QuickBASIC automatically assigns the current system time to *TIME$* and the current system date to *DATE$.*

You can assign a value to a string variable in the same way that you assign a value to a numeric variable. Use the New Program option on the File menu to clear the View window (do this with each new program), and then enter the following program. This program assigns a value to the variable *FirstName$* and prints the value of *FirstName$* on the Output screen.

```
CLS
FirstName$ = "George"

PRINT FirstName$
```

Now change the program to assign a last name to *LastName$* and print it. One possible program is shown here:

```
CLS
FirstName$ = "George"
LastName$ = "Firedrake"

PRINT FirstName$
PRINT LastName$
```

Using INPUT with String Variables

You can assign a value to a string variable when a program is running with the INPUT keyword. You can use an INPUT statement with string variables just as you have already done with numeric variables. The following program prints the current date and time and then assigns the name typed during program execution to the variable *MyName$* and prints it on the screen.

```
CLS
PRINT "The date is "; DATE$
PRINT "The time is "; TIME$
PRINT

INPUT "What is your name"; MyName$

PRINT "Your name is "; MyName$
```

Note that *DATE$* and *TIME$* are automatically assigned values by Quick-BASIC. As you learned in an earlier chapter, however, you can reset the current date and time by assigning new values to those variables just as you would to any other string variable. The next program, QBME0501.BAS, asks for the current date and time, and assigns those values to *DATE$* and *TIME$*. It then asks your name and address, and prints them in the middle of the screen.

```
REM ** QBME0501.BAS ***
'    ** 1/1/90 **
'    ** Input String Variables Program **
'    ** Practice assigning and printing string
'        variables **
' QuickBASIC Made Easy, Chapter 5
' Microsoft QuickBASIC 4.5

REM ** Clear screen, print date and time **
CLS
PRINT "The date is "; DATE$
PRINT "The time is "; TIME$
PRINT

REM ** Ask date and time **
INPUT "The new date is"; NewDate$
INPUT "The new time is"; NewTime$

REM ** Assign new current date and time **
DATE$ = NewDate$
TIME$ = NewTime$

REM ** Ask name and address **
INPUT "What is your name"; MyName$
INPUT "What is your address - line 1"; AddressLine1$
INPUT "What is your address - line 2"; AddressLine2$

REM ** Print new date and time, name and address **
PRINT
PRINT
PRINT "The new date is ";DATE$
PRINT "The new time is ";TIME$
PRINT
PRINT TAB(35); MyName$
PRINT TAB(35); AddressLine1$
PRINT TAB(35); AddressLine2$
```

A sample run of this program is shown here:

```
The date is 01-01-1990
The time is 08:19:05

The new date is? 01-01-1990
The new time is? 10:30
What is your name? George Firedrake
What is your address - line 1? 303 Red Road
What is your address - line 2? Somewhere
```

```
The new date is 01-01-1990
The new time is 10:30:22
```

```
                         George Firedrake
                         303 Red Road
                         Somewhere
```

```
Press any key to continue
```

Run it several times, changing it to ask for other information, such as telephone number and birthday. Experiment with the appearance of the Output screen; try clearing the screen again after the INPUT statement, or printing each line with different TAB values.

THE DO...LOOP STRUCTURE

The programs that you have written so far execute one line at a time, with each line in the program processed only once. In this section, you will learn how to make programs that "loop back" and repeat, so that parts of the program are executed several times. This feature can be very useful, especially when the same process must be executed more than once to produce the desired result. One of the structures you can use to make parts of a program repeat is DO...LOOP. DO...LOOP causes all or part of a program to be repeated until you interrupt it or instruct it to stop.

Simple DO...LOOP Structures

Enter the following simple program.

```
DO
  PRINT "Hold down CTRL and press BREAK to stop"
LOOP
```

(If you are using one of the Tandy 1000 computers, replace BREAK with HOLD.)

It is a very good practice to indent the lines within a DO...LOOP structure, although it is not necessary to do so. When those line are indented, the program is much easier to read and understand; this will become clear later when you use the DO...LOOP structure in more complex programs. In this book, lines that appear between DO and LOOP will always be indented.

Now run the program you just entered. The screen quickly fills with the message in the PRINT statement. Look at the bottom line of the screen: it flickers. The flicker is caused by the rapid scrolling of the message up the screen. When a new message is printed at the bottom of the screen, the others are pushed one line up and the top line disappears, just as commands entered in the Immediate window disappear when new commands are entered. This happens so fast that you cannot see the scrolling; only the flicker indicates that it is occurring.

The PRINT statement between DO and LOOP will be repeated until you stop the program. To stop the program you must press CTRL and BREAK simultaneously (CTRL + HOLD on Tandy 1000 computers).

Press:
CTRL

and then, while still pressing CTRL,

Press:
BREAK

This will interrupt the program. You will see a screen similar to the one shown in Figure 5-1.

When you interrupt a program by pressing CTRL + BREAK, you are returned to QuickBASIC Control; the instruction that was being executed when you interrupted the program is highlighted. In this short program, the word "LOOP" is most likely to be highlighted.

The program you have entered in the View window is a very simple example of a DO...LOOP structure. The program that follows is another example of a simple DO...LOOP structure. This program continuously prints the time until you interrupt it.

```
DO
  PRINT TIME$
LOOP
```

If you watch as the program runs, you will see the seconds, minutes, and hours change. Notice the lines scrolling as new information is printed at the bottom of the screen.

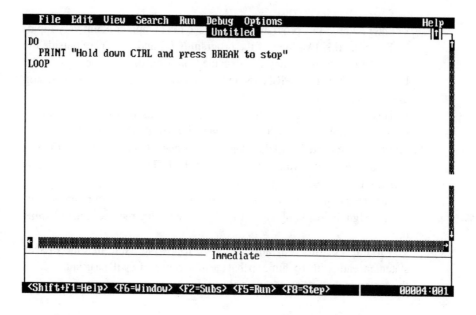

FIGURE 5-1   DO...LOOP program in View window after CTRL + BREAK

Multiple-Line DO...LOOP Structures

The two programs involving DO...LOOP structures that you have just entered and run have only one line between the DO statement and the LOOP statement. A DO...LOOP structure can, however, contain any number of lines between the DO and LOOP statements. In the following program, a two-line DO...LOOP structure is used to count consecutively. This program prints the values 1, 2, 3, 4, 5, and so on, until it is interrupted.

```
CLS

x = 1

DO
  PRINT x
  x = x + 1
LOOP
```

Enter and run this program; you will see the computer count very rapidly. Since the first two lines of the program (CLS and x = 1) are outside the DO...LOOP structure, they are executed only once. The lines inside the DO...LOOP structure (PRINT x and x = x + 1) are repeated until you stop the program.

This program first clears the screen (CLS) and assigns the value 1 to the numeric variable x ($x = 1$). The two statements inside the DO...LOOP structure are then repeated until the program is stopped. Each time DO...LOOP is executed, the current value of x is printed (PRINT x), then the value of x is increased by 1 ($x = x + 1$).

The statement $x = x + 1$ tells the computer to add 1 to the current value of x and assign the resulting value to x. This new value replaces the old value of x.

Variations of this program are shown following. Note that the PRINT statement ends with a comma so that the new values of x will be printed across the screen in the five standard print positions.

```
Variation #1.        Print the odd integers (1, 3, 5, etc.)

CLS

x = 1

DO
  PRINT x,
  x = x + 2
LOOP


*********************************************************

Variation #2. Print the even integers (2, 4, 6, etc.)

CLS

x = 2

DO
  PRINT x,
  x = x + 2
LOOP


*********************************************************

Variation #3. Count by tens (10, 20, 30, etc.)

CLS
```

```
x = 10

DO
  PRINT x,
  x = x + 10
LOOP
***********************************************************

Variation #4. Count by hundreds (100, 200, 300, etc.)

CLS

x = 100
DO
  PRINT x,
  x = x + 100
LOOP
```

Enter and run each of these programs; press CTRL + BREAK to interrupt them. Note that the four programs are very similar, differing only in the initial value assigned to *x*, and the number added to *x* in the DO...LOOP.

FREEZING AND UNFREEZING THE SCREEN Sometimes it is helpful to "freeze" the screen so that you can study the results of a program without breaking out of it and returning to QuickBASIC Control.

Press:
SCROLL LOCK

(Press HOLD on Tandy 1000 computers.)
Run the program that is currently in the View window; then press SCROLL LOCK to freeze the screen. Use the same key to "unfreeze" the screen and resume running the program,

Press:
SCROLL LOCK

(Press HOLD again on Tandy 1000 computers.)
Press SCROLL LOCK again now and the program will continue running. Practice using SCROLL LOCK to stop and start the program; when ready, press CTRL + BREAK to return to QuickBASIC Control.

A Sales Tax Program with DO...LOOP

The sales tax programs that you wrote in Chapter 4, "Number Crunching," can easily be modified to be more convenient to use. Through the use of a DO...LOOP structure, the sales tax for several different sales amounts can be calculated without returning to QuickBASIC Control and running the program again for each amount. Program QBME0502.BAS, Sales Tax Program with DO...LOOP, is a modification of program QBME0407.BAS, Sales Tax Program.

```
REM ** QBME0502.BAS **
'    ** 1/1/90 **
'    ** Sales Tax Program with DO...LOOP **
' QuickBASIC Made Easy, Chapter 5
' Microsoft QuickBASIC 4.5

CLS
TaxRate = .06

REM ** Use a DO...LOOP to do repeated calculations **
DO
  INPUT "Amount of sale"; SalesAmount
  SalesTax = SalesAmount * TaxRate
  TotalAmount = SalesAmount + SalesTax

  PRINT
  PRINT "Amount of sale is"; TAB(40);
  PRINT USING "#####.##"; SalesAmount
  PRINT "Amount of sales tax is"; TAB(40);
  PRINT USING "#####.##"; SalesTax

  PRINT "Total amount is"; TAB(40);
  PRINT USING "#####.##"; TotalAmount
  PRINT
LOOP
```

The following sample run shows the results from three different sales amounts.

```
Amount of sale? 169.95

Amount of sale is              169.95
Amount of sales tax is          10.20
Total amount is                180.15
```

```
Amount of sale? 225
Amount of sale is                    225.00

Amount of sales tax is                13.50
Total amount is                      238.50

Amount of sale? 349.95

Amount of sale is                    349.95
Amount of sales tax is                21.00
Total amount is                      370.95

Amount of sale? _
```

Since DO...LOOP is still executing, the computer is again waiting for a sales amount to be entered.

Interrupt the program now by pressing CTRL + BREAK. You will return to QuickBASIC Control with the INPUT statement highlighted and the cursor on the I of INPUT as shown in Figure 5-2. This is a helpful feature of QuickBASIC—it highlights the statement that was executing when the program was interrupted.

THE LPRINT KEYWORD   It is often helpful to print the results of a

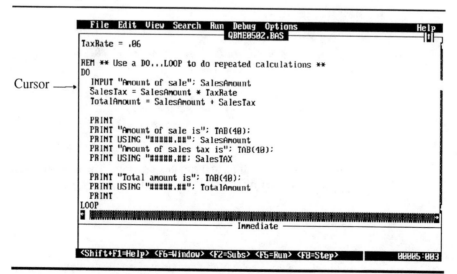

FIGURE 5-2   INPUT highlighted after program interruption

program on paper rather than on the screen. There is a very simple way to do this: use the LPRINT keyword rather than the PRINT keyword in any line in the program in which the output should appear on paper.

The following program, QBME0503.BAS, is a modification of program QBME0502.BAS, Sales Tax Program with DO...LOOP. Some of the PRINT statements have been changed to LPRINT statements, and some of the variables have been changed to double precision variables in order to handle much larger sales amounts correctly.

```
REM ** QBME0503.BAS **
'    ** 1/1/90 **
'    ** Sales Tax Program with DO...LOOP **
' QuickBASIC Made Easy, Chapter 5
' Microsoft QuickBASIC 4.5

CLS
TaxRate = .06

REM ** Use a DO...LOOP to do repeated calculations **
DO
   INPUT "Amount of sale"; SalesAmount#
   PRINT

   SalesTax# = SalesAmount# * TaxRate
   TotalAmount# = SalesAmount# + SalesTax#

   LPRINT
   LPRINT "Amount of sale is"; TAB(40);
   LPRINT USING "###########,.##"; SalesAmount#

   LPRINT "Amount of sales tax is"; TAB(40);
   LPRINT USING "###########,.##"; SalesTax#

   LPRINT "Total amount is"; TAB(40);
   LPRINT USING "###########,.##"; TotalAmount#
   LPRINT
LOOP
```

If you have a printer, turn it on and run this program. The following is a sample run of QBME0503.BAS, as displayed in the Output Screen.

```
Amount of sale? 500
Amount of sale? _
```

The following shows the results of this run printed on the printer.

```
Amount of sale is              500.00
```

```
Amount of sales tax is              30.00
Total amount is                    530.00
```

You can improve program QBME0503.BAS further. For example, you might add two dollar signs to the PRINT USING statements so that dollar signs are printed before each dollar amount. (You used this PRINT USING format previously in QBME0407.BAS.) You might also change this program so that the user assigns the value of *TaxRate* each time the program is run.

Value of Stocks with DO...LOOP

If your portfolio contains several stocks, you can use the next program to compute the value of each block of shares and keep a running total of the stocks entered. Look at the following sample run and think about how you might write the program.

```
The date is 01-01-1990
The time is 12:29:17

Number of shares? 1
Price per share? 2.125
The value of these shares is               $2.13
The total value so far is                  $2.13

Number of shares? 1000000
Price per share? 257.75
The value of these shares is     $25,775,000.00
The total value so far is        $25,775,002.13

Number of shares?
```

It is a good idea to write an outline of the program in REM statements first. A REM outline of program QBME0504.BAS is shown next:

```
REM ** QBME0504.BAS **
'    ** 1/1/90 **
'     ** Value of Stocks with DO...LOOP **
' QuickBASIC Made Easy, Chapter 5
' Microsoft QuickBASIC 4.5

REM ** Print the date and time **

REM ** Set the total value of all stocks to zero **
```

```
REM ** DO...LOOP **
    ' Get number of shares & price per share
    ' Compute value and add to total value
    ' Print value this stock and total value so far
```

Study the sample run and the REM outline. Much of the overall program design is finished once you decide how you want the output to look and have written an outline of the program. Now try completing the program; one possible version of program QBME0504.BAS follows:

```
REM ** QBME0504.BAS **
'    ** 1/1/90 **
'    ** Value of Stocks with DO...LOOP **
' QuickBASIC Made Easy, Chapter 5
' Microsoft QuickBASIC 4.5

REM ** Print the date and time **
CLS
PRINT "The date is "; DATE$
PRINT "The time is "; TIME$

REM ** Set the total value of all stocks to zero **
TotalValue# = 0

REM ** DO...LOOP **
DO

    ' Get number of shares & price per share
    INPUT "Number of shares"; NumberOfShares#
    INPUT "Price per share"; PricePerShare#
    ' Compute value and add to total value
    Value# = NumberOfShares# * PricePerShare#
    TotalValue# = TotalValue# + Value#

    ' Print value of this stock and total value so far
    PRINT "The value of these shares is ";
    PRINT USING "$$#########,.##"; Value#
    PRINT "The total value so far is     ";
    PRINT USING "$$#########,.##"; TotalValue#
    PRINT
LOOP
```

Notice the indentation of the DO...LOOP structure, the explanatory REM statement above each block, and the blank lines in the program. Programs are much more readable, and thus more easily understood, when blocks of related material are set off in some way.

A Graceful Exit from DO...LOOP

The DO...LOOP structures shown so far must be interrupted by pressing CTRL + BREAK. DO...LOOP structures can, however, be modified so that the loop stops automatically. The following shows a run of a program for figuring the value of stocks that has a built-in exit from DO...LOOP.

```
The date is 01-01-1990
The time is 12:57:39

Number of shares (0 to quit)? 500
Price per share              ? 5.875

The value of these shares is        $2,937.50

Number of shares (0 to quit)? 1500
Price per share              ? 114

The value of these shares is        $171,000.00

Number of shares (0 to quit)? 0

The total value of all stocks is        $173,937.50



Press any key to continue
```

Notice that when a zero (0) was entered for the number of shares, the program printed the total value of all stocks entered and then ended automatically.

In the REM outline that follows, note that the block that prints the total value of all stocks follows the DO...LOOP block. The total value is therefore printed only once, at the end of the program. Also note that the DO...LOOP structure includes a construct that you have not used before: IF...THEN. IF...THEN statements are *conditional statements*. They are used to test for a certain condition, specified by "IF"; if that condition exists, what follows "THEN" is executed. IF...THEN statements are among the most useful and powerful features of QuickBASIC. Study this program's REM outline and think about how you might use an IF...THEN statement to exit from DO...LOOP.

```
REM ** QBME0505.BAS **
'    ** 1/1/90 **
'    ** Value of Stocks with DO...LOOP & Graceful Exit **
' QuickBASIC Made Easy, Chapter 5
' Microsoft QuickBASIC 4.5

REM ** Print the date and time **

REM ** Set the total value of all stocks to zero **

REM ** DO...LOOP with IF...THEN and EXIT DO **
  ' Get number of shares (0 to quit) & price per share
  ' Compute value and add to total value
  ' Print value of this stock

REM ** Print total value of all stocks **
```

The completed program QBME0505.BAS, which follows, uses the new IF...THEN... construct and introduces the new keywords IF, THEN, and EXIT. They are used in the conditional statement, which tests the number of shares entered and, if zero, exits from the DO...LOOP structure.

```
REM ** QBME0505.BAS **
'    ** 1/1/90 **
'    ** Value of Stocks with DO...LOOP & Graceful Exit **
' QuickBASIC Made Easy, Chapter 5
' Microsoft QuickBASIC 4.5

REM ** Print the date and time **
CLS
PRINT "The date is "; DATE$
PRINT "The time is "; TIME$
PRINT

REM ** Set the total value of all stocks to zero **
TotalValue# = 0

REM ** DO...LOOP with IF...THEN and EXIT DO **
DO

  ' Get number of shares (0 to quit) & price per share
  INPUT "Number of shares (0 to quit)"; NumberOfShares#
  IF NumberOfShares# = 0 THEN EXIT DO
  INPUT "Price per share              "; PricePerShare#
  PRINT

  ' Compute value and add to total value
  Value# = NumberOfShares# * PricePerShare#
  TotalValue# = TotalValue# + Value#
```

```
' Print value of this stock
PRINT "The value of these shares is"; TAB(40);
PRINT USING "$$#########,.##"; Value#
PRINT

LOOP

REM ** Print total value of all stocks **
PRINT
PRINT "The total value of all stocks is"; TAB(40);
PRINT USING "$$#########,.##"; TotalValue#

END
```

The IF...THEN statement tests to see if the value entered for *NumberOf-Shares#* is zero, and if it is, stops the program from looping. After exiting the loop, the program resumes with the first line following the DO...LOOP structure. If, however, *NumberOfShares#* is not equal to zero, then the program continues executing the loop with the line following the IF...THEN statement.

The statement IF NumberOfShares# = 0 THEN EXIT DO tells the computer this: If the value entered for *NumberOfShares#* is zero, exit from DO...LOOP; continue executing the program with the line following LOOP. If the value entered for *NumberOfShares#* is not zero, continue with the line following the IF...THEN statement. The program continues to loop until *NumberOfShares#* equals zero and it has exited from DO...LOOP.

This program illustrates another important concept in addition to the IF...THEN statement: how to keep a running total. In this program, the variable *TotalValue#* is a running total. Just before the DO...LOOP structure, *TotalValue#* is set to zero. Then, every time DO...LOOP is executed, the value of the stocks, *Value#*, is added to *TotalValue#*. When the program exits from DO...LOOP, the total value of all stocks, *TotalValue#*, is printed. Run this program several times; experiment with different numbers of stocks and their values before exiting the loop. Notice that the total value printed is the sum of all the stock values from each run.

FUTURE VALUE—COMPOUND INTEREST WITH EXIT FROM DO...LOOP If your money is invested in a bank, savings and loan, or other place that pays interest compounded regularly, you can use the next program, QBME0506.BAS, to calculate the future value of your investment. Here is a REM outline of the program.

```
REM ** QBME0506.BAS **
'    ** 1/1/90 **
'    ** Future Value--Compound Interest with DO...LOOP **
  ' QuickBASIC Made Easy, Chapter 5
  ' Microsoft QuickBASIC 4.5

REM ** Clear screen, print date & time **

REM ** DO...LOOP with IF...THEN EXIT DO **
  ' Enter data -- quit if principal is zero
  ' Compute & print future value of investment **
```

Think about how you might write this program; one possible version follows.

```
REM ** QBME0506.BAS ***

'    ** 1/1/90 **
'    ** Future Value--Compound Interest with DO...LOOP **
' QuickBASIC Made Easy, Chapter 5
' Microsoft QuickBASIC 4.5

REM ** Clear screen, print date & time **
CLS
PRINT "The date is   "; DATE$
PRINT "The time is   "; TIME$
PRINT

REM ** DO...LOOP with IF...THEN EXIT DO **
DO
  ' Enter data -- quit if principal is zero
  INPUT "Principal amount invested ($)"; Principal#
  IF Principal# = 0 THEN EXIT DO
  INPUT "Interest rate per year (%)   "; InterestRate!
  INPUT "Interest periods per year    "; PeriodsPerYear&
  INPUT "Number of interest periods   "; NbrOfPds&

  ' Compute & print future value of investment **
  PdRate! = InterestRate! / PeriodsPerYear& / 100
  FutureValue# = Principal# * (1 + PdRate!) ^ NbrOfPds&
  PRINT "At maturity, the value will be ";
  PRINT USING "$$############,.##"; FutureValue#
  PRINT

LOOP

END
```

Perhaps you are thinking of putting your money in Erosion Savings and Loan for 6% per year, compounded monthly. How long will it take to double your money? The following shows the future value of an original investment (principal) of $1000 for 60 months (5 years), 120 months (10 years), and 180 months (15 years).

```
The date is 01-01-1990
The time is 11:30:04

Principal amount invested ($)? 1000
Interest rate per year (%)    ? 6
Interest periods per year     ? 12
Number of interest periods    ? 60
At maturity, the value will be          $1,348.85

Principal amount invested ($)? 1000
Interest rate per year (%)    ? 6
Interest periods per year     ? 12
Number of interest periods    ? 120
At maturity, the value will be          $1,819.40

Principal amount invested ($)? 1000
Interest rate per year (%)    ? 6
Interest periods per year     ? 12
Number of interest periods    ? 180
At maturity, the value will be          $2,454.09

Principal amount invested ($)? 0


Press any key to continue
```

Your investment doubles at some time between 120 and 180 months (between 10 and 15 years). If you are willing to accept more risk, you might find a place to invest your nest egg at, say, 12%. As shown here, you can double your money in about 6 years (72 months).

```
The date is 01-01-1990
The time is 11:35:21

Principal amount invested ($)? 1000
Interest rate per year (%)    ? 12
Interest periods per year     ? 12
Number of interest periods    ? 36
At maturity, the value will be          $1,430.77
```

```
Principal amount invested ($)? 1000
Interest rate per year (%)    ? 12
Interest periods per year     ? 12
Number of interest periods    ? 72
At maturity, the value will be              $2,047.10

Principal amount invested ($)? 0




Press any key to continue
```

Another Exit from DO...LOOP

The following program introduces a new IF...THEN statement, which tells
the program to exit from a DO...LOOP structure when SPACEBAR is pressed.
Compare this IF...THEN statement with the IF...THEN statement used in
program QBME0506.BAS.

```
DO
  PRINT "Press SPACEBAR to stop"
  IF INKEY$ = " " THEN EXIT DO
LOOP
```

This program uses a new keyword: INKEY$. If a key has been pressed,
the value of INKEY$ is that character. If no key has been pressed, the value
of INKEY$ is the null (or empty) string. The null string is represented as a
pair of quotation marks with nothing between them (""). This is not the same
as a pair of quotation marks that enclose a space (" "), as in this IF...THEN
statement.

```
IF INKEY$ = " " THEN EXIT DO
```

This statement tells the computer the following: If SPACEBAR is pressed (that
is, if the value of INKEY$ is a space), exit from DO...LOOP. If no key is
pressed, or any key other than SPACEBAR is pressed, continue executing
DO...LOOP.

Enter and run this program. The screen quickly fills with the message in
the PRINT statement. Press several keys other than SPACEBAR—the program
continues to run. Press SPACEBAR—the program exits from DO...LOOP and
stops.

Experiment with the INKEY$ function. Try modifying this program so that it exits from DO...LOOP when some other key is pressed, or so that it prints the value of INKEY$ when a key is pressed.

More Exits from DO...LOOP

As you have just seen, DO...LOOP can be exited by including an IF...THEN EXIT DO statement in the loop. You can also specify an exit from DO...LOOP with the UNTIL keyword. The following program illustrates this exit.

```
DO UNTIL INKEY$ = " "
  PRINT "Press the SPACEBAR to stop"
LOOP
```

Enter and run this program. Notice that the program continues to run until you press SPACEBAR. The following DO...LOOP structure will also run until you press SPACEBAR.

```
DO
  PRINT "Press the SPACEBAR to stop"
LOOP UNTIL INKEY$ = " "
```

Two other equivalent DO...LOOP structures are shown next. Both will run until you type a lowercase q.

```
DO UNTIL INKEY$ = "q"
PRINT "Press q to stop"
LOOP
```

* *

```
DO
  PRINT "Press q to stop"
LOOP UNTIL INKEY$ = "q"
```

The DO...LOOP structures shown next will run until you type an upper-case Q (press SHIFT + Q, or press CAPS LOCK).

```
DO UNTIL INKEY$ = "Q"
  PRINT "Type Q to stop"
LOOP
```

* *

```
DO
  PRINT "Type Q to stop"
LOOP UNTIL INKEY$ = "Q"
```

You can change these DO...LOOP structures so that they can be exited if either a lowercase or an uppercase letter is typed. To do this, use the UCASE$ string function.

```
DO UNTIL UCASE$(INKEY$) = "Q"
PRINT "Type q or Q to stop"
LOOP
```

```
* * * * * * * * * * * * * * * * * * * * * * * * * * * * * * * * * * * * * * * * * * * * * * * * * * * * * * * * *
```

```
DO
  PRINT "Type q or Q to stop"
LOOP UNTIL UCASE$(INKEY$) = "Q"
```

UCASE$ converts any lowercase letters in a string to uppercase letters, but does nothing to uppercase letters. Therefore, if you type a lowercase letter while this program is running, the value of UCASE$(INKEY$) will be the uppercase equivalent of the letter you typed.

The DO...LOOP structures that you have seen so far continue until some condition is true. For example, until the value of INKEY$ is a space or the letter "q." You can also write a DO...LOOP structure that continues until some condition is not true. For example, consider the following two DO...LOOP structures:

```
DO UNTIL INKEY$  < >""
  PRINT "Press any key to stop"
LOOP
```

```
* * * * * * * * * * * * * * * * * * * * * * * * * * * * * * * * * * * * * * * * * * * * * * * * * * * * * * * * *
```

```
DO
  PRINT "Press any key to stop"
LOOP UNTIL INKEY$ < > ""
```

The symbol < > means "not equal to," so this loop will continue to execute until the value of INKEY$ is not the null string (""), in other words, until a key is pressed.

Practice by writing several DO...LOOP structures with different exit statements. Use both loops that continue until some condition is true, as well as loops that continue until some condition is not true.

The Final Exit from DO...LOOP

The DO UNTIL...LOOP and DO...LOOP UNTIL loops determine when a given condition occurs, then stop executing. The DO WHILE...LOOP and DO...LOOP WHILE loops are very similar and equally useful. The next program is a modification of a simple DO UNTIL...LOOP structure, which you wrote earlier.

```
DO WHILE INKEY$ = ""
  PRINT "Press any key to stop"
LOOP
```

This loop will be executed as long as INKEY$ is the null string, that is, while no key is pressed. When a key is pressed, INKEY$ no longer equals the null string, so the program exits from the loop.

The following two programs are also modifications of programs that you wrote earlier. They illustrate the difference that the location of the exit test can make.

```
REM ** Count by tens (10, 20, 30, etc.) **
'    ** Exit when x is greater than 100 **

CLS

x = 10

DO WHILE x < 100
  PRINT x,
x = x + 10
LOOP
PRINT x
```

You can also write the program like this:

```
REM ** Count by tens (10, 20, 30, etc.) **
'    ** Exit when x is greater than 100 **

CLS

x = 10

DO
  PRINT x,
  x = x + 10
LOOP WHILE x < 100
PRINT x
```

Enter and run both of these programs. Notice that the final value of *x* differs in the two programs. This is because of the different location of the test to continue the loop. If the test is at the beginning of the loop (first example), the loop is executed one more time than if the test is at the end of the loop (second example). Study the two programs—can you see why they produce slightly different results?

THE QuickBASIC RAINBOW

If your computer has a Color Graphics Adaptor (CGA) or other color capabilities, you can change the color of the text or the background of the Output screen. Ordinarily, the text on the Output screen is white against a black background. You can use the COLOR keyword to select from 16 colors to print text in; you can select from 8 colors for the background.

Changing the Text Color

The 16 colors in which text can be printed and their color numbers are listed in Table 5-1. The color numbers 0 to 15 specify nonblinking text; the color numbers 16 to 31 specify blinking text. The program that follows prints text in the color you choose.

```
CLS

INPUT "Text color number (0 to 31)"; kolor%
COLOR kolor%

DO
  PRINT "The text color number is"; kolor%
  PRINT "Press SPACEBAR to stop"
LOOP UNTIL INKEY$ = " "
```

The variable *kolor%* is an integer, since possible color numbers are in the range −32,768 to 32,767. This variable is used in the COLOR statement, which changes the color in which text is printed.

The statement COLOR *kolor%* tells the computer to set the foreground screen color to the color specified by the variable *kolor%*. Text printed on the screen is then printed in the specified color. The background color remains black.

Color	Color Number Not Blinking	Color Number Blinking
Black	0	16
Blue	1	17
Green	2	18
Cyan	3	19
Red	4	20
Magenta	5	21
Brown	6	22
White	7	23
Gray	8	24
Light blue	9	25
Light green	10	26
Light cyan	11	27
Light red	12	28
Light magenta	13	29
Yellow	14	30
Bright white	15	31

TABLE 5-1   Foreground Colors and Color Numbers

Enter and run the program. Type the color number of your choice. Press SPACEBAR to stop the program, and then press any key to return to Quick-BASIC Control. Note that if you enter 0 or 16 you will see a blank, black Output screen because black is also the background color. If you enter a non-integer, the number will be rounded to the nearest whole number; the rounded value is then used to set the color.

If you enter a negative number or a number greater than 31, you will see the Illegal Function Call dialog box in the View window. If you see that dialog box, explore the help available, then clear the dialog box.

Changing the Background Color

In addition to changing the foreground color, you can use the COLOR keyword to change the background color. The background colors and their color numbers are listed in Table 5-2.

Color	Color Number
Black	0
Blue	1
Green	2
Cyan	3
Red	4
Magenta	5
Brown	6
White	7

TABLE 5-2   Background Colors and Color Numbers

Background color numbers are in the range 0 to 7. If you use a background color number between 8 and 15, the number is treated as though it were in the 0 to 7 range and no illegal function call error is triggered. A number outside the range 0 to 15, however, will generate an illegal function call error.

The following COLOR statement tells the computer to print text in black (color 0), on a white background (color 7)—the reverse of the normal screen colors. The number before the comma is the foreground color; the number after the comma is the background color.

```
COLOR 0,7
      ↑ ↑_____ Background color (white)
      |_____ Foreground color (black)
```

Use the following program, QBME0507.BAS, to try various combinations of foreground and background colors.

```
REM ** QBME0507.BAS **
'    ** 1/1/90 **
'    ** COLOR Demonstrator **
' QuickBASIC Made Easy, Chapter 5
' Microsoft QuickBASIC 4.5
```

```
CLS
INPUT "Foreground color (0 to 31)"; foreground%
PRINT
INPUT "Background color (0 to 7) "; background%

COLOR foreground%, background%

DO
  PRINT "The foreground number is "; foreground%
  PRINT "The background number is "; background%
  PRINT "Press SPACEBAR to stop"
LOOP UNTIL INKEY$ = " "
```

The next program chooses a random number in the range 0 to 15, sets the foreground color to that number, and prints Mariko's name in that color.

```
DO
  COLOR INT(16 * RND)
  PRINT "Mariko  ";
LOOP UNTIL INKEY$ = " "
```

This program introduces two QuickBASIC keywords: RND and INT. RND generates a single precision random number between 0 and 1, but never 0 or 1. That is, RND is a random number greater than 0 and less than 1.

$$0 < \text{RND} < 1$$

To select a color number between 0 and 15, the random number generated by RND is multiplied by 16. 16 * RND is a random number between 0 and 16, but never 0 or 16. That is, 16 * RND is a random number greater than 0 and less than 16.

$$0 < 16 * \text{RND} < 16$$

Although 16 * RND is always less than 16, it may equal 16 when it is rounded by the COLOR statement. Also, 16 * RND will never equal 0, so that color will not be chosen. The INT function solves this problem. INT(16 * RND) is the integer part of 16 * RND. For example, if 16 * RND is 7.32086, then INT(16 * RND) is 7. If 16 * RND is .54127, INT(16 * RND) is 0. INT(16 * RND) is therefore a random integer in the range 0 to 15, inclusive.

$$0 <= \text{INT}(16 * \text{RND}) <= 15$$

The statement PRINT "Mariko "; tells the computer to print Mariko's name, followed by two spaces, in the current foreground color. Note the semi-colon (;) at the end of the statement. Mariko's name will be printed on the same line across the screen until the line is filled.

To see Mariko's name (or any name) in blinking and nonblinking colors, change the COLOR statement to generate a number in the range 0 to 31, as follows:

COLOR INT(32 * RND)

To see the name only in blinking colors, change the COLOR statement to generate a number from 0 to 15, and then add 16 to the result, as follows.

COLOR INT(16 * RND) + 16

You can also randomly set the background color. Practice writing programs that reset both the foreground and background colors using randomly generated numbers.

MAKING MUSIC

As you learned earlier, you can use the keyword BEEP to make the computer beep. Every beep sounds the same, and lasts for the same length of time. You can make more interesting sounds than simple beeps by using the SOUND keyword. The SOUND keyword lets you control the *frequency* (or *pitch*) of the sound, as well as the *duration* (the length of time the sound is heard). For example, the following SOUND statement causes the computer to play the note middle C for 18 *ticks*, or about one second (18.2 ticks equal one second).

```
SOUND 262, 18
        ↑    ↑__ Duration
   Frequency
```

Enter this SOUND statement as a command in the Immediate window; you will hear middle C for about one second. Then enter and run the following program, which plays two tones alternately until you press SPACEBAR.

Note	Frequency	Note	Frequency
C	130.81	C	523.25
D	146.83	D	587.33
E	164.81	E	659.26
F	174.61	F	698.46
G	196.00	G	783.99
A	220.00	A	880.00
B	246.94	B	987.77
C	261.63	C	1046.50
D	293.66	D	1174.70
E	329.63	E	1318.50
F	349.23	F	1396.90
G	392.00	G	1568.00
A	440.00	A	1760.00
B	493.88	B	1975.50

TABLE 5-3   Frequencies for Musical Notes

```
DO
  SOUND 262, 9
  SOUND 440, 9
  PRINT "Press SPACEBAR to stop"
  IF INKEY$ = " " THEN EXIT DO
LOOP
```

The statement SOUND 262, 9 tells the computer to sound a tone of frequency 262 Hertz (Hz), or cycles per second for a duration of 9 ticks, or about one-half second. That tone is middle C.

The statement SOUND 440, 9 tells the computer to sound a tone of frequency 440 Hz for a duration of 9 ticks, or about one-half second. That tone is A above middle C.

Table 5-3 lists the frequencies for musical notes for four octaves in the scale of C.

Add another SOUND statement inside the DO...LOOP structure. Choose any frequency to play, but it must be a number from 37 to 32,767. You probably will not be able to hear the very high notes. The duration may be a number from 0 to 65,535.

You can sound any of the notes in Table 5-3, or other frequencies of your choice, by entering and running program QBME0508.BAS, SOUND Demonstration.

```
REM ** QBME0508.BAS **
'   ** 1/1/90 **
'    ** SOUND Demonstration **
' QuickBASIC Made Easy, Chapter 5
' Microsoft QuickBASIC 4.5

CLS

DO
  INPUT "Frequency"; frequency
  IF frequency = 0 THEN EXIT DO
  INPUT "Duration "; duration
  PRINT
  SOUND frequency, duration
LOOP
```

An annotated run is shown in Table 5-4.

Frequency? 262 Duration ? 18	Middle C for about one second.
Frequency? 294 Duration ? 36	D for about two seconds.
Frequency? 330 Duration ? 54	E for about three seconds.
Frequency? 0	Enter zero to quit.

TABLE 5-4   An Annotated Run of Program QBME0508.BAS

Sound Off in the Scale of C

The musical scale of C consists of the notes C, D, E, F, G, A, B, and C (an octave above the first C). You can use program QBME0509.BAS, Scale of C with Notes, to hear and see the scale of C.

```
REM ** QBME0509.BAS **
'    ** 1/1/90 **
'    ** Scale of C with Notes **
' QuickBASIC Made Easy, Chapter 5
' Microsoft QuickBASIC 4.5

REM ** Scale of C with C, D, E, ... **

duration = 18    ' 18 ticks, about 1 second
DO
  CLS : PRINT "Scale of C with Notes":
  PRINT
  SOUND 262, duration: PRINT "C"
  SOUND 294, duration: PRINT "D"
  SOUND 330, duration: PRINT "E"
  SOUND 349, duration: PRINT "F"
  SOUND 392, duration: PRINT "G"
  SOUND 440, duration: PRINT "A"
  SOUND 494, duration: PRINT "B"
  SOUND 523, duration: PRINT "C"
  PRINT
  PRINT "Press any key to repeat or CTRL+BREAK to stop"
  anykey$ = INPUT$(1)
LOOP
```

QBME0509.BAS introduces the INPUT$() string function. The INPUT$() function waits for the number of keys specified in the parentheses to be typed before executing the next statement in the program. This program will loop after one key is typed. Compare this function with the INKEY$ function: INPUT$() waits until a key is pressed before continuing; INKEY$ does not wait before looping—if no key is pressed, INKEY$ is the null string.

Notice that some of the lines in this program consist of two statements separated by a colon (:). Any line in a program may consist of multiple statements; multiple statements are always separated by a colon. Multiple statement lines are processed as though the statements were on separate lines. You can use multiple statements to make a program easier to read, or, as in this program, to group related statements.

The line CLS : PRINT "Scale of C with Notes" consists of two statements. The first statement (CLS) tells the computer to clear the Output screen. The second statement (PRINT "Scale of C with Notes") tells the computer to print the string enclosed in quotation marks.

The line SOUND 262, duration: PRINT "C" also has two statements. The first statement (SOUND 262, duration) tells the computer to play a sound of frequency 262 Hz for the length of time specified by the value of duration. The second statement (PRINT "C") tells the computer to print a C on the Output screen.

A sample run of QBME0509.BAS is shown here:

```
Scale of C with Notes

C
D
E
F
G
A
B
C

Press any key to repeat or CTRL+BREAK to stop
```

As each note is printed, the corresponding tone is heard. Note how the INPUT$() function works in the last line: you can press almost any single key (SPACEBAR is a good choice) to repeat the scale, or press CTRL + BREAK to stop.

The statement *anykey$* = INPUT$(1) tells the computer to wait for someone to type a single character. This becomes the value of INPUT$(1) and is then assigned as the value of the string variable *anykey$*. As soon as you press a key, the program continues to the next line, which is LOOP, and loops back to repeat the lines inside the DO...LOOP structure.

The keyword INPUT$(1) tells the computer to wait for keyboard input of one character. You can specify the number of characters by putting the desired number inside the parentheses. For example, if you want the computer to wait for two characters to be typed, use INPUT$(2).

Program QBME0510.BAS, Sound Effects with DO...LOOP & UNTIL lets you enter two frequencies and one duration. It then plays "music" until you press almost any key.

```
REM ** QBME0510.BAS **
'    ** 1/1/90 **
'    ** Sound Effects with DO...LOOP & UNTIL **
' QuickBASIC Made Easy, Chapter 5
' Microsoft QuickBASIC 4.5
```

```
REM ** Get low frequency, high frequency,
'      and duration **
CLS
INPUT "Low frequency (Hz) ": LoTone
PRINT
INPUT "High frequency (Hz)"; HiTone
PRINT
INPUT "Duration in ticks  "; duration
PRINT
PRINT "Press any key to stop the 'music'"

REM ** Play 'music' until a key is pressed **

DO UNTIL INKEY$  < >  ""
  frequency = (HiTone - LoTone) * RND + LoTone
  SOUND frequency, duration
LOOP
```

The statement *frequency = (HiTone − LoTone)* ∗ RND + *LoTone* tells the computer to compute a random number between the values of *HiTone* and *LoTone* and assign it as the value of *frequency*. Here is a sample run of the program.

```
Low frequency (Hz)  ? 37

High frequency (Hz)? 32767

Duration in ticks  ? 1

Press any key to stop the 'music'




Press any key to continue
```

This program produces strange music, including some sounds you cannot hear and some the computer's speaker cannot reproduce. Press any key to stop the program and run it again with another frequency. Use a high frequency of 20000 or 15000 or 12000. What is the highest frequency you can hear? Try a very short duration, as shown here:

```
Low frequency (Hz)  ? 100

High frequency (Hz)? 3000

Duration in ticks  ? .125
```

```
Press any key to stop the 'music'
```

```
Press any key to continue
```

Listen to the "music," which sounds a bit like some arcade game sound effects.

String variables are variables that store character information, rather than numbers. They can be used, for example, to store names, addresses, or school transcripts. INKEY$ is a string function that stores the value of a key when it is pressed; if no key is pressed, the value of INKEY$ is the null (or empty) string. INPUT$() is a string function that waits for the number of keys specified in the parentheses to be pressed before continuing with the next line.

DO...LOOP structures are used to control the execution of a program; they allow portions of a program to be executed repeatedly. DO...LOOP structures can be exited in several ways: an IF...THEN EXIT DO construct within the loop; DO UNTIL...LOOP and DO...LOOP UNTIL contructs; and DO WHILE...LOOP and DO...LOOP WHILE constructs.

You can print output on your printer as well as on the screen. Use the LPRINT keyword to print on paper; use the PRINT keyword to print on the screen.

You can change the foreground and background color of the screen with the COLOR keyword. You can make "music" on your computer with the SOUND keyword.

6

EDITING AND DYNAMIC DEBUGGING

Editing
Dynamic Debugging

In this chapter you will learn to use some of QuickBASIC's editing tools. In doing so, you will also learn to use some of the powerful debugging tools that are provided in QuickBASIC. In particular, you will

- Learn to use the Cut option on the Edit menu to remove sections of a program

- Learn to use the Copy option on the Edit menu to copy sections of a program from one place to another

- Learn to use the Paste option on the Edit menu to copy sections from one program to another

- Learn to use the Add Watch... option on the Debug menu to watch the values of certain variables while a program is executing

- Learn to use the Delete Watch... option on the Debug menu to delete watchpoints

- Learn about the Instant Watch... option on the Debug menu, which displays the value of a variable or the condition of an expression in a dialog box

- Learn to step through an executing program, one line at a time

- Learn about the Toggle Breakpoint and Clear All Breakpoints options on the Debug menu

EDITING

When you write programs, especially long or complex programs, you often need to edit them. Editing ranges from simple one-letter changes to removing or copying a portion of a program. QuickBASIC provides several useful and powerful editing tools to simplify and enhance your programming.

You have already used some editing keys: BACKSPACE, DEL, LEFT ARROW, RIGHT ARROW, UP ARROW, and DOWN ARROW. Now you will learn to use other helpful editing keys, as well as the options on the Edit menu.

Editing Keys

In addition to the editing keys just mentioned, there are other simple yet powerful keys you can use to make changes quickly in a program. Table 6-1 lists some of the editing keys that you will find useful when writing programs.

Many of the editing keys included in Table 6-1 are self-explanatory. For example, pressing HOME moves the cursor to the beginning of the line, and pressing END moves the cursor to the end of the line. Others, however, are more complex and require some discussion.

The QuickBASIC Control Center is divided into two windows: the View window, and the Immediate window. When a program is too large to be displayed in the View window, as much of it as possible is displayed; this is a window-full. To see the next window-full, press PGDN. To see the previous window-full, press PGUP. PGDN and PGUP, then, allow you to scroll your program within the View window, one window-full at a time.

You may also want to scroll up or down one line at a time in order to display lines that are out of sight above or below the window. To scroll down

Cursor Controls	**Keys**
Left one character	LEFT ARROW
Right one character	RIGHT ARROW
Left one word	CTRL + LEFT ARROW
Right one word	CTRL + RIGHT ARROW
Up one line	UP ARROW
Down one line	DOWN ARROW
Beginning of the line	HOME
Beginning of next line	CTRL + ENTER
End of the line	END
Beginning of the program	CTRL + HOME
End of the program	CTRL + END

Scrolling Controls	**Keys**
Up one page (window)	PGUP
Down one page (window)	PGDN
Left one window	CTRL + PGUP
Right one window	CTRL + PGDN
Move the window up one line*	CTRL + UP ARROW
Move the window down one line**	CTRL + DOWN ARROW

*   That is, scroll the text down one line

** That is, scroll the text up one line

TABLE 6-1   Cursor and Scrolling Control Keys

one line, press CTRL + UP ARROW. To scroll up one line, press CTRL + DOWN arrow.

A program may not only be too long to be displayed in a single window, it may also be too wide. If it contains lines that are more than 79 characters wide, only 79 characters are displayed in the View window at one time. To move the window so that you can see the "hidden" part of this line to the right, press CTRL + PGDN. To move the window to the left, press CTRL + PGUP.

As you write more, larger programs, these editing features will become increasingly useful. Experiment with various editing keys as you write and modify your programs. Refer to Table 12.2 in *Learning to Use QuickBASIC*, one of the two Quickmanuals in your QuickBASIC package, for more editing keys.

USING THE EDITING KEYS   Enter QBME0001.BAS, QuickBASIC
Made Easy Program File Names, including any errors. You might even make
more mistakes than are included here.

```
REM ** QBME0001.BAS **
REM ** 1/1/90 **
REM ** QuickBASIC Made Easy Program File Names **
' REM program - contains programm file names, descriptions
' QuickBASIC Made Easy, Chapter 6
' Microsorft QuickBASIC 4.5

REM ** Chapter 3. Introduction to Programming
' QBME0301.BAS  Date, Time, and Nome

REM ** Chapter 4. Number Crunching
' QBME0401.BAS  Sales Tax with INPUT

REM ** Chapter 5. Making Programs More Useful

REM ** Chapter 6. Editing and Dynmaic Debugging
```

Notice that this program consists only of REM statements and therefore
has no executable statements. It is named QBME0001.BAS so that it will always appear at the beginning of the list of programs displayed in the Open
Program Files box. As you write more programs, this REM program will become increasingly useful. When you want to review or use a particular
program, you can use QBME0001.BAS to determine the correct program
name to load.

Now, using some of the edit keys listed in Table 6-1, correct the errors in
this program. Press CTRL + HOME (press CTRL and then press HOME) to move
the cursor to the beginning of the program. The first mistake occurs in the
fourth line of the program, so press DOWN ARROW until the cursor is on this
line:

```
' REM program-contains programm file names, descriptions
```

The word "programm" in this line needs to be changed to "program." Press
CTRL+RIGHT ARROW until the cursor is on "programm," and then press RIGHT
ARROW until the cursor is under the second "m" of the word "programm."
You could also press CTRL + RIGHT ARROW until the cursor is on "file" and
then press LEFT ARROW until the cursor is on the second "m" in "programm."
In either case, when the cursor is on the extra "m," press DEL to delete that
letter.

Press HOME to move the cursor to the beginning of the line and then press DOWN ARROW to move the cursor to the line that contains the next error :

```
' Microsorft QuickBASIC 4.5
```

Use any combination of editing keys you wish to correct the spelling to "Microsoft." You could put the cursor under the second "r" in "Microsorft" and press DEL; or you could put the cursor under the "f " in "Microsorft" and press BACKSPACE. When this line has been corrected, press DOWN ARROW until the cursor is on the next line that contains an error:

```
' QBME0301.BAS  Date, Time, and Nome
```

Press END; the cursor will move to the end of the line. Press LEFT ARROW to move the cursor to the "o" in the word "Nome," delete that letter, and type an "a" to spell the correct word, "Name."

The last error in this program occurs in the last line:

```
REM ** Chapter 6. Editing and Dynmaic Debugging
```

Change "Dynmaic" to "Dynamic" and then save this program.

Experiment with the cursor and scrolling keys for a while. Next you will learn to use other editing keys to delete one line or an entire block from a program.

INSERTING LINES   Before learning how to delete, add a few "throwaway" lines to QBME0001.BAS. Later, you will delete these lines. To insert new lines, first create space in your program for those lines. Move the cursor until it is just below the line that lists QBME0401.BAS, like this:

```
REM ** Chapter 4.  Number Crunching
' QBME0401.BAS  Sales Tax with INPUT
_ ←—————————— Cursor
REM ** Chapter 5.  Making Programs More Useful
```

Now press ENTER; a blank line has been added to the program:

```
REM ** Chapter 4. Number Crunching
' QBME0401.BAS  Sales Tax with INPUT

REM ** Chapter 5. Making Programs More Useful
```

Enter the following lines.

```
' Throw away line #1
' Throw away line #2
' Throw away line #3
```

Use this technique of adding blank lines to open up space in your programs whenever you need to insert new lines.

DELETING LINES   To delete a single line from your program, move the cursor to the line that is to be deleted and press CTRL + Y. Delete the following line, which you just inserted:

```
' Throw away line #3
```

Put the cursor anywhere on this line and press CTRL + Y. The line will disappear.

It is also possible to delete an entire block without having to press CTRL + Y several times. This involves a technique known as *selecting*. To select a block for deletion, move the cursor to the beginning of the first line to be deleted. Press and hold SHIFT and then press DOWN ARROW until all of the lines to be deleted have been highlighted. The highlighted text is the selected text.

Select the remaining two lines that you just inserted. Move the cursor to the beginning of this line:

```
' Throw away line #1
```

Press and hold SHIFT and then press DOWN ARROW. That line is now highlighted. Press DOWN ARROW again to highlight both lines being deleted:

```
' Throw away line #1
' Throw away line #2
```

Those lines have now been selected. Figure 6-1 shows the selected text in the View window. To delete those lines, simply press DEL. The selected text disappears from the View window.

The Edit Menu

The Edit menu has three options: Cut, Copy, and Paste. Cut is used to delete blocks of text from a program; Copy is used to copy text without having to re-enter it; and Paste is used to "paste" text that has previously been cut or

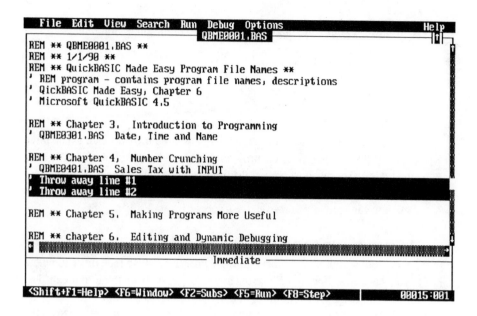

FIGURE 6-1   Selected text in the View window

copied to a new place in a program. Each of these options makes use of the
clipboard, a temporary file in which the text just cut or copied is placed so
that it can be used again. The clipboard contains only the text from the most
recent Cut or Copy.

CUTTING   Insert these three lines back into program QBME0001.BAS:

```
' Throw away line #1
' Throw away line #2
' Throw away line #3
```

To delete the three lines that you just inserted in your program, you will
use the Cut option on the Edit menu. Before using that option, you must first
select the text to be deleted. To select the three lines that you just inserted,
move the cursor to the beginning of the following line:

```
' Throw away line #1
```

Press SHIFT while pressing DOWN ARROW to highlight all three lines:

```
' Throw away line #1
' Throw away line #2
' Throw away line #3
```

The highlighted lines have now been selected.

To delete these lines, choose the Cut option on the Edit menu. The three lines will be deleted from the program and placed in the clipboard. The clipboard is one of the most powerful editing tools of QuickBASIC. You can cut any lines you wish from a program and, if you decide you need them after all, you can recover them from the clipboard.

CUTTING AND PASTING   To confirm that the lines you just cut are in the clipboard, paste them back into the program. Move the cursor to where you want these lines to be inserted and select Paste from the Edit menu. The lines will reappear in your program, as shown in Figure 6-2.

Experiment with cutting and pasting. For example, cut a block from the middle of the program and paste it at the bottom. Next you will learn how to copy portions of a program from one place to another.

COPYING   Since you have just been experimenting with deleting and pasting, load QBME0001.BAS from the disk before proceeding. It should look like this:

```
REM ** QBME0001.BAS **
REM ** 1/1/90 **
REM ** QuickBASIC Made Easy Program File Names **
' REM program - contains program file names, descriptions
' QuickBASIC Made Easy, Chapter 6
' Microsoft QuickBASIC 4.5

REM ** Chapter 3. Introduction to Programming
' QBME0301.BAS  Date, Time, and Name

REM ** Chapter 4. Number Crunching
' QBME0401.BAS  Sales Tax with INPUT

REM ** Chapter 5. Making Programs More Useful

REM ** Chapter 6. Editing and Dynamic Debugging
```

You will use the Copy and Paste options on the Edit menu to complete this program. When you use the Copy option on the Edit menu, the line or block of text being copied must first be selected. Select the following line:

```
' QBME0401.BAS  Sales Tax with INPUT
```

Now choose Copy from the Edit menu. Notice that the text is no longer highlighted and is still in the program. Copy copies the selected text to the clipboard, but otherwise leaves the program untouched. Note that the clipboard only contains the text from the most recent cut or copy. Therefore, the clipboard no longer contains the three lines that you cut previously; it only contains the one line that you just copied. To make use of the text in the clipboard, it must be pasted into the program.

COPYING AND PASTING   Paste inserts the contents of the clipboard to the right of the cursor, so move the cursor to where the new line is to be in-

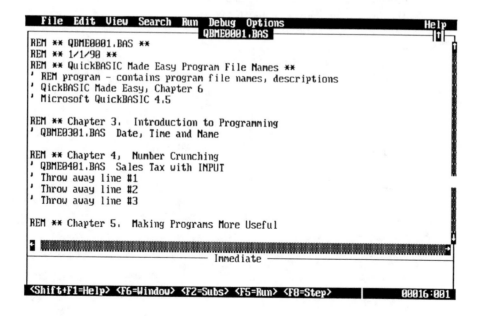

FIGURE 6-2   Text pasted into program from clipboard

inserted, below the line you just copied.

```
REM ** Chapter 4.  Number Crunching
' QBME0401.BAS  Sales Tax with INPUT
_ ←——————————— Cursor
REM ** Chapter 5.  Making Programs More Useful
```

Select Paste from the Edit menu. The line is now in the program twice.

```
REM ** Chapter 4. Number Crunching
' QBME0401.BAS  Sales Tax with INPUT
' QBME0401.BAS  Sales Tax with INPUT

REM ** Chapter 5. Making Programs More Useful
```

Modify the line you just pasted into the program so that it looks like this:

```
' QBME0402.BAS  Sales Tax with Enhanced INPUT
```

Move the cursor down one line and select Paste from the Edit menu again. The block should now look like the following:

```
REM ** Chapter 4. Number Crunching
' QBME0401.BAS  Sales Tax with INPUT
' QBME0402.BAS  Sales Tax with enhanced INPUT
' QBME0401.BAS  Sales Tax with INPUT

REM ** Chapter 5. Making Programs More Useful
```

Modify the last line you pasted to look like this line:

```
' QBME0403.BAS  Sales Tax with labeled OUTPUT
```

This block should now look like the following block:

```
REM ** Chapter 4. Number Crunching
' QBME0401.BAS  Sales Tax with INPUT
' QBME0402.BAS  Sales Tax with enhanced INPUT
' QBME0403.BAS  Sales Tax with labeled OUTPUT

REM ** Chapter 5. Making Programs More Useful
```

Continue copying and pasting QBME0001.BAS until you complete the list of programs included in each chapter. The program should then be similar to the following:

```
REM ** QBME0001.BAS **
REM ** 1/1/90 **
REM ** QuickBASIC Made Easy Program File Names **
' REM program - contains program file names, descriptions
' QuickBASIC Made Easy, Chapter 6
' Microsoft QuickBASIC 4.5

REM ** Chapter 3. Introduction to Programming
' QBME0301.BAS  Date, Time, and Name

REM ** Chapter 4. Number Crunching
' QBME0401.BAS  Sales Tax with INPUT
' QBME0402.BAS  Sales Tax with enhanced INPUT
' QBME0403.BAS  Sales Tax with labeled OUTPUT
' QBME0404.BAS  Sales Tax Modifiable for printer output
' QBME0405.BAS  Sales Tax with PRINT USING
' QBME0406.BAS  Sales Tax with PRINT USING
' QBME0407.BAS  Sales Tax with REMs
' QBME0408.BAS  Value of Stocks
' QBME0409.BAS  Value of Stocks with double precision
' QBME0410.BAS  Future Value of Money -- Compound Interest
' QBME0411.BAS  Future Value of Money -- Compound Interest
' QBME0412.BAS  Future Value of Money -- Compound Interest


REM ** Chapter 5. Making Programs More Useful
' QBME0501.BAS  Demonstrate INPUT with string variables
' QBME0502.BAS  Sales Tax Program with DO...LOOP
' QBME0503.BAS  Sales Tax Program with DO...LOOP
' QBME0504.BAS  Value of Stocks with DO...LOOP
' QBME0505.BAS  Value of Stocks, DO...LOOP & graceful exit
' QBME0506.BAS  Future Value, Compound Interest, DO...LOOP
' QBME0507.BAS  COLOR Demonstrator
' QBME0508.BAS  SOUND Demonstrator
' QBME0509.BAS  Scale of C with notes
' QBME0510.BAS  Sound Effects with DO...LOOP & UNTIL

REM ** Chapter 6. Editing and Dynamic Debugging
' QBME0001.BAS  QuickBASIC Made Easy Program File Names

REM ** Chapter 7. Function Junction

REM ** Chapter 8. Arrays

REM ** Chapter 9. Unstructured Sequential Files

REM ** Chapter 10. Structured Sequential Files

REM ** Chapter 11. Random-Access Files

REM ** Chapter 12. FUNCTION and SUB Procedures
```

Use as many of the editing keys and editing tools as you wish when completing this program. Remember to save the program when you have finished as QBME0001.BAS. After you have saved the completed program, experiment further with the editing tools provided by QuickBASIC.

More Editing

Since the clipboard retains its contents until a new Cut or Copy is executed or until you exit from QuickBASIC, you can use it to copy portions of one program to another program. This means that you can select text from one program, copy it to the clipboard, load a different program in the View window, and paste the contents of the clipboard to the second program.

Use the Copy and Paste options on the Edit menu to create program QBME0002.BAS, "QuickBASIC Made Easy Program File Names." Program QBME0002.BAS contains the programs created in each chapter in the book, as well as the QuickBASIC keywords used in each program. It can be especially helpful when you need an example of how to use a particular keyword or how to write a particular block of a program.

Select the entire QBME0001.BAS program. Since it does not matter whether the selected text remains in the View window, you can use either Cut or Copy to copy to the clipboard. After the program has been copied to the clipboard, choose New Program from the File menu to clear the View window. Now select Paste from the Edit menu; the program will reappear in the View window. Although it is unlikely that you would copy an entire program, you can see how useful and powerful Cut, Copy, and Paste are. Using this technique can save a lot of time (and prevent mistakes).

Modify this program. Change the program name to QBME0002.BAS and add the keywords used in each program, as in the following example.

```
REM ** QBME0002.BAS **
REM ** 1/1/90 **
REM ** QuickBASIC Made Easy Program File Names **
' REM program - contains program file names, descriptions,
' and keywords used in each program
' QuickBASIC Made Easy, Chapter 6
' Microsoft QuickBASIC 4.5

REM ** Chapter 3. Introduction to Programming
' QBME0301.BAS  Date, Time, and Name
'               CLS, INPUT, PRINT

REM ** Chapter 4. Number Crunching
' QBME0401.BAS  Sales Tax with INPUT
```

```
'              CLS, INPUT, PRINT
' QBME0402.BAS  Sales Tax with enhanced INPUT
'              CLS, INPUT, PRINT
' QBME0403.BAS  Sales Tax with labeled OUTPUT
'              CLS, INPUT, PRINT, TAB
' QBME0404.BAS  Sales Tax Modifiable for printer output
'              CLS, INPUT, PRINT, TAB
' QBME0405.BAS  Sales Tax with PRINT USING
'              CLS, INPUT, PRINT, TAB, PRINT USING
' QBME0406.BAS  Sales Tax with PRINT USING
'              CLS, INPUT, PRINT, TAB, PRINT USING
' QBME0407.BAS  Sales Tax with REMs
'              REM, CLS, INPUT, PRINT, TAB, PRINT USING
' QBME0408.BAS  Value of Stocks
'              REM, CLS, INPUT, PRINT, PRINT USING
' QBME0409.BAS  Value of Stocks with double precision
'              REM, CLS, INPUT, PRINT, TAB, PRINT USING
' QBME0410.BAS  Future Value of Money -- Compound Interest
'              REM, CLS, INPUT, PRINT, PRINT USING
' QBME0411.BAS  Future Value of Money -- Compound Interest
'              REM, CLS, INPUT, PRINT, PRINT USING
' QBME0412.BAS  Future Value of Money -- Compound Interest
'              REM, CLS, INPUT, PRINT, PRINT USING

REM ** Chapter 5. Making Programs More Useful
' QBME0501.BAS  Demonstrate INPUT with string variables
'              REM, CLS, PRINT, DATE$, TIME$, INPUT, TAB
' QBME0502.BAS  Sales Tax Program with DO...LOOP
'              REM, CLS, DO, INPUT, PRINT, TAB,
'              PRINT USING, LOOP
' QBME0503.BAS  Sales Tax Program with DO...LOOP
'              REM, CLS, DO, INPUT, PRINT, LPRINT, TAB,
'              LPRINT USING, LOOP
' QBME0504.BAS  Value of Stocks with DO...LOOP
'              REM, CLS, PRINT, DATE$, TIME$, DO, INPUT,
'              PRINT USING, LOOP
' QBME0505.BAS  Value of Stocks, DO...LOOP & graceful exit
'              REM, CLS, PRINT, DATE$, TIME$, DO, INPUT,
'              IF...THEN, EXIT, TAB, PRINT USING, LOOP, END
' QBME0506.BAS  Future Value, Compound Interest, DO...LOOP
'              REM, CLS, PRINT, DATE$, TIME$, DO, INPUT,
'              IF...THEN, EXIT, PRINT USING, LOOP, END
' QBME0507.BAS  COLOR Demonstrator
'              REM, CLS, INPUT, PRINT, COLOR, DO, LOOP,
'              UNTIL, INKEY$
' QBME0508.BAS  SOUND Demonstrator
'              REM, CLS, DO, INPUT, IF...THEN, EXIT, PRINT,
'              SOUND, LOOP
' QBME0509.BAS  Scale of C with notes
'              REM, DO, CLS, PRINT, SOUND, INPUT$, LOOP
' QBME0510.BAS  Sound Effects with DO...LOOP & UNTIL
```

```
  '                    REM, CLS, INPUT, PRINT, DO, UNTIL, INKEY$,
  '                    RND, SOUND, LOOP

REM ** Chapter 6. Editing and Dynamic Debugging
  ' QBME0001.BAS  QuickBASIC Made Easy Program File Names
  '                    REM

REM ** Chapter 7. Function Junction

REM ** Chapter 8. Arrays

REM ** Chapter 9. Unstructured Sequential Files

REM ** Chapter 10. Structured Sequential Files

REM ** Chapter 11. Random-Access Files

REM ** Chapter 12. FUNCTION and SUB Procedures
```

Again, use as many editing keys and editing tools as you wish to create this program. Many programs include keywords that are nearly the same, so you may find it easier to use Copy and Paste to enter some of the lines than to retype them.

Add the names of the programs that you write in this book to both QBME0001.BAS and QBME0002.BAS. Only if these programs are updated will they be the helpful tool they ought to be.

DYNAMIC DEBUGGING

It is very easy, especially when writing large and complex programs, to make errors that are not so easily identified as the errors that you have just been correcting. You will often not know what error has occurred until you check the value of certain variables during program execution. This is known as *dynamic debugging*.

Debugging is the term used to refer to the trial-and-error process of finding all the errors in long programs. Bugs occur in programs for a myriad of reasons. They are usually caused by simple oversights and typographical errors, but sometimes they occur because of the programmer's misunderstanding of how the program is to accomplish its task.

QuickBASIC provides some powerful dynamic debugging tools: watch expressions and breakpoints. In the sections that follow, you will learn to use both of them.

Watch Expressions

A *watch expression* is a variable or expression whose value you wish to watch during program execution. The circumstances under which you will need to monitor the value of certain variables will depend on the program you are writing; so this section simply tells you how to use watch expressions and gives you hints on when they might be useful.

ADDING WATCH EXPRESSIONS   To watch the value of a variable while a program is running, you must first add that variable as a watch expression. The New Program and Open Program... options on the File menu both clear any watch expressions you might previously have declared. Select New Program from the File menu now to clear the View window.

To add a watch expression, select Add Watch... on the Debug menu. You will then see the Add Watch dialog box shown in Figure 6-3. Enter the name of the variable whose value you are going to watch and press ENTER. For now, you will watch the computer's time, so do the following.

Type:
TIME$
and press ENTER

You will then return to the QuickBASIC Control Center, as shown in Figure 6-4. This screen, however, is slightly different from the usual QuickBASIC Control Center screen. The Watch window has appeared just above the View window, and within it you can see the name of the current program, Untitled; the variable to be watched, *TIME$,* followed by a colon (:); and the last value this variable had when it was watched, as shown here:

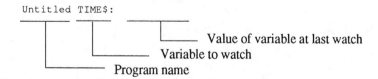

Since *TIME$* has not yet been watched, no value appears in the Watch window. For a variable to have a watch value, a program must be executed after the variable is added to the watch list. Therefore, enter and run the following simple program:

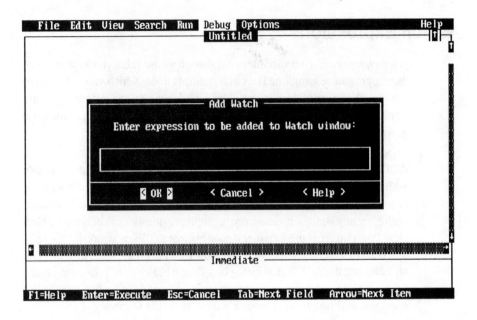

FIGURE 6-3   Add Watch dialog box

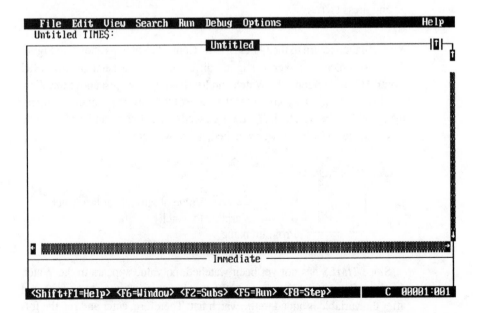

FIGURE 6-4   QuickBASIC Control Center with Watch window

```
CLS
PRINT TIME$
```

Note the time printed on the Output screen and then press any key to return to QuickBASIC Control. The Watch window now shows the value of *TIME$*; this is the same time that you just saw on the Output screen. Notice that although time is passing, the value of *TIME$* remains unchanged in the Watch window. This is because the values displayed in the Watch window are the values from the most recent program execution. Run this two-line program again. Note the new time and then return to the Control Center. What value for *TIME$* appears in the Watch window? You will see the most recent value of *TIME$*, which was displayed on the Output screen.

You can watch the value of several variables in the Watch window at once. Add a second variable, *TIMER*, to the watch list. To do so, select Add Watch... from the Debug menu, and you will again see the Add Watch dialog box.

Type:
TIMER
and press ENTER

This adds the variable to the Watch window. The Watch window now contains both variables, as shown here:

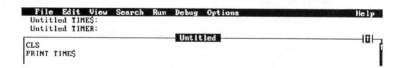

When you add a watch expression to the watch list, the values of all watched variables are cleared, so neither variable shows a current value. Now run the two-line program once more; again note the time displayed on the output screen and then return to the Control Center. The Watch window now has values for both *TIME$* and *TIMER*.

Notice that although *TIMER* was not used in the program, it now has a watch value. This is because *TIMER* is a QuickBASIC keyword (as is *TIME$*) whose value is assigned automatically. If you are watching a variable that is not also a QuickBASIC keyword, it will show a value of zero (or the null string if you are watching a string variable) until it is used in a program.

To illustrate this, add the variable *x* to the watch list; the Watch window should now include three variables: *TIME$, TIMER*, and *x*. Now run the program and then return to QuickBASIC Control. The values of *TIME$* and *TIMER* have changed, but the value of *x* is zero (0), as shown here:

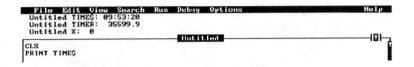

Add the following line to the program in the View window:

$$x = 3$$

Run this program and then check the values now appearing in the Watch window. The variable *x* now shows a value of 3.

DELETING WATCH EXPRESSIONS   As mentioned earlier, the New program and Open Program... options on the File menu both clear all watch expressions. Sometimes, however, you may wish to clear only one or two watch expressions, rather than clearing them all. Or, you may wish to clear all watch expressions but retain the current program in the View window.

To delete a watch expression, select Delete Watch... from the Debug menu. You will then see the Delete Watch dialog box with the current list of watch expressions, as shown in Figure 6-5. The last item in the watch list is highlighted. QuickBASIC assumes that the watch expression that was added most recently is the expression you wish to delete.

To delete another expression in the watch list, press UP ARROW to highlight the next item up on the list. When the item you wish to delete is highlighted, press ENTER. That expression no longer appears in the Watch window.

Figure 6-6 shows the Watch window with only two watch expressions; the second item on the previous watch list, *TIMER*, has been deleted. Notice that the program remains in the View window, unaffected by the addition or deletion of items from the watch list.

Delete the remaining two items from the watch list. Each time an item is deleted from the list, the Watch window becomes smaller, showing fewer watch expressions. When the last watch expression has been deleted, the Watch window disappears entirely.

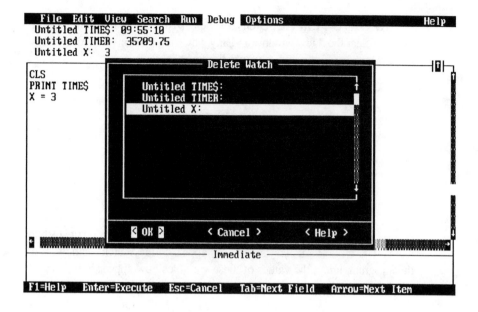

FIGURE 6-5   Delete Watch dialog box

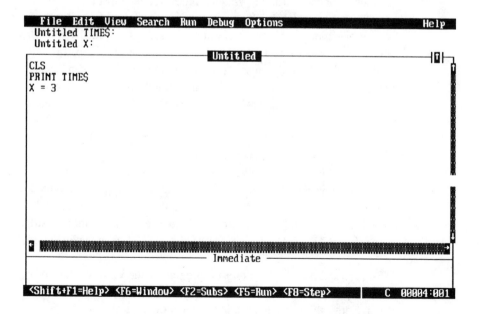

FIGURE 6-6   Watch window after deleting a watch expression

USING WATCH EXPRESSIONS   Select New Program from the File menu to clear the View window and any watch expressions that may still be in the watch list. Enter and run the following program:

```
CLS
x = 1
x = 22
x = 333
a$ = "Hi"
a$ = "there,"
a$ = "Mariko"
PRINT x
PRINT a$
```

Add *x* and *a$* to the watch list with the Add Watch... option on the Debug menu. These two variables should now appear in the Watch window. Run this program again; the values of these variables now appear in the Watch window, as follows:

```
Untitled x: 333
Untitled a$: Mariko
```

The values that appear in the Watch window are the most recent values assigned to each watched variable.

You can also monitor the values of watched variables continually, as each statement is executed, rather than just when a program is stopped or has finished executing. To do so, press F8 (the function 8 key). The screen flashes, the values of the variables being watched are cleared, and the next line to be executed is highlighted. Figure 6-7 shows the Watch and View windows after F8 has been pressed.

Press F8 again; the screen flashes as the first statement (CLS) is executed. The values in the Watch window remain untouched, and the next line to be executed (*x* = 1) is now highlighted. Press F8; *x* now shows a value of 1 in the Watch window, and the next line to be executed (*x* = 22) is highlighted.

Press F8 again; *x* now shows a value of 22 in the Watch window, and the next line in the program (*x* = 333) is highlighted. Press F8 twice more; *x* still shows a value of 333, and *a$* now shows a value of "Hi," as shown in Figure 6-8.

As you can see, pressing F8 causes the program in the View window to be executed one line at a time. Press F8 until each line in the program has been executed. Notice that when the last line in the program is executed, you can see the run of the program on the Output screen. This is because the last line

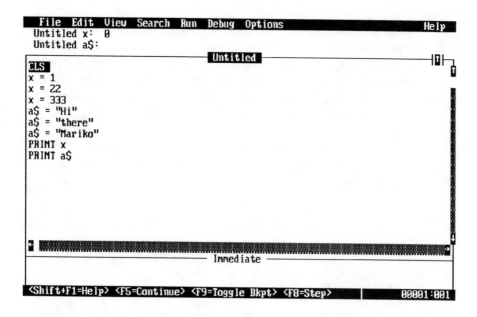

FIGURE 6-7 Watch and View windows after pressing F8

```
 File  Edit  View  Search  Run  Debug  Options                    Help
 Untitled x:   333
 Untitled a$: Hi
┌──────────────────────────── Untitled ────────────────────────────┤▌├─┐
│CLS                                                                    ▲│
│x = 1                                                                  █│
│x = 22                                                                 █│
│x = 333                                                                █│
│a$ = "Hi"                                                              █│
│a$ = "there"                                                           █│
│a$ = "Mariko"                                                          █│
│PRINT x                                                                █│
│PRINT a$                                                               █│
│                                                                       █│
│                                                                       █│
│                                                                       █│
│                                                                       █│
│                                                                       █│
│◄█████████████████████████████████████████████████████████████████►  ▼│
├──────────────────────────── Immediate ───────────────────────────────┤
│                                                                        │
└────────────────────────────────────────────────────────────────────┘
 <Shift+F1=Help>  <F5=Continue>  <F9=Toggle Bkpt>  <F8=Step>     00006:001
```

FIGURE 6-8 Watch and View windows after pressing F8 several times

in the program is a PRINT statement (PRINT *a$*), which causes the value of *a$* to be displayed on the Output screen.

Press F8 once more; the screen flashes as it did the first time you pressed F8, and the values of the watch expressions in the Watch window are again cleared. The next line in the program to be executed (CLS) is again highlighted. Pressing F8 again starts another line-by-line execution of the program.

Now try another example. Clear the watch expressions and the View window by selecting New Program from the File menu. Enter the following simple program:

```
CLS
x = 0
DO
  x = x + 1
  PRINT x
LOOP
```

Add *x* to the watch expression list and run this program. Press CTRL + BREAK to stop it. Notice the value of *x* in the Watch window. Now run this program one line at a time by pressing F8; watch the value of *x* increase as you continue to execute the program line by line.

This line-by-line execution of a program is referred to as stepping through a program. The ability to step through a program while watching key variables is one of the most useful features available to you when debugging programs.

INSTANT WATCH   Instant Watch displays the value of a variable or expression when program execution has been stopped. It is convenient to use when you do not need to monitor a variable continually, but do wish to check its value at certain times when the program is no longer running. Instant Watch is most appropriate for long or complex programs. You will therefore not use the feature in this book, though it is described briefly in this section.

To use Instant Watch, select the variable or expression in your program whose value you wish to display. To select that variable, place the cursor at the beginning of the variable name, press and hold the SHIFT key, and press RIGHT ARROW until the entire variable name is highlighted. Then choose Instant Watch... from the Debug menu. The variable or expression you just highlighted appears in the Expression box, and its current value appears in the Value box, as shown in Figure 6-9.

As you write more complex programs, you will find Instant Watch increasingly useful. You can suspend program execution, check the values of

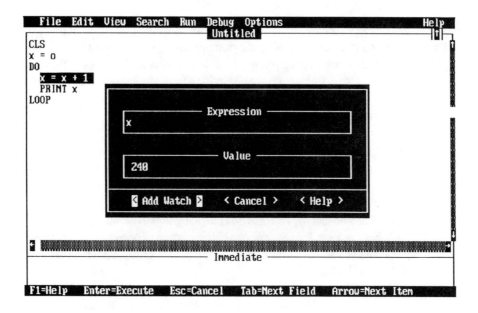

FIGURE 6-9   Instant Watch dialog box with *x* being watched

certain key variables, and then continue running the program. Or you can stop a program, check the values of important variables with Instant Watch, and add those variables to the watch list.

Experiment with Instant Watch: load and run one of the more complex programs you wrote in a previous chapter. Press CTRL + BREAK to stop the program and select (highlight) a variable to watch. Then choose Instant Watch... from the Debug menu. You should see the variable name and its current value in the Instant Watch dialog box. Continue running this program and then stop it again. Select another variable to watch.

You can see that this process of running a program and then using Instant Watch to check certain variable values can be very useful, especially when you are trying to figure out why a program isn't doing what it is supposed to be doing. Refer to the QuickBASIC manuals for more detail on Instant Watch.

Breakpoints

A *breakpoint* is a place in your program at which you want to stop program execution. Typically, you will use breakpoints when you need to check the value of key variables at a certain point in a program. Using a breakpoint allows you to control precisely the point at which you will check your variables, rather than hoping you will be able to press CTRL + BREAK at the right moment. The sections that follow describe how to toggle and clear any breakpoints you set. Practice using breakpoints on various programs until you feel comfortable with them.

TOGGLING BREAKPOINTS   Toggling breakpoints means using a "toggle switch" to turn breakpoints on if they are off, or off if they are on. To turn a breakpoint on, move the cursor to the line at which you want the program to stop executing and select Toggle Breakpoint from the Debug menu. The line that the cursor is on is then highlighted to show that a breakpoint has been set. Run the program; the program executes up to the breakpoint, and you are then returned to QuickBASIC Control, with the cursor on the breakpoint line.

When the program has stopped at a breakpoint, you can check the values of variables in the Watch window, or use Instant Watch to check variables that are not included in the watch list. When you are ready to proceed, select Continue from the Run menu, and the program will resume execution from the breakpoint.

If the breakpoint you set is within a loop, the program will stop each time it encounters the breakpoint in repeating the loop. To toggle such a breakpoint off, place the cursor on the breakpoint you wish to turn off, and choose Toggle Breakpoint from the Debug menu. The breakpoint is turned off, and that line is no longer highlighted. Run the program again or select Continue from the Run menu to resume program execution.

You can set as many breakpoints as you wish in a program. Practice using breakpoints in various programs. Try setting several breakpoints, and toggling one or two of them on and off to see how they behave.

CLEARING ALL BREAKPOINTS   Clear all Breakpoints is an option on the Debug menu. It will clear all breakpoints from the program in the View window so that when you run the program again the program will only stop when it is finished, or when it is stopped by pressing CTRL + BREAK.

The New Program and Open Program... options on the File menu will also clear all breakpoints.

There are several powerful editing features of QuickBASIC. You can use editing keys to move the cursor within a program, or to move a program within the View window. You can also use editing keys to modify a program.

For example, press CTRL + Y to delete the line that the cursor is on. Or, select (highlight) a block of text and press DEL to delete it.

The Edit menu has three options: Cut, Copy, and Paste. Each of these options makes use of the clipboard, where text that has been cut or copied is placed. The clipboard contains only the text from the most recent Cut or Copy. The Cut option deletes the selected (highlighted) text from the program and places it in the clipboard. The Copy option copies the selected text from the program to the clipboard, leaving the selected text untouched in the program. The Paste option puts the contents of the clipboard in the program to the right of the cursor.

The Debug menu has three options for monitoring the value of variables (Add Watch..., Delete Watch..., and Instant Watch...). Watched variable values are displayed in the Watch window in the QuickBASIC Control Center.

The Debug menu has two options for setting breakpoints (Toggle Breakpoint and Clear All Breakpoints). A breakpoint is a place in the program at which execution stops to allow you to check certain variable values. There are no restrictions on the number or placement of breakpoints in a program.

7

FUNCTION JUNCTION

Built-in Functions
User-defined Functions
Some New Control Structures

In this chapter you will learn about some of the functions that are built in to QuickBASIC, as well as how to write your own user-defined functions. You will also learn about two new control structures. In particular you will

- Learn how to use the simple functions TIMER, RND, DATE$, TIME$

- Learn to use functions with arguments, including TAB, INT, FIX, INPUT$, LCASE$, UCASE$, MID$, and LEFT$

- Learn to write and use your own user-defined functions

- Learn about the SELECT CASE program structure

- Learn about the FOR...NEXT loop program structure

BUILT-IN FUNCTIONS

QuickBASIC has a rich selection of built-in *functions*. A function is a keyword that, when used, returns a *value;* this value is the result computed by the function. QuickBASIC has both *numeric functions* and *string functions*. The value of a numeric function is a number; the value of a string function is a string. In other words, if the function is a numeric function, a number value is returned; if the function is a string function, a string value is returned. String function names end with a dollar sign ($), just as string variable names do.

In addition, some functions use arguments and some do not. Functions that have no arguments are called *simple functions*. As you read and learn about the functions described in this chapter, try writing your own programs, in addition to trying the sample programs, which explore how each function works.

Simple Functions

A simple function is a function that does not require any arguments. A simple function can be either a numeric or a string function. Some useful simple functions are described next.

TIMER FUNCTION   TIMER is a numeric function. The TIMER function returns the number of seconds since midnight. At midnight, the value of TIMER is zero (0). At high noon, the value of TIMER is 43200. At one minute before midnight, the value of TIMER is 86340. To see TIMER change value, run program QBME0701.BAS, Demonstrate TIMER Numeric Function.

```
REM ** QBME0701.BAS **
REM ** 1/1/90 **
REM ** Demonstrate TIMER Numeric Function **
' QuickBASIC Made Easy, Chapter 7
' Microsoft QuickBASIC 4.5

TIME$ = "23:59"     'One minute before midnight

REM ** DO...LOOP. Press a key to stop **
DO
  PRINT TIMER,
LOOP WHILE INKEY$ = ""   'Loop while no key press
```

```
86399.33   86399.33   86399.33   86399.33   86399.39
86399.39   86399.39   86399.39   86399.33   86399.39
86399.44   86399.44   86399.44   86399.44   86399.44
86399.5    86399.5    86399.5    86399.5    86399.5
86399.5    86399.5    86399.55   86399.55   86399.55
86399.55   86399.55   86399.55   86399.55   86399.61
86399.61   86399.61   86399.61   86399.61   86399.61
86399.66   86399.66   86399.66   86399.66   86399.66
86399.66   86399.72   86399.72   86399.72   86399.72
86399.72   86399.72   86399.72   86399.77   86399.77
86399.77   86399.77   86399.77   86399.77   86399.83
86399.83   86399.83   86399.83   86399.83   86399.83
86399.88   86399.88   88399.88   86399.88   86399.88
86399.88   86399.94   86399.94   86399.94   86399.94
86399.94   86399.94   86399.94   0          0
0          0          0          0          0
.05        .05        .05        .05        .05
.05        .05        .1         .1         .1
.1         .1         .1         .16        .16
.16        .16        .16        .16        .16
.21        .21        .21        .21        .21
.27        .27        .27        .27        .27
.32        .32        .32        .32        .32
.32        .32
```

```
Press any key to continue
```

FIGURE 7-1   Value of TIMER numeric function

Figure 7-1 shows a sample run of program QBME0701.BAS; this program was stopped after midnight, when the value of TIMER reached 0.

RND FUNCTION   RND is a numeric function. Its value is a "random number" between zero and one. The numbers generated by the RND function are not truly random, as are numbers obtained, for example, by rolling dice. Rather, RND generates pseudo-random numbers. To see the difference between truly random and pseudo-random numbers, run the following short program at least twice.

```
CLS
PRINT RND, RND, RND, RND, RND
```

Two sample runs are shown next. Notice that both runs produced the same set of numbers.

```
.7107346   .99058   .8523988   .3503776   4.363585E-02
.7107346   .99058   .8523988   .3503776   4.363585E-02
```

RND generates the same numbers each time the program is run. These numbers are pseudo-random; if RND generated truly random numbers, different numbers would be produced each time the program was run.

You can avoid this replication of so-called random numbers by using the RANDOMIZE statement with the TIMER function, as shown in the program below. RANDOMIZE TIMER is needed only once in each program. To ensure that each random number generated is unpredictable, this statement must precede the first RND function in the program.

```
CLS
RANDOMIZE TIMER
PRINT RND, RND, RND, RND, RND
```

Two runs of this program are shown next. Notice that these two runs produced different sets of random numbers.

```
.3151505    .8492073  .2608918  .1717735  .4388232
.1946366    .3044991  .6137666  .9568992  .552196
```

Now run the program several times. You will see a different set of numbers each time it is run.

DATE\$ and TIME\$ FUNCTIONS   DATE\$ and TIME\$ can be used either as string functions or as statements. You have used DATE\$ and TIME\$ in previous chapters as both functions and statements. Examples of function and statement usage are shown here:

```
Used as statements:    DATE$ = "1/1/90"
                       TIME$ = "7:30"


Used as functions:     PRINT DATE$
                       PRINT TIME$
```

When DATE$ or TIME$ are used as statements, you can assign a value to them. When they are being used as functions, they return string values, that is, the current date or time.

INKEY$ FUNCTION   INKEY$ is a string function. You also used this function in an earlier chapter. INKEY$ scans the keyboard for a key press. If any key has been pressed, the value of INKEY$ is that character. If no key has been pressed, the value of INKEY$ is the null, or empty, string (""). INKEY$ does not wait for a key to be pressed, as does the INPUT$ function, described later in this section.

Remember: QuickBASIC has two kinds of functions, numeric functions and string functions. The name of a string function ends in a dollar sign ($). The value of a numeric function is a number; the value of a string function is a string. Some names of functions are listed here.

Numeric functions:	RND	TIMER	
String functions:	DATE$	INKEY$	TIME$

Functions That Require Arguments

Many QuickBASIC functions operate on arguments to compute the value of the function. The argument is enclosed in parentheses, and follows the name of the function. This section describes several useful functions that require arguments.

TAB FUNCTION   TAB is another function that you should recognize from earlier chapters. TAB is a numeric function that uses an argument; the argument specifies the column in which the next output will be printed. TAB(40), for example, specifies the print column as 40; the number 40 is the argument of the function and is enclosed in parentheses.

```
TAB(40)

 ↑   ↑
 │    Argument
Function name
```

TAB can only be used in PRINT and LPRINT statements. The following small program illustrates how you might use TAB.

```
CLS

PRINT TAB(10); "This text begins at column 10"
PRINT TAB(20); "This test begins at column 20"

PRINT TAB(10); "Column 1"; TAB(30); "Column 2";
PRINT TAB(50); "Column 3"
```

INT FUNCTION   The INT function is a numeric function that returns the integer value of the argument enclosed in parentheses. More precisely, INT(*number*) is the greatest integer that is less than or equal to the value of *number*. For example, INT(6 * RND) returns the integer value of the argument, (6 * RND). Thus, if the value of RND is .3151505, then the value of 6 * RND is 1.890903, and the value of INT(6 * RND) is 1. Some examples of the INT function are shown next.

```
Non-negative numbers:   INT(0) = 0      INT(3.142) = 3

Negative numbers:       INT(-1) = -1    INT(-3.14) = -4
```

In this book, most applications of INT involve non-negative numbers. If you want to compute the integer part of a number, regardless of its sign, you can use another function, called FIX.

FIX FUNCTION   FIX is a numeric function that returns the integer part of its numeric argument. More precisely, if *number* is positive, FIX(*number*) returns the first integer which is less than or equal to *number;* if *number* is negative, FIX returns the first integer which is greater than or equal to *number*. For example:

```
FIX(0) = 0        FIX(3.14) = 3          FIX(-3.14) = -3
```

Compare this example with the results, using the same arguments, with the INT function. Use program QBME0702.BAS, Demonstrate FIX and INT Numeric Functions, to learn more about FIX and INT.

```
REM ** QBME0702.BAS **
REM ** 1/1/90 **
REM ** Demonstrate FIX and INT Numeric Functions **
' QuickBASIC Made Easy, Chapter 7
' Microsoft QuickBASIC 4.5
```

```
CLS

REM ** DO...LOOP to print FIX and INT of a number **

DO
  INPUT "Argument, please"; argument
  PRINT "FIX(argument) is "; FIX(argument)
  PRINT "INT(argument) is "; INT(argument)
  PRINT
LOOP
```

A sample run is shown in Figure 7-2. You can use the program to verify that, for integer arguments, FIX and INT are the same. They are also the same for positive noninteger arguments. For negative noninteger arguments, however, the values differ by one.

INPUT$ FUNCTION   INPUT$($n$) is a string function with a numeric argument. INPUT$($n$) tells the computer to wait for a string of n characters to be entered from the keyboard. Program QBME0703.BAS, Demonstrate INPUT$ String Function, waits for one character to be entered, and then prints the character that was just entered.

```
Argument, please? 1
FIX(argument) is  1
INT(argument) is  1

Argument, please? -1
FIX(argument) is  -1
INT(argument) is  -1

Argument, please? .123
FIX(argument) is  0
INT(argument) is  0

Argument, please? -.123
FIX(argument) is  0
INT(argument) is  -1

Argument, please?
```

FIGURE 7-2   Results of INT and FIX functions

```
REM ** QBME0703.BAS ***
REM ** 1/1/90 **
REM ** Demonstrate INPUT$ String Function **
' QuickBASIC Made Easy, Chapter 7
' Microsoft QuickBASIC 4.5

CLS

REM ** DO...LOOP to get & print value of INPUT$(1) **

DO
  PRINT "Press a key"
  anykey$ = INPUT$(1)
  PRINT "You pressed "; anykey$
  IF LCASE$(anykey$) = "q" THEN EXIT DO
  PRINT
LOOP
```

Figure 7-3 shows an annotated run of program QBME0703.BAS. Note that some keys, such as ENTER, are nonprinting characters. Try pressing ENTER when you run this program and see what happens.

LCASE\$ AND UCASE\$ FUNCTIONS   LCASE$ and UCASE$ are string functions with string arguments. The argument can be a string enclosed in quotation marks, a string variable, a string function, or a string expression. LCASE$ returns a string with all of the letters converted to lowercase. UCASE$ returns a string with all of the letters converted to uppercase. For example:

```
LCASE$("ABC 123") = "abc 123"
LCASE$("aBc 123") = "abc 123"

UCASE$("abc 123") = "ABC 123"
UCASE$("ABc 123") = "ABC 123"
```

Arguments of these functions can also be string variables. LCASE$(*anykey$*) is the value of the string variable *anykey$* with all letters changed to lowercase. UCASE$(*word$*) is the value of the string variable *word$* with all letters changed to uppercase. Use program QBME0704.BAS, Demonstrate LCASE$ and UCASE$ String Functions, to learn more about LCASE$ and UCASE$.

```
REM ** QBME0704.BAS **
REM ** 1/1/90 **
REM ** Demonstrate LCASE$ and UCASE$ String Functions **
' QuickBASIC Made Easy, Chapter 7
```

```
' Microsoft QuickBASIC 4.5

CLS

REM ** DO...LOOP to get string, print LCASE$, UCASE$ **
' Press ENTER to stop

DO
  LINE INPUT "String, please? "; anystring$
  PRINT "The LCASE$ is:  "; LCASE$(anystring$)
  PRINT "The UCASE$ is:  "; UCASE$(anystring$)
  PRINT
LOOP UNTIL anystring$ = ""    ' "" is the null string
```

Figure 7-4 shows a run of QBME0704.BAS. To stop this program, press ENTER without typing any characters. This assigns the null string ("") as the value of *anystring$*. Note that QBME0704.BAS uses a LINE INPUT statement rather than an INPUT statement. LINE INPUT accepts all characters entered, including commas, and assigns them to a string variable. LINE INPUT does not automatically print a question mark following the prompt

```
    Press a key
    You pressed a

    Press a key
    You pressed A

    Press a key
    You pressed 8

    Press a key
    You pressed *

    Press a key              (ENTER was pressed)
    You pressed

    Press a key
    You pressed q


    Press any key to continue
```

FIGURE 7-3   An annotated run of QBME0703.BAS

string. A question mark has therefore been included within it, as shown in the next example.

```
LINE INPUT "String, please? "; anystring$
```

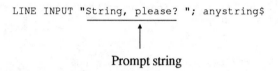

Prompt string

Remember: A function returns one value and may or may not require an argument. The functions described so far are shown here:

```
Numeric functions:     RND
                       TIMER
                       FIX(number)
                       INT(number)
                       TAB(number)

String functions:      DATE$
                       TIME$
                       INKEY$
                       INPUT$(number)
                       LCASE$(string$)
                       UCASE$(string$)
```

```
String, please? Agent 007
The LCASE$ is:  agent 007
The UCASE$ is:  AGENT 007

String, please? LCASE$ and UCASE$ change only LEtTeRs!!
The LCASE$ is:  lcase$ and ucase$ change only letters!!
The UCASE$ is:  LCASE$ AND UCASE$ CHANGE ONLY LETTERS!!

String, please? 1, 2, 3
The LCASE$ is:  1, 2, 3
The UCASE$ is:  1, 2, 3

String, please?                          (ENTER was pressed)
The LCASE$ is:
The UCASE$ is:

Press any key to continue
```

FIGURE 7-4   Demonstration of LCASE$ and UCASE$ functions

USER-DEFINED FUNCTIONS

You can write and use your own functions, in addition to using the functions that are built in to QuickBASIC. Functions that you write are called *user-defined* functions. In this section, you will learn how to name, define, and use single-line user-defined functions. Later in this chapter you will learn how to name, define, and use multi-line user-defined functions.

To define and name your own function, you will use the DEF FN statement. To define an integer function to "roll" one six-sided die, enter the following function:

```
DEF FNrollD6% = INT(6 * RND) + 1
```

The name of this function is FNrollD6%. Since its name ends with a percent symbol (%), this function is defined to be an integer function. A user-defined function can be either numeric or string. Numeric user-defined functions, like numeric variables, can be integer, long integer, single precision, or double precision functions.

The function definition is to the right of the equal sign (=). The function FNrollD6% has no argument. In program QBME0705.BAS, Roll Two Six-sided Dice, FNrollD6% is used twice.

```
REM ** QBME0705.BAS **
REM ** 1/1/90 **
REM ** Roll Two Six-sided Dice (Roll 2D6) **
' QuickBASIC Made Easy, Chapter 7
' Microsoft QuickBASIC 4.5

REM ** Define FNrollD6%, a function to roll D6 **
' Returns an integer from 1 to 6
DEF FNrollD6% = INT(6 * RND) + 1

REM ** Set up **
CLS
RANDOMIZE TIMER

DO
  BEEP
  PRINT "Press the SPACE BAR to roll, or 'Q' to quit"
  k$ = INPUT$(1)
  IF UCASE$(k$) = "Q" THEN EXIT DO
  IF k$=" " THEN PRINT "The roll is"; FNrollD6% + FNrollD6%
  PRINT
LOOP
```

A sample run of QBME0705.BAS is shown in Figure 7-5. SPACEBAR was pressed three times to produce three simulated rolls of the dice; Q was then pressed to exit the DO...LOOP structure. Of course, you could define a single function to simulate the rolling of two dice, and then use it only once in your program. Modify QBME0705.BAS to define the function FNroll2D6%, as shown next.

```
DEF FNroll2D6% = INT(6 * RND) + INT(6 + RND) + 2
```

Run the modified program; notice that it produces results similar to the original, QBME0705.BAS. Program QBME0706.BAS, Roll Three Six-sided Dice, uses the function FNroll3D6% to simulate rolling three six-sided dice.

```
REM ** QBME0706.BAS **
REM ** 1/1/90 **
REM ** Roll Three Six-sided Dice (Roll 3D6) **
' QuickBASIC Made Easy, Chapter 7
' Microsoft QuickBASIC 4.5

REM ** Define FNroll3D6%, a function to roll 3D6 **
' Returns integer from 3 to 12, not equally probable
DEF FNroll3D6% = INT(6*RND) + INT(6*RND) + INT(6*RND) + 3

REM ** Set up **
CLS
RANDOMIZE TIMER

REM ** DO...LOOP to roll three six-sided dice **
DO
  BEEP: PRINT "Press SPACEBAR to roll 3D6, or 'Q' to quit"
  anykey$ = INPUT$(1)
  IF UCASE$(anykey$) = "Q" THEN EXIT DO
  IF anykey$ = " " THEN PRINT "The roll is"; FNroll3D6%
  PRINT
LOOP
```

You can change this program to define a function that simulates the roll of as many dice as you choose. Try modifying FNrollD6% to simulate the flipping of one and two coins.

User-defined Functions with Arguments

The user-defined functions that you have used so far have not used any arguments. You can also define functions, however, that do have arguments.

```
Press the SPACEBAR to roll, or 'Q' to quit
The roll is 10

Press SPACEBAR to roll, or 'Q' to quit
The roll is 6

Press SPACEBAR to roll, or 'Q' to quit
The roll is 7

Press SPACEBAR to roll, or 'Q' to quit


Press any key to continue
```

FIGURE 7-5   Demonstrate use of FNrolld6% function

Again, as with the built-in functions, the argument is enclosed in parentheses. The function FNrndint%, shown next, is an integer function with an argument, $n\%$. The value of FNrndint%($n\%$) is a random integer in the range 1 to $n\%$.

```
DEF FNrndint%(n%) = INT(n% * RND) + 1
```

The argument ($n\%$) is a *local variable;* that is, the value of $n\%$ has no meaning outside the function definition. You may use the variable name $n\%$ elsewhere in the program without affecting this function. The argument $n\%$ was chosen arbitrarily. You can replace $n\%$ on both sides of the equal sign with any appropriate variable of your choice. For example:

```
DEF FNrndint%(range%) = INT(range% * RND) + 1
```

Program QBME0707.BAS, Coin Flipping, uses the function FNrndint% to generate a random integer, 1 or 2, which is then used to print HEADS or TAILS.

```
REM ** QBME0707.BAS **
REM ** 1/1/90 **
REM ** Coin Flipping **
' QuickBASIC Made Easy, Chapter 7
' Microsoft QuickBASIC 4.5
```

```
REM ** Define FNrndint%, a random integer function **
' Returns integer in range 1 to n%, equally probable
DEF FNrndint% (n%) = INT(n% * RND) + 1

REM ** Set up **
CLS
RANDOMIZE TIMER

REM ** DO...LOOP to flip coin. Press "Q" to quit **
DO
  BEEP:PRINT "Press SPACEBAR to flip coin or 'Q' to quit"
  anykey$ = INPUT$(1)

  ' Block IF structure does the flip if anykey$ is a space
  IF anykey$ = " " THEN
    OneOrTwo% = FNrndint%(2)
    IF OneOrTwo% = 1 THEN PRINT "The flip is HEADS"
    IF OneOrTwo% = 2 THEN PRINT "The flip is TAILS"
  END IF

  PRINT
LOOP UNTIL UCASE$(anykey$) = "Q"
```

QBME0707.BAS introduces a new program structure, QuickBASIC's powerful Block IF...END IF structure shown below.

```
IF anykey$ = " " THEN
  OneOrTwo% = FNrndint%(2)
  IF OneOrTwo% = 1 THEN PRINT "The flip is HEADS"
  IF OneOrTwo% = 2 THEN PRINT "The flip is TAILS"
END IF
```

A Block IF...END IF structure begins with an IF statement and ends with an END IF statement. A Block IF...END IF structure can have any number of lines between the IF statement and the END IF statement. This Block IF...END IF structure begins with this IF statement

```
IF anykey$ = " " THEN
```

and ends with the statement

```
END IF
```

If the value of *anykey$* is a space, the three lines between the IF and END IF statements are executed. The value of *OneOrTwo%* is a random integer, 1 or 2. The two IF...THEN statements select one of the two possible messages to be printed, depending on the value of *OneOrTwo%*.

```
Press SPACEBAR to flip coin or 'Q' to quit
The flip is TAILS

Press SPACEBAR to flip coin or 'Q' to quit
The flip is TAILS

Press SPACEBAR to flip coin or 'Q' to quit
The flip is HEADS

Press SPACEBAR to flip coin or 'Q' to quit
```

FIGURE 7-6   A sample run of coin flipping program

A partial sample run is shown in Figure 7-6. The SPACEBAR was pressed three times, resulting in TAILS, TAILS, and HEADS. The computer is waiting for another key press. If SPACEBAR is pressed, HEADS or TAILS will again be printed. If Q is pressed, the program will stop. If any other key is pressed, the computer will beep and wait for SPACEBAR or Q to be pressed.

WORD MAKER PROGRAM   Suppose you want to name a new product, or even a new venture company. Or perhaps you are writing a novel and want to create unusual names for characters or places. Why not use your computer to help you invent names? How would you write a program to print names that are pronounceable, but seem exotic, or even fantastic?

The key to this task is the QuickBASIC MID$ function. MID$ is a string function with three arguments—one string argument and two numeric arguments. When a function has more than one argument, the arguments are separated by commas. MID$ is used to select a portion of a string (a substring) from within a string. To see why the MID$ function is so useful, consider the word "proverb." It contains these shorter words.

pro   prove   rove   rover   over   verb

You can use MID$ to select portions of a word or string.
Enter and run the following program.

```
CLS

word$ = "proverb"

PRINT MID$(word$, 1, 3)
PRINT MID$(word$, 1, 5)
PRINT MID$(word$, 1, 6)
PRINT MID$(word$, 1, 7)
PRINT MID$(word$, 2, 4)
PRINT MID$(word$, 2, 5)
PRINT MID$(word$, 3, 4)
PRINT MID$(word$, 4, 4)
```

A run of this program produces the following "words within words."

```
pro
prove
prover
proverb
rove
rover
over
verb
```

The value of of the MID$ function is a substring of the function's first argument. The second argument is numeric; it specifies the position within the string (the first argument) at which to begin. The third argument is also numeric; it specifies how many characters to select, counting from where the substring begins (the second argument). The following example illustrates this.

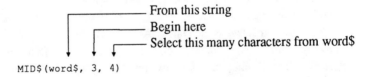

```
MID$(word$, 3, 4)
```

Since the value of *word$* is "proverb," the value of MID$(*word$, 3, 4*) is obtained by starting at the third character of "proverb" ("o"), and selecting four characters. Thus, MID$(*word$, 3, 4*) is "over."

Program QBME0708.BAS, Word Maker, generates random five-letter words of this form: consonant, vowel, consonant, vowel, consonant (cvcvc). In this program, the letter "y" can appear as either a consonant or vowel. Here are some possible random words.

kilam   losas   zilog   conan   dymax

QBME0708.BAS uses MID$ and FNrndint% to select random consonants from the string *consonant$* and random vowels from the string *vowel$*.

```
REM ** QBME0708.BAS **
REM ** 1/1/90 **
REM ** Word Maker (cvcvc) **
' QuickBASIC Made Easy, Chapter 7
' Microsoft QuickBASIC 4.5

REM ** Define FNrndint%, a random integer function **
' Returns integer in range 1 to n%, equally probable
DEF FNrndint% (n%) = INT(n% * RND) + 1

REM ** Set up **
CLS
RANDOMIZE TIMER
consonant$ = "bcdfghjklmnpqrstvwxyz"   '21 consonants
vowel$ = "aeiouy"                      '6 vowels, plus y

REM ** DO...LOOP to make cvcvc words. Press "Q" to quit **

DO

  BEEP: PRINT "Press SPACEBAR for a word or 'Q' to quit"
  anykey$ = INPUT$(1)

  ' If anykey$ is a space, make a word. Start with empty
  ' string  and add (+) consonant, vowel, consonant,
  ' vowel, consonant.
  IF anykey$ = " " THEN
    word$ = ""
    word$ = word$ + MID$(consonant$, FNrndint%(21), 1)
    word$ = word$ + MID$(vowel$, FNrndint%(6), 1)
    word$ = word$ + MID$(consonant$, FNrndint%(21), 1)
    word$ = word$ + MID$(vowel$, FNrndint%(6), 1)
    word$ = word$ + MID$(consonant$, FNrndint%(21), 1)
    PRINT "Your random cvcvc word is:"; TAB(43); word$
    PRINT
  END IF

LOOP UNTIL LCASE$(anykey$) = "q"
```

The string variables *consonant$* and *vowel$* are assigned during the setup block of the program. The program also uses a Block IF...END IF structure to generate the five-letter word. If the value of *anykey$* is a space (" "), the statements between the IF statement and the END IF statement are executed.

The statement *word$* = "" tells the computer to assign the null string as the value of *word$*. Each time the loop is repeated, *word$* is reset to the null string, thus erasing any earlier value it may contain.

The statement *word$* = *word$* + MID$(*consonant$*, FNrndint%(21), 1) tells the computer to select one random letter from the string variable *consonant$* and append it to the value of *word$*. When used with strings, the plus sign (+) means concatenate, or put together with, or attach to. The following MID$ function illustrates how this single letter is selected from *consonant$*.

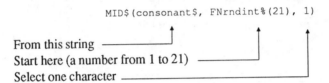

```
                        MID$(consonant$, FNrndint%(21), 1)
```

From this string
Start here (a number from 1 to 21)
Select one character

The statement *word$* = *word$* + MID$(*vowel$*, FNrndint%(6), 1) tells the computer to concancenate a random letter from *vowel$* and to the value of *word$*.

Another consonant, another vowel, and finally another consonant are added to *word$*. After the randomly generated five-letter word is displayed, you can generate another word or exit the loop by pressing Q.

A sample run of this program is shown in Figure 7-7. When you run this program, the words generated will probably be different, since the letters in the words are randomly selected.

In programming, you can almost always do things in more than one way. Program QBME0709.BAS, Word Maker with Random Character Function, uses a defined function called FNrndchr$ to generate random words. The value of FNrndchr$ is a single character selected at random from a string argument.

```
REM ** QBME0709.BAS **
REM ** 1/1/90 **
REM ** Word Maker with Random Character Function **
' QuickBASIC Made Easy, Chapter 7
' Microsoft QuickBASIC 4.5

REM ** Define FNrndchr$, a random character function **
' Returns one random character from a string argument
DEF FNrndchr$(strng$) = MID$(strng$, INT(LEN(strng$)*RND)+1,1)
```

```
REM ** Set up **
CLS
RANDOMIZE TIMER
consonant$ = "bcdfghjklmnpqrstvwxyz"    '21 consonants
vowel$ = "aeiouy"                        '6 vowels, plus y

REM ** DO...LOOP to make cvcvc words. Press "Q" to quit **

DO

   BEEP: PRINT "Press SPACEBAR for a word or 'Q' to quit"
   anykey$ = INPUT$(1)

   ' If anykey$ = " ", make a word. Start with empty string;
   ' add (+) consonant, vowel, consonant, vowel, consonant.

   IF anykey$ = " " THEN
     word$ = ""
     word$ = word$ + FNrndchr$(consonant$)
     word$ = word$ + FNrndchr$(vowel$)
     word$ = word$ + FNrndchr$(consonant$)
     word$ = word$ + FNrndchr$(vowel$)
     word$ = word$ + FNrndchr$(consonant$)
     PRINT "Your random cvcvc word is:"; TAB(43); word$
     PRINT
   END IF

LOOP UNTIL LCASE$(anykey$) = "q"
```

```
Press SPACEBAR for a word or Q to quit
Your random cvcvc word is:              lonis

Press SPACEBAR for a word or Q to quit
Your random cvcvc word is:              tytuj

Press SPACEBAR for a word or Q to quit
Your random cvcvc word is:              rewik

Press SPACEBAR for a word or Q to quit
Your random cvcvc word is:              nabez

Press SPACEBAR for a word or Q to quit
Your random cvcvc word is:              vuyod

Press SPACEBAR for a word or Q to quit
```

FIGURE 7-7   A sample run of Word Maker program

The definition of FNrndchr$ uses four built-in functions: MID$, INT, LEN, and RND. You have already used MID$, INT, and RND; LEN is introduced here.

The value of LEN(*strng$*) is the length of *strng$*. That is, LEN(*strng$*) is the number of characters in the string *strng$*. For example, *consonant$* is a string consisting of 21 consonants. LEN(*consonant$*) is therefore 21. The variable *vowel$* is a string consisting of 6 vowels. LEN(*vowel$*) is therefore 6.

The value of INT(LEN(*strng$*) * RND) + 1 is a random integer from 1 to the length of *strng$*. This value is then used in the MID$ function as the starting point of a substring one character long. This one-character long substring is the value of FNrndchr$(*strng$*). The value of FNrndchr$(*consonant$*) is therefore one random character selected from *consonant$*. The value of FNrndchr$(*vowel$*) is one random character selected from the value of *vowel$*.

Multi-Line User-defined Functions

The multi-line function definition provides a way for you to define functions that are too complex or too long to be written in a single line. A multi-line function begins with a DEF FN statement containing the name of the function and ends with an END DEF statement. You can write as many lines between the DEF FN and END DEF statements as necessary to define the function.

MULTI-LINE USER-DEFINED FUNCTIONS WITH NO ARGUMENTS   Program QBME0710.BAS, Coin Flipping with Multi-Line Defined Function, uses a function called FNflip$ to simulate the flipping of a coin. FNflip$ is a simple function—it has no arguments. The value of FNflip$ is "H" or "T," selected at random.

```
REM ** QBME0710.BAS **
REM ** 1/1/90 **
REM ** Coin Flipping with Multi-Line Defined Function **
' QuickBASIC Made Easy, Chapter 7
' Microsoft QuickBASIC 4.5

DEF FNflip$
' Returns "H" or "T" selected at random
  ZeroOrOne% = INT(2 * RND)
  IF ZeroOrOne% = 0 THEN flip$ = "H"
  IF ZeroOrOne% = 1 THEN flip$ = "T"
  FNflip$ = flip$
```

```
END DEF

REM ** Set up **
CLS
RANDOMIZE TIMER

REM ** DO...LOOP to 'flip' three coins **
DO
  BEEP: PRINT "Press SPACEBAR to flip 3 coins or 'Q' to quit"
  anykey$ = INPUT$(1)
  IF anykey$ = " " THEN PRINT FNflip$, FNflip$, FNflip$
  PRINT
LOOP UNTIL UCASE$(anykey$) = "Q"
```

The beginning of a sample run is shown in Figure 7-8. In Figure 7-8, four flips of three coins were made, and the computer is waiting for another key press. The definition of the function FNflip$ is shown next.

```
DEF FNflip$
  ' Returns "H" or "T" selected at random
  ZeroOrOne% = INT(2 * RND)
  IF ZeroOrOne% = 0 THEN flip$ = "H"
  IF ZeroOrOne% = 1 THEN flip$ = "T"
  FNflip$ = flip$
END DEF
```

```
Press SPACEBAR to flip 3 coins or 'Q' to quit
T              H              T

Press SPACEBAR to flip 3 coins or 'Q' to quit
T              H              H

Press SPACEBAR to flip 3 coins or 'Q' to quit
T              H              T

Press SPACEBAR to flip 3 coins or 'Q' to quit
T              T              T

Press SPACEBAR to flip 3 coins or 'Q' to quit
```

FIGURE 7-8   A sample run of Coin-Flipping with Multi-Line Defined Function program

The definition begins with the DEF FNflip$ statement and ends with the END DEF statement.

The statement ZeroOrOne% = INT(2 * RND) assigns a random integer, 0 or 1, to the integer variable ZeroOrOne%. No other values are possible.

The two IF...THEN statements test the value of ZeroOrOne% and assign "H" or "T" as the value of flip$.

The statement FNflip$ = flip$ assigns flip$ as the value of the function. Every multi-line defined function must have a statement of this type to actually define the value of the function.

The two IF...THEN statements can also be combined in a single IF...THEN...ELSE statement, as shown in the following alternative definition of FNflip$.

```
DEF FNflip$
' Returns "H" or "T" selected at random
  ZeroOrOne% = INT(2 * RND)
  IF ZeroOrOne% = 0 THEN flip$ = "H" ELSE flip$ = "T"
  FNflip$ = flip$
END DEF
```

MULTI-LINE USER-DEFINED FUNCTIONS WITH ARGUMENTS

If a multi-line function requires an argument, it is shown in the first line, the DEF FN statement, of the definition. This is illustrated in the definition of FNDaysInMonth% in program QBME0711.BAS, Number of Days in a Month.

```
REM ** QBME0711.BAS **
REM ** 1/1/90 **
REM ** Number of Days in a Month **
' QuickBASIC Made Easy, Chapter 7
' Microsoft QuickBASIC 4.5

REM ** Define FNDaysInMonth%, number of days in a month **
' Returns the number of days in month% (month% = 1 to 12)
' Returns 0 if the value of month% is not 1 to 12
DEF FNDaysInMonth% (month%)
  days% = 0
  IF month% = 1 THEN days% = 31    'January
  IF month% = 2 THEN days% = 28    'February
  IF month% = 3 THEN days% = 31    'March
  IF month% = 4 THEN days% = 30    'April
  IF month% = 5 THEN days% = 31    'May
  IF month% = 6 THEN days% = 30    'June
  IF month% = 7 THEN days% = 31    'July
  IF month% = 8 THEN days% = 31    'August
  IF month% = 9 THEN days% = 30    'September
```

```
   IF month% = 10 THEN days% = 31   'October
   IF month% = 11 THEN days% = 30   'November
   IF month% = 12 THEN days% = 31   'December
   FNDaysInMonth% = days%
END DEF

REM ** Demonstrate FNDaysInMonth% function **
CLS
DO
   INPUT "Month number (1 to 12 or 0 to quit)"; month%
   IF month% = 0 THEN EXIT DO
   PRINT "That month has"; FNDaysInMonth%(month%); "days."
   PRINT
LOOP
```

A sample run of this program is shown in Figure 7-9. In this run, the computer is waiting for a month number or 0 to quit. When you run this program, try entering some unexpected values. What happens if you enter **13**? **3.14**? **3.9**? All values entered are rounded to integers when they are input, because *month%* is an integer variable.

SOME NEW CONTROL STRUCTURES

This section introduces two new program control structures: the SELECT CASE structure and the FOR...NEXT loop. These structures provide you with some very useful and powerful program control statements.

```
Month number (1 to 12 or 0 to quit)? 1
That month has 31 days.

Month number (1 to 12 or 0 to quit)? 2
That month has 28 days.

Month number (1 to 12 or 0 to quit)? 4
That month has 30 days.

Month number (1 to 12 or 0 to quit)? 12
That month has 31 days.

Month number (1 to 12 or 0 to quit)? _
```

FIGURE 7-9   A sample run of Number of Days in Month program

The SELECT CASE Structure

SELECT CASE is a multiple-choice decision structure. Depending on the value of the variable used in the SELECT CASE statement, one of several blocks in the structure is executed. A simple example of SELECT CASE follows.

```
SELECT CASE number
   CASE 1
     PRINT "one"
   CASE 2
     PRINT "two"
   CASE ELSE
     PRINT "not one or two"
END SELECT
```

There are three blocks that might be executed based on the value of *number:* CASE 1, CASE 2, or CASE ELSE. For any value of *number,* only one CASE block will be executed. If the value of *number* is 1, the CASE 1 block is executed, and the computer will print the word "one." If the value of *number* is 2, the CASE 2 block will be executed and the computer will print "two." For any value of *number* other than 1 or 2, the CASE ELSE block is executed and the computer will print "not one or two."

Here is another example:

```
SELECT CASE NumberName$
   CASE "one"
     PRINT 1
   CASE "two"
     PRINT 2
   CASE ELSE
     PRINT "not 'one' or 'two'"
END SELECT
```

Note that in this example, the variable following SELECT CASE is a string variable. The case values used to determine which block to execute are therefore also strings. If the value of *NumberName$* is "one," the computer will print the numeral 1. If the value of *NumberName$* is "two," the computer will print the numeral 2. For any value of *NumberName$* other than "one" or "two," the computer will print "not 'one' or 'two'."

A SELECT CASE structure usually includes a CASE ELSE clause, which is executed if none of the other cases occur. A CASE clause can specify a single comparison value, as in the previous examples, or a list of comparison values, as shown in the following example:

```
SELECT CASE number
  CASE 0, 2, 4, 6, 8
    PRINT "even decimal digit"
  CASE 1, 3, 5, 7, 9
    PRINT "odd decimal digit"
  CASE ELSE
    PRINT "not a decimal digit"
END SELECT
```

Program QBME0712.BAS, Number of Days in a Month (SELECT CASE), uses a SELECT CASE structure in the definition of the function FNDaysInMonth%.

```
REM ** QBME0712.BAS **
REM ** 1/1/90 **
REM ** Number of Days in a Month (SELECT CASE) **
' QuickBASIC Made Easy, Chapter 7
' Microsoft QuickBASIC 4.5

REM ** Define FNDaysInMonth%, number of days in a month **
' Returns the number of days in month% (month% = 1 to 12)
' Returns 0 if the value of month% is not 1 to 12
DEF FNDaysInMonth% (month%)
  SELECT CASE month%
    CASE 1, 3, 5, 7, 8, 10, 12  'Jan Mar May Jul Aug Oct Dec
      days% = 31
    CASE 4, 6, 9, 11            'Apr Jun Sep Nov
      days% = 30
    CASE 2                      'Feb (not a leap year)
      days% = 28
    CASE ELSE                   'value of month% not 1 to 12
      days% = 0
  END SELECT
  FNDaysInMonth% = days%
END DEF

REM ** Demonstrate FNDaysInMonth% function **
CLS
DO
  INPUT "Month number (1 to 12 or 0 to quit)"; month%
  IF month% = 0 THEN EXIT DO
  PRINT "That month has"; FNDaysInMonth%(month%); "days."
  PRINT
LOOP
```

Program QBME0713.BAS, Number of Days in a Month with Alpha Input, is a variation of QBME0712.BAS. In this program, you enter at least the first three letters of the name of a month; the first three letters of your entry are then used as the argument of FNDaysInMonth%. Note that the argument for

FNDaysInMonth% is a string argument (*month$*). Before looking at the program, study the sample run shown in Figure 7-10.

```
REM ** QBME0713.BAS **
REM ** 1/1/90 **
REM ** Number of Days in a Month with Alpha Input **
' QuickBASIC Made Easy, Chapter 7
' Microsoft QuickBASIC 4.5

REM ** Define FNDaysInMonth%, number of days in a month **
' Returns the number of days in month$ (jan, feb, ..., dec)
' Returns 0 if the value of month$ is not understood
DEF FNDaysInMonth%(month$)
  SELECT CASE LCASE$(LEFT$(month$, 3))
    CASE "jan", "mar", "may", "jul", "aug", "oct", "dec"
      days% = 31
    CASE "apr", "jun", "sep", "nov"
      days% = 30
    CASE "feb"        'Not a leap year
      days% = 28
    CASE ELSE         'Value of month$ not "jan", "feb", ...
      days% = 0
  END SELECT
  FNDaysInMonth% = days%
END DEF

REM ** Demonstrate FNDaysInMonth% function **
CLS
DO
  INPUT "Month name (or 'ENTER' to quit)"; month$
  IF month$ = "" THEN EXIT DO
  PRINT "That month has"; FNDaysInMonth%(month$); "days."
  PRINT
LOOP
```

Note the use of the LEFT$ function. The statement LEFT$(*month$*, 3) selects the first three characters from the variable *month$*. The LCASE$ function is used to ensure that the three letters selected by LEFT$ are lowercase letters. For example:

```
LCASE$(LEFT$("January", 3)) = "jan"
LCASE$(LEFT$("MARCH", 3)) = "mar"
```

If the string argument of the LEFT$ function has fewer than three characters, all characters are selected. For example:

```
LCASE$(LEFT$("Ap", 3)) = "ap"
```

```
Month (1st 3 or more letters or 'ENTER' to quit)? January
That month has 31 days.

Month (1st 3 or more letters or 'ENTER' to quit)? feb
That month has 28 days.

Month (1st 3 or more letters or 'ENTER' to quit)? March
That month has 31 days.

Month (1st 3 or more letters or 'ENTER' to quit)? Bobuary
That month has 0 days.

Month (1st 3 or more letters or 'ENTER' to quit)? April
That month has 30 days.

Month (1st 3 or more letters or 'ENTER' to quit)?
```

FIGURE 7-10   A sample run of Number of Days in a Month with Alpha Input
program

The FOR...NEXT Loop

The FOR...NEXT loop is a program control structure that repeats a loop the number of times specified in the FOR statement. A FOR...NEXT loop begins with a FOR statement and ends with a NEXT statement, and may have any number of statements between the two statements. An example of a simple FOR...NEXT loop follows.

```
FOR word% = 1 TO NumberOfWords%
  PRINT FNrndword$(wordform$),
NEXT word%
```

Note that the same variable name occurs after the FOR and the NEXT keywords. This variable must be a numeric variable. Since a FOR...NEXT loop is a counting loop, numeric variables are used to specify the number of times a loop is to be repeated. This FOR...NEXT loop tells the computer to begin at 1 and count consecutively to the value of *NumberOfWords%*.

The statements FOR *word%* = 1 TO *NumberOfWords%* and NEXT *word%* tell the computer to set *word%* to 1 and execute the FOR...NEXT loop up to the NEXT statement. When the NEXT statement is executed, 1 is added to *word%* and the value of *word%* is compared to the value of *NumberOfWords%*. If *word%* is less than or equal to *NumberOfWords%*, the loop is executed again; if *word%* is now greater than *NumberOfWords%*, the loop is exited automatically. Program execution then continues with the line following the NEXT statement.

In this example, *word%* increases from 1 to *NumberOfWords%*. The PRINT statement between the FOR and NEXT statements is executed for each value of *word%*.

Program QBME0714.BAS, Word Maker with Word Structure Entry, uses one FOR...NEXT loop to generate a word and a second FOR...NEXT loop to print the words as they are generated. This program also lets you select the consonant-vowel sequence of the word to be generated: enter **c** for a consonant and **v** for a vowel. You choose how many words are to be generated.

```
REM ** QBME0714.BAS **
REM ** 1/1/90 **
REM ** Word Maker. You Enter the Word Structure **
' QuickBASIC Made Easy, Chapter 7
' Microsoft QuickBASIC 4.5

REM ** Define FNrndword$(wordform$), random word function **
' Returns a random word of the form defined by the value of
' wordform$. For example, if wordform$ is "cvc", the random
' word is of the form: consonant, vowel, consonant.
DEF FNrndword$ (wordform$)
  consonant$ = "bcdfghjklmnpqrstvwxyz"  '21 consonants
  vowel$ = "aeiouy"              '6 vowels, plus y

  word$ = ""                          'start with empty string

  ' FOR...NEXT loop to make one word
  FOR CharacterPosition% = 1 TO LEN(wordform$)
    CorV$ = UCASE$(MID$(wordform$, CharacterPosition%, 1))
    ' SELECT CASE to add a constant or vowel to word$
    SELECT CASE CorV$
      CASE "C"
        rc% = INT(21 * RND) + 1
        word$ = word$ + MID$(consonant$, rc%, 1)
      CASE "V"
        rv% = INT(6 * RND) + 1
        word$ = word$ + MID$(vowel$, rv%, 1)
      CASE ELSE
    END SELECT
  NEXT CharacterPosition%

  FNrndword$ = word$
```

```
END DEF

REM ** Set up **
CLS
RANDOMIZE TIMER

REM ** Word structure and number of words to make **
INPUT "Word form (string of c's and v's)"; wordform$
PRINT
INPUT "How many random words"; NumberOfWords%
PRINT

REM ** Make and print the words **
PRINT "Here are your random '"; wordform$; "' words:"
PRINT
FOR word% = 1 TO NumberOfWords%
  PRINT FNrndword$(wordform$),
NEXT word%
END
```

A sample run of this program is shown in Figure 7-11.

Notice the longer and more complicated FOR...NEXT loop that is used in the definition of the function FNrndword%.

```
FOR CharacterPosition% = 1 TO LEN(wordform$)
  CorV$ = UCASE$(MID$(wordform$, CharacterPosition%, 1))
  ' SELECT CASE to add a consonant or vowel to word$
  SELECT CASE CorV$


    CASE "C"
      rc% = INT(21 * RND) + 1
      word$ = word$ + MID$(consonant$, rc%, 1)
    CASE "V"
      rv% = INT(6 * RND) + 1
      word$ = word$ + MID$(vowel$, rv%, 1)
    CASE ELSE
  END SELECT
NEXT CharacterPosition%
```

This FOR...NEXT loop is repeated for each value of the variable *CharacterPosition%*: 1, 2, 3, and so on, up to the length of *wordform$*. For example, if *wordform$* is "cvc," the loop is executed three times.

Note that the loop's controlling variable, *CharacterPosition%*, is used within the loop itself to select the next "c" or "v" from *wordform$*. Since *CharacterPosition%* goes from 1 to LEN(*wordform$*), its value is 2 when the second "c" or "v" is selected from *wordform$*, 3 when the third "c" or "v" is selected from *wordform$*, and so on.

```
Word form (string of c's and v's)? cvc

How many random words? 25

Here are your random 'cvc' words:

cyg         dar         qax         zyt         nef
daj         ziz         kok         fiq         jab
giv         kaz         yah         buk         boc
syp         typ         ceq         lur         dat
cat         myl         duh         say         vol


Press any key to continue
```

FIGURE 7-11   A sample run of Word Maker program

QuickBASIC has many built-in functions. A function may be either string or numeric; numeric functions, like numeric variables, can be integer, long integer, single precision, or double precision functions. A function returns a value: a string function returns a string value; a numeric function returns a number. In addition, some functions require arguments and others do not.

The built-in numeric and string functions discussed in this chapter are listed next:

```
Numeric functions:     RND
                       TIMER
                       FIX(number)
                       INT(number)
                       TAB(number)


String functions:      DATE$
                       TIME$
                       INKEY$
                       INPUT$(number)
                       LCASE$(string$)
                       UCASE$(string$)
                       MID$(string$, From, NumberOfChar)
                       LEFT$(string$, NumberOfCharacters)
```

You can write your own user-defined functions. A user-defined function can be numeric or string, one line or many lines. All user-defined functions begin with a DEF FN statement. Multi-line user-defined functions end with a DEF END statement. A user-defined function may or may not require an argument.

The SELECT CASE structure selects variables to make comparisons with and then executes only one CASE block; which one depends on the value of the variable selected.

The FOR...NEXT loop repeats the lines between the FOR statement and NEXT statement the number of times specified in the FOR statement. This structure can be very useful, especially when the variable that controls the FOR...NEXT loop is used in some way within the loop itself.

8

ARRAYS

Array Variables
Programming with Arrays
Manipulating Arrays

In this chapter you will learn about arrays—how to use them and how to manipulate them. In particular you will

- Learn about array dimensions and subscripts

- Learn to use the DIM statement to set the size of an array

- Learn to use the LBOUND and UBOUND functions to determine the lowest and highest subscripts of an array

- Learn to use the DEFINT keyword to define all numeric variables as integers, unless specified otherwise

- Learn to use two or three related arrays to calculate and print line items and dot products

- Learn to use the SWAP keyword to exchange values in an array

- Learn to use a bubble sort to sort both numeric and string arrays

ARRAYS

In previous chapters you have used simple numeric and string variables. Now you will learn about *array* variables, also called arrays. An array is a set of related variables, each of which is referenced by the same variable name. Each individual value of an array is called an *element*. An array element is referenced by the array variable name followed by a subscript. Here are some examples of both simple and subscripted array variables:

```
Simple Numeric
    Variables:    number     TaxRate!       Principal#

Simple String
    Variables:    anystring$     word$

Numeric Array
    Variables:    DayOfMonth%(12)     temperature!(5)

String Array
    Variables:    word$(2)     FirstName$(300)
```

Notice that arrays, like simple variables, can be either numeric or string. Also, like simple numeric variables, numeric arrays can be integer, long integer, single precision, or double precision arrays. The subscript is the number in parentheses following the variable name, as shown next.

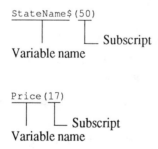

Array Dimensions

The default size of an array is 11 elements, *Array(0)* through *Array(10)*. The smallest default array subscript is 0; the largest default array subscript is 10. A numeric array with four elements is shown here. Note that the subscripts begin with 0, followed by 1, 2, and 3.

Price(0)   Price(1)   Price(2)   Price(3)

A string array with five elements is shown next. The subscripts are 0, 1, 2, 3, and 4.

word$(0)   word$(1)   word$(2)   word$(3)   word$(4)

THE DIM STATEMENT   The DIM statement is used to specify the size of an array. If the DIM statement is not used, then an array defaults to 11 elements (0 to 10). You can use the DIM statement to specify different smallest and largest subscripts. The keyword DIM is a shortened form of the word "dimension." When you use the DIM statement, you are establishing the dimensions of an array. In this book, all programs that use arrays will contain a DIM statement. Some examples of DIM statements are shown following.

```
DIM temperature!(1 TO 7)

DIM DaysInMonth%(1 TO 12)

DIM StateName$(1 TO 50)

DIM Description$(15)
```

The statement DIM *temperature!(1 TO 7)* defines a single precision numeric array of seven elements, *temperature!(1)* through *temperature!(7);* 1 is the smallest array subscript, 7 is the largest array subscript.

The statement DIM *DaysInMonth%(1 TO 12)* defines an integer array of twelve elements, *DaysInMonth%(1)* through *DaysInMonth%(12)*. *DaysInMonth%(1)* contains the number of days in the first month, January. *DaysInMonth%(12)* contains the number of days in the 12th month, December.

The statement DIM *StateName$(1 TO 50)* defines a string array of 50 elements, numbered 1 through 50. *StateName$(1)* contains the name of the first state, *StateName$(25)* contains the name of the 25th state, and so on.

The statement DIM *Description$(15)* defines a string array of 16 elements, 0 through 15. In this DIM statement, the smallest array subscript defaults to 0, and the largest subscript is 15. *Description$(0)* is the smallest subscript and the first element in this array; *Description$(15)* is the largest subscript and 16th element in this array.

In this book, an array name followed by an empty set of parentheses is used to refer to an entire array. This convention is used so you can easily dis-

$$
\text{DaysInMonth\%()}\left\{\begin{array}{l}
\texttt{DaysInMonth\%(1)} \\
\texttt{DaysInMonth\%(2)} \\
\texttt{DaysInMonth\%(3)} \\
\texttt{DaysInMonth\%(4)} \\
\texttt{DaysInMonth\%(5)} \\
\texttt{DaysInMonth\%(6)} \\
\texttt{DaysInMonth\%(7)} \\
\texttt{DaysInMonth\%(8)} \\
\texttt{DaysInMonth\%(9)} \\
\texttt{DaysInMonth\%(10)} \\
\texttt{DaysInMonth\%(11)} \\
\texttt{DaysInMonth\%(12)}
\end{array}\right.
$$

FIGURE 8-1   The array *DaysInMonth%( )*

tinguish an array from a simple, nonsubscripted variable, as demonstrated here.

```
Simple variables:   Price      word$

        Arrays:   Price()    word$()
```

For example, *DaysInMonth%()* is an integer array defined by the following DIM statement.

```
DIM DaysInMonth%(1 TO 12)
```

DaysInMonth%(), then, refers to the entire array consisting of 12 elements, as shown in Figure 8-1. The array *temperature!()* is a single precision array defined by this DIM statement.

```
DIM temperature!(1 TO 7)
```

Figure 8-2 shows the array *temperature!(),* defined by this DIM statement.

Array Subscripts

An array subscript can be a number, a numeric variable, or a numeric expression consisting of any legal combination of numbers, numeric variables, and numeric functions. For example, a subscript can be a simple number:

temperature!(7)

In this case, the subscript is the number 7.

A subscript can also be a numeric variable:

Word$(WordNumber%)

WordNumber% is an integer variable; its value specifies the element in this array that is to be manipulated.

A subscript can also be a numeric expression.

*Number(INT(49 * RND) + 1)*

The array element referenced here is the number that INT(49 * RND) + 1) equals. An array subscript is always an integer value; if the variable or numeric expression used to represent an array subscript is not an integer value, then its value is rounded to the nearest integer.

THE LBOUND AND UBOUND FUNCTIONS   Once an array has been dimensioned, you can use the LBOUND and UBOUND functions to determine the smallest (LBOUND) and the largest (UBOUND) array subscripts. LBOUND, meaning lower bound, shows the smallest array subscript. UBOUND, meaning upper bound, shows the largest array subscript. The following program prints the smallest and largest subscripts of the array *temperature!()*.

```
                                   ⎧  temperature! (1)
                                   ⎪  temperature! (2)
                                   ⎪  temperature! (3)
         temperature! ()        ⎨  temperature! (4)
                                   ⎪  temperature! (5)
                                   ⎪  temperature! (6)
                                   ⎩  temperature! (7)
```

FIGURE 8-2   The array *temperature!( )*

```
CLS

DIM temperature!(1 TO 7)

PRINT "The smallest subscript is"; LBOUND(temperature!)
PRINT "The largest subscript is "; UBOUND(temperature!)
```

For the array *DaysInMonth%()*,

```
LBOUND(DaysInMonth%) = 1
UBOUND(DaysinMonth%) = 12
```

PROGRAMMING WITH ARRAYS

Arrays are used in programs in much the same way that simple variables are. In fact, an array is a set of related variables. Programs that use arrays can, however, be much more powerful and useful than programs that use only simple variables. Programs that use arrays can also be much easier to write, as you will see in the sections that follow.

High, Low, and Average Temperature

The program QBME0801.BAS, High, Low, and Average Temperature, uses the array *temperature!()* to store the temperatures for each of the seven days of the week, Sunday through Saturday. The values of *temperature!(1)* through *temperature!(7)* are input, and the program calculates and prints the high, low, and average temperatures for the week.

```
REM ** QBME0801.BAS **
REM ** 1/1/90 **
REM ** High, Low, and Average Temperature **
' QuickBASIC Made Easy, Chapter 8
' Microsoft QuickBASIC 4.5

REM ** Define all numeric variables as short integers **
' Use &, !, # to designate other numeric variable types
DEFINT A-Z

REM ** Dim single precision array temperature!() **
DIM temperature!(1 TO 7)
```

```
REM ** Get temperature data for one week **
CLS
PRINT "Enter the temperature for each day of the week."
PRINT
INPUT "Sunday    "; temperature!(1)
INPUT "Monday    "; temperature!(2)
INPUT "Tuesday   "; temperature!(3)
INPUT "Wednesday"; temperature!(4)
INPUT "Thursday "; temperature!(5)
INPUT "Friday    "; temperature!(6)
INPUT "Saturday "; temperature!(7)
PRINT

REM ** Find high temperature **
High! = temperature!(1)
FOR k = 2 TO 7
  IF temperature!(k) > High! THEN High! = temperature!(k)
NEXT k

REM ** Find low temperature **
Low! = temperature!(1)
FOR k = 2 TO 7
  IF temperature!(k) < Low! THEN Low! = temperature!(k)
NEXT k

REM ** Compute average temperature **
' Sum the seven temperatures and divide total by 7
Total! = 0
FOR k = 1 TO 7
  Total! = Total! + temperature!(k)
NEXT k
Average! = Total! / 7

REM ** Print high, low, and average temperature **
PRINT "High:    "; High!
PRINT "Low:     "; Low!
PRINT "Average:"; Average!
END
```

A test run of program QBME0801.BAS is shown in Figure 8-3. The temperatures entered in this run are very low, so that the program can be verified easily. As you will see if you check the program yourself, the answers are correct. As a further test of the program, Figure 8-4 shows another run of the program with the same numbers, but in scrambled order; again the results were correct. A more realistic application of this program is shown in the sample run in Figure 8-5; the temperatures entered in this run were taken at noon each day.

```
Enter the temperature for each day of the week.

Sunday    ? 1
Monday    ? 2
Tuesday   ? 3
Wednesday? 4
Thursday  ? 5
Friday    ? 6
Saturday  ? 7

High:    7
Low:     1
Average: 4
```

FIGURE 8-3   Test run of High, Low, and Average Temperature program

Program QBME0801.BAS introduces a new keyword, DEFINT. A-Z DEFINT defines all numeric variables as short integer variables, unless explicitly specified otherwise as long integer (&), single precision (!), or double precision (#) variables. The DEFINT statement appears near the beginning of the program, in the program block shown next.

```
Enter the temperature for each day of the week.

Sunday    ? 3
Monday    ? 6
Tuesday   ? 1
Wednesday? 5
Thursday  ? 7
Friday    ? 2
Saturday  ? 4

High:    7
Low:     1
Average: 4
```

FIGURE 8-4   Second test run of High, Low, and Average Temperature program

```
Enter the temperature for each day of the week.

Sunday    ? 68
Monday    ? 67
Tuesday   ? 70
Wednesday? 72
Thursday ? 75
Friday    ? 80
Saturday ? 77

High:     80
Low:      67
Average: 72.71429
```

FIGURE 8-5   Practical run of High, Low, and Average Temperature program

```
REM ** Define all numeric variables as short integers **
' Use &, !, # to designate other numeric variable types
DEFINT A-Z
```

The statement DEFINT A-Z tells the computer to regard all variables beginning with the letters A to Z as short integer variables. Since uppercase and lowercase letters are considered by the program to be the same (in variable names) and all variables must begin with a letter, this statement defines all numeric variables as short integers. You can use variable type designators to specify individual numeric variable names as other than short integer: & for long integer, ! for single precision, and # for double precision variables.

The next block in the program defines the array *temperature!()* as a single precision array with seven elements, or subscripts.

```
REM ** Dim single precision array temperature!() **
DIM temperature!(1 TO 7)
```

The values of the seven elements of *temperature!()*, *temperature!(1)* through *temperature!(7)*, are assigned during program execution with seven INPUT statements.

```
INPUT "Sunday   "; temperature!(1)
INPUT "Monday   "; temperature!(2)
INPUT "Tuesday  "; temperature!(3)
INPUT "Wednesday"; temperature!(4)
```

```
INPUT "Thursday "; temperature!(5)
INPUT "Friday   "; temperature!(6)
INPUT "Saturday "; temperature!(7)
```

The values of *temperature!(1)* through *temperature!(7)* entered in the third sample run of QBME0801.BAS (Figure 8-5) are shown in Table 8-1.

The fourth block in the program uses a FOR...NEXT loop to search *temperature!()* for the highest temperature of the week, and assign it as the value of *High!*.

```
REM ** Find high temperature **
High! = temperature!(1)
FOR k = 2 TO 7
  IF temperature!(k) > High! THEN High! = temperature!(k)
NEXT k
```

The value of *High!* is set equal to the value of *temperature!(1)*, the first element in the array. The FOR...NEXT loop then searches the rest of the array (subscripts 2 through 7). If any value in the array is greater than the value of *High!*, it is assigned as the new value of *High!*. A similar method is used to find the lowest temperature of the week and assign it as the value of *Low!*, as follows:

```
REM ** Find low temperature **
Low! = temperature!(1)
FOR k = 2 TO 7
  IF temperature!(k) < Low! THEN Low! = temperature!(k)
NEXT k
```

Array Element	Value
temperature!(1)	68
temperature!(2)	67
temperature!(3)	70
temperature!(4)	72
temperature!(5)	75
temperature!(6)	80
temperature!(7)	77

TABLE 8-1   Values of Array Elements, Third Sample Run

A third FOR...NEXT loop uses the variable *Total!* to add up the week's temperatures. *Total!* is first set to zero. Each value in *temperature!()* is then added to *Total!,* one at a time, as the value of *k* goes from 1 to 7. *Total!* is then divided by seven (the number of elements) to obtain the average (*Average!*) temperature.

```
REM ** Compute average temperature **
' Sum the seven temperatures and divide total by 7
Total! = 0
FOR k = 1 TO 7
  Total! = Total! + temperature!(k)
NEXT k
Average! = Total! / 7
```

Remember, the variable *k,* used in each of the FOR...NEXT loops in this program, is an integer variable; the DEFINT statement in the first block of the program defines all variables as integers, unless specified otherwise.

In the third sample run (Figure 8-5), the value of *Average!* is 72.71429. You can use a PRINT USING statement to round this value to the nearest degree or nearest 10th of a degree. To round *Average!* to the nearest degree, use a statement like this.

```
PRINT "Average:"; : PRINT USING "###"; Average!
```

To round *Average!* to the nearest tenth of a degree, use this PRINT USING statement:

```
PRINT "Average"; : PRINT USING "###.#"; Average!
```

A More General High, Low, and Average Temperature Program

Program QBME0801.BAS is adequate if you have exactly seven temperatures to process. However, if you wished to average the temperatures for a length of time other than 7 days (10 days, a month, a year) you could not do so. Program QBME0802.BAS, High, Low, and Average Temperature, allows you to enter the number of temperatures to be averaged, and then dimensions the *temperature!()* array to that number of days.

```
REM ** QBME0802.BAS **
REM ** 1/1/90 **
REM ** High, Low, and Average Temperature **
```

```
' QuickBASIC Made Easy, Chapter 8
' Microsoft QuickBASIC 4.5

REM ** Define all numeric variables as short integers **
' Use &, !, # to designate other numeric variable types
DEFINT A-Z

REM ** Get number of temperatures to process **
CLS
PRINT "High, Low, and Average Temperature Program."
PRINT
INPUT "How many temperatures"; NumberOfElements
PRINT

REM ** Dim single precision array temperature!() **
DIM temperature!(1 TO NumberOfElements)

REM ** Get temperature data **
PRINT "Enter the temperatures:"
PRINT
FOR k = 1 TO NumberOfElements
  PRINT "Temperature #"; k; : INPUT temperature!(k)
NEXT k
PRINT

REM ** Find high temperature **
High! = temperature!(1)
FOR k = 2 TO NumberOfElements
  IF temperature!(k) > High! THEN High! = temperature!(k)
NEXT k

REM ** Find low temperature **
Low! = temperature!(1)
FOR k = 2 TO NumberOfElements
  IF temperature!(k) < Low! THEN Low! = temperature!(k)
NEXT k

REM ** Compute average temperature **
' Add temperatures and divide by number of temperatures
Total! = 0
FOR k = 1 TO NumberOfElements
  Total! = Total! + temperature!(k)
NEXT k
Average! = Total! / NumberOfElements

REM ** Print high, low, and average temperature **
PRINT "High:    "; High!
PRINT "Low:     "; Low!
PRINT "Average:"; Average!
END
```

Compare QBME0801.BAS with QBME0802.BAS. Notice in program QBME0802.BAS that *temperature!()* is dimensioned from 1 to *NumberOf-Elements*. An array can be dimensioned using explicit numbers (as in QBME0801.BAS) or variables (as in QBME0802.BAS). Program QBME0802.BAS first requests the number of temperatures to process (*NumberOf Elements*). Again, because of the previous DEFINT statement, *NumberOf Elements* is an integer variable. The array *temperature!()* is then dimensioned as a single precision array with *NumberOf Elements* subscripts, *temperature!(1)* through *temperature!(NumberOf Elements)*, as shown next.

```
REM ** Dim single precision array temperature!() **
DIM temperature!(1 TO NumberOfElements)
```

The value for each element in *temperature!()* is then input within a FOR...NEXT loop, as shown in the following program block. Note that the value of *k* goes from 1 to *NumberOf Elements*.

```
REM ** Get temperature data **
PRINT "Enter the temperatures:"
PRINT
FOR k = 1 TO NumberOfElements
  PRINT "Temperature #"; k; : INPUT temperature!(k)
NEXT k
PRINT
```

The rest of program QBME0802.BAS is the same as program QBME0801.BAS, except for the upper limit of the three FOR...NEXT loops.

```
Program QBME0801: FOR k = 2 TO 7
                  FOR k = 1 TO 7
                  Average! = Total! / 7

Program QBME0802: FOR k = 2 TO NumberOfElements
                  FOR k = 1 TO NumberOfElements
                  Average! = Total! / NumberOfElements
```

In QBME0801.BAS, *temperature!()* consists of seven elements; thus the upper limit of the FOR...NEXT loops is seven. In QBME0802.BAS, however, *temperature!()* consists of *NumberOf Elements* elements; the upper limit of these FOR...NEXT loops is therefore *NumberOfElements*.

Two sample runs of program QBME0802.BAS are shown in Figure 8-6 and Figure 8-7.

```
High, Low, and Average Temperature Program.

How many temperatures? 7

Enter the temperatures:

Temperature #  1  ?  68
Temperature #  2  ?  67
Temperature #  3  ?  70
Temperature #  4  ?  72
Temperature #  5  ?  75
Temperature #  6  ?  80
Temperature #  7  ?  77


High:     80
Low:      67
Average: 72.71429
```

FIGURE 8-6   Sample run of General High, Low, and Average Temperature program

```
High, Low, and Average Temperature Program.

How many temperatures? 12

Enter the temperatures:

Temperature #  1  ?  36
Temperature #  2  ?  38
Temperature #  3  ?  43
Temperature #  4  ?  43
Temperature #  5  ?  39
Temperature #  6  ?  37
Temperature #  7  ?  34
Temperature #  8  ?  27
Temperature #  9  ?  25
Temperature #  10 ?  22
Temperature #  11 ?  23
Temperature #  12 ?  19


High:     43
Low:      19
Average: 32.16667
```

FIGURE 8-7   Second sample of General High, Low, and Average Temperature program

Dot Product of Two Arrays

The dot product of two arrays is the sum of the products of corresponding elements of the two arrays. The dot product of two arrays, *array1()* and *array2()*, each dimensioned with three elements, is *array1(1) * array2(1) + array1(2) * array2(2) + array1(3) * array2(3)*. The dot product of two arrays can be a very useful value. Consider, for example, the order for camping equipment shown in Table 8-2.

This order has five line items. For each line, the Quantity and Price Each are multiplied to produce the line total. The five line totals are added to get the total amount of the order. The total amount of the order is the dot product. Program QBME0803.BAS, Dot Product of Two Arrays, computes and prints the dot product of two arrays, *Quantity&()* and *PriceEach#()*.

```
REM ** QBME0803.BAS **
REM ** 1/1/90 **
REM ** Dot Product of Two Arrays **
' QuickBASIC Made Easy, Chapter 8
' Microsoft QuickBASIC 4.5

REM ** Define all numeric variables as short integers **
' Use &, !, # to designate other numeric variable types
DEFINT A-Z

REM ** Get number of array elements **
CLS
PRINT "Dot Product of Two Arrays,"
PRINT "Quantity&() and PriceEach#()"
PRINT
```

Item	Quantity	Price Each	Line Total
sleeping bag	1	89.95	89.95
stuff bags	3	4.50	13.50
stove	1	21.99	21.99
fuel cartridges	6	1.75	10.50
waterproof matches, boxes	4	.35	1.40
Total amount (dot product)			137.34

TABLE 8-2   An Order for Camping Equipment

```
INPUT "How many line items"; NumberOfElements
PRINT

REM ** Dimension arrays Quantity&() and PriceEach#() **
DIM Quantity&(1 TO NumberOfElements)
DIM PriceEach#(1 TO NumberOfElements)

REM ** Get data for Quantity&() and PriceEach#() **
PRINT "Enter data as requested."
PRINT
FOR k = 1 TO NumberOfElements
  PRINT "Quantity   #"; k; : INPUT Quantity&(k)
  PRINT "Price each #"; k; : INPUT PriceEach#(k)
  PRINT
NEXT k

REM ** Compute dot product of Quantity&() and
'       PriceEach#() **
DotProduct# = 0
FOR k = 1 TO NumberOfElements
  DotProduct# = DotProduct# + Quantity&(k) * PriceEach#(k)
NEXT k

REM ** Print dot product of Quantity&() and
'       PriceEach#() **
PRINT "The Dot Product is"; DotProduct#
END
```

Again, the DEFINT statement in the first program block defines all numeric variables as integers. The noninteger numeric variables used in this program include the following:

Quantity&() A long integer array
PriceEach#() A double precision array
DotProduct# A double precision variable

The values for both arrays are entered within the following FOR...NEXT loop.

```
REM ** Get data for arrays Quantity&() and
'       PriceEach#() **
PRINT "Enter data as requested."
PRINT
FOR k = 1 TO NumberOfElements
  PRINT "Quantity   #"; k; : INPUT Quantity&(k)
  PRINT "Price each #"; k; : INPUT PriceEach#(k)
  PRINT
NEXT k
```

The array values are entered in the order *Quantity&(1)* and *PriceEach#(1),* *Quantity&(2)* and *PriceEach#(2), Quantity&(3)* and *PriceEach#(3),* and so on, as *k* increases from 1 to the value of *NumberOf Elements.*

The dot product is computed by the next block. *DotProduct#* is first set to zero. Then, within another FOR...NEXT loop, the corresponding elements of the two arrays are multiplied and added to *DotProduct#*.

```
REM ** Compute dot product of Quantity&() and
'       PriceEach#() **
DotProduct# = 0
FOR k = 1 TO NumberOfElements
  DotProduct# = DotProduct# + Quantity&(k) * PriceEach#(k)
NEXT k
```

Two sample runs are shown in Figure 8-8. Notice that the line item totals are not printed in this program, although they are computed. Small quantities and prices were chosen for these examples to enable the user to verify easily that the program is running correctly.

Dot Product with Line Item Printout

Program QBME0804.BAS, Dot Product with Line Item Printout, is an expanded version of program QBME0803.BAS. It allows you to enter the name of each item, as well as the quantity and price. The item names are stored in the string array *ItemName$()*. After all information has been entered, the computer prints "Press a key and I'll print the answers," and then waits for a key to be pressed. After you press a key, each line item and line total is printed, followed by the grand total, or dot product.

```
REM ** QBME0804.BAS **
REM ** 1/1/90 **
REM ** Dot Product of Two Arrays with Line Item Printout **
' QuickBASIC Made Easy, Chapter 8
' Microsoft QuickBASIC 4.5

REM ** Define all numeric variables as integers **
' Use &, !, # to designate other numeric variable types
DEFINT A-Z

REM ** Get number of array elements **
CLS
PRINT "Dot Product of Two Arrays with Line Items"
PRINT
INPUT "How many line items"; NumberOfElements
PRINT
```

```
Dot Product of Two Arrays, Quantity&() and PriceEach#()

How many items (quantity and price)? 3

Enter data as requested.

Quantity   # 1 ? 1
Price each # 1 ? 1

Quantity   # 2 ? 1
Price each # 2 ? 2

Quantity   # 3 ? 1
Price each # 3 ? 3

The Dot Product is 6


Press any key to continue

Dot Product of Two Arrays, Quantity&() and PriceEach#()

How many items (quantity and price)? 3

Enter data as requested.

Quantity   # 1 ? 1
Price each # 1 ? 1

Quantity   # 2 ? 2
Price each # 2 ? 1

Quantity   # 3 ? 3
Price each # 3 ? 1

The Dot Product is 6
```

FIGURE 8-8   Sample run of Dot Product program

```
REM ** Dim ItemName$(), Quantity&(), and PriceEach#() **
DIM ItemName$(1 TO NumberOfElements)
DIM Quantity&(1 TO NumberOfElements)
DIM PriceEach#(1 TO NumberOfElements)
```

```
REM ** Get data for ItemName$(), Quantity&(),
'       PriceEach#() **
PRINT "Enter data as requested."
PRINT
FOR k = 1 TO NumberOfElements
  PRINT "Item name  #"; k; :LINE INPUT "? "; ItemName$(k)
  PRINT "Quantity   #"; k; :INPUT Quantity&(k)
  PRINT "Price each #"; k; :INPUT PriceEach#(k)
  PRINT
NEXT k
PRINT "Press a key and I'll print the answers"
anykey$ = INPUT$(1)

REM ** Print headings **
CLS
PRINT "Item"; TAB(30); "Quantity";
PRINT TAB(44); "Price each"; TAB(64); "Line total"
PRINT

REM ** Print name of item, quantity, price, and line
'       total **
' While doing so, also compute dot product
DotProduct# = 0
FOR k = 1 TO NumberOfElements
  LineTotal# = Quantity&(k) * PriceEach#(k)
  DotProduct# = DotProduct# + LineTotal#
  PRINT LEFT$(ItemName$(k), 20);
  PRINT USING "#########,"; TAB(28); Quantity&(k);
  PRINT USING "#########,.##"; TAB(40); PriceEach#(k);
  PRINT USING "#########,.##"; TAB(60); LineTotal#
NEXT k
PRINT

REM ** Print dot product of Quantity&() and
'       PriceEach#() **
PRINT TAB(27); "Total amount (dot product):";
PRINT USING "##########,.##"; TAB(60); DotProduct#
END
```

Figure 8-9 shows the appearance of the screen during the data entry portion of a run. In this example, five items are entered, and therefore some information has scrolled off the top of the screen. This scrolling does not affect the data stored in each array—all data entered for *ItemName$()*, *Quantity&()*, and *PriceEach#()* are retained, regardless of any screen scrolling. Figure 8-10 shows the results printed following a key press.

Note that part of the name of the fifth item name was not printed. The string function LEFT$ was used to print only the first 20 characters of *Item-Name$()*, thus truncating any element in *ItemName$()* that is longer than 20

```
Enter data as requested.

Item name  # 1 ? sleeping bag
Quantity   # 1 ? 1
Price each # 1 ? 89.95

Item name  # 2 ? stuff bags
Quantity   # 2 ? 3
Price each # 2 ? 4.50

Item name  # 3 ? stove
Quantity   # 3 ? 1
Price each # 3 ? 21.99

Item name  # 4 ? fuel cartridges
Quantity   # 4 ? 6
Price each # 4 ? 1.75

Item name  # 5 ? waterproof matches, boxes
Quantity   # 5 ? 4
Price each # 5 ? .35

Press a key and I'll print the answers
```

FIGURE 8-9   Data entry of Dot Product with Line Item program

characters. This is done so that long names like *ItemName$(5)* will not encroach on the space reserved for Quantity.

```
Item                 Quantity  Price Each    Line Total

sleeping bag            1        89.95          89.95
stuff bags              3         4.50          13.50
stove                   1        21.99          21.99
fuel cartridge          6         1.75          10.50
waterproof matches      4          .35           1.40

Total amount (dot product)                     137.34
```

FIGURE 8-10   Printout of Dot Product with Line Item program

MANIPULATING ARRAYS

Arrays can be used to store and print item descriptions and values, as in the preceding programs. Arrays can also be used to manipulate information more easily. For example, arrays are often used to sort lists of numbers or names. Sorting involves putting array values in least-to-greatest or greatest-to-least order.

Scramble an Array of Numbers

Sometimes, especially when creating computer simulations or games, you may want to scramble a list, or array, of numbers. For example, you can use an array of numbers 1 to 52 to represent the 52 cards in a deck of cards, then "shuffle the deck" by scrambling the array. The following is a REM outline of a program to scramble an array of numbers.

```
REM ** QBME0805.BAS **
REM ** 1/1/90 **
REM ** Scramble an Array of Numbers **
' QuickBASIC Made Easy, Chapter 8
' Microsoft QuickBASIC 4.5

REM ** Scramble an Array of Numbers **

REM ** Set up **

REM ** Get number of array elements and
'       dimension array **

REM ** Generate the original (unscrambled) array **

REM ** Print the original (unscrambled) array **

REM ** Scramble the array **

REM ** Print the scrambled array **
```

The REM outline provides an overall design of the program. It is helpful to consider how you want the screen to appear before you write or run the program. Figure 8-11 shows the Ouput screen after a test run of program QBME0805.BAS. Each time you run the program and ask for seven numbers, the program is likely to produce seven different numbers. Program QBME0805.BAS, Scramble an Array of Numbers, follows.

```
REM ** QBME0805.BAS **
REM ** 1/1/90 **
REM ** Scramble an Array of Numbers **
' QuickBASIC Made Easy, Chapter 8
' Microsoft QuickBASIC 4.5

REM ** Set up **
DEFINT A-Z              'Define numeric variables as integer
RANDOMIZE TIMER

REM ** Get number of array elements and dim array **
CLS
PRINT "Scramble an Array of Numbers"
PRINT
INPUT "How many numbers shall I scramble"; NbrOfElements
PRINT
DIM array(1 TO NbrOfElements)

REM ** Generate the original (unscrambled) array **
FOR i = 1 TO NbrOfElements
  array(i) = i
NEXT i

REM ** Print the original (unscrambled) array **
PRINT "Here are the original (unscrambled) numbers:"
PRINT
```

```
Scramble an Array of Numbers

How many numbers shall I scramble?

Here are the original (unscrambled) numbers:

  1          2          3          4          5
  6          7

Here are the mixed-up numbers:

  5          3          6          4          2
  7          1
```

FIGURE 8-11   Screen appearance of Scramble an Array program

```
FOR i = 1 TO NbrOfElements
  PRINT array(i),          'Comma prints 5 numbers/line
NEXT i
PRINT : PRINT

REM ** Scramble the array **
FOR i = 1 TO NbrOfElements
  RandomSubscript = INT(NbrOfElements * RND) + 1
  SWAP array(i), array(RandomSubscript)
NEXT i

REM ** Print the scrambled array **
PRINT "Here are the mixed-up numbers:"
PRINT
FOR i = 1 TO NbrOfElements
  PRINT array(i),          'Comma prints 5 numbers/line
NEXT i

END
```

The original, unscrambled array is generated by assigning 1 to *array(1)*, 2 to *array(2)*, 3 to *array(3)*, and so on. If *NbrOfElements* equals 7, the unscrambled array will contain the values shown in Table 8-3. This array is then scrambled by the program block shown below. Within the FOR...NEXT loop, the value of each array element is exchanged, or swapped, for the value of a randomly selected array element.

A value is assigned to *RandomSubscript*, and then the value of *array(1)* is exchanged for the value of *array(RandomSubscript)*; a new value is assigned to *RandomSubscript*, and then the value of *array(2)* is exchanged for

Array Element	Value
array(1)	1
array(2)	2
array(3)	3
array(4)	4
array(5)	5
array(6)	6
array(7)	7

TABLE 8-3   Values of Elements in Unscrambled Array

the value of *array(RandomSubscript)*. This sequence continues until *array(NbrOfElements)* has been exchanged for *array(RandomSubscript)*.

```
REM ** Scramble the array **
FOR i = 1 TO NbrOfElements
   RandomSubscript = INT(NbrOfElements * RND) + 1
   SWAP array(i), array(RandomSubscript)
NEXT i
```

The statement *RandomSubscript* = INT(*NbrOfElements* * RND) + 1 tells the computer to generate a random integer between 1 and *NbrOfElements*. The SWAP keyword is then used to exchange the value of *array(Random-Subscript)* with the value of *array(i)*.

The statement SWAP *array(i)*, *array(RandomSubscript)* tells the computer to exchange the value of *array(i)* with the value of *array(Random-Subscript)*. For example, if *array(i)* = 4 and *array(RandomSubscript)* = 7 before their values are swapped, then after being swapped *array(i)* = 7 and *array(RandomSubscript)* = 4.

Scramble and Sort an Array of Numbers

The converse of scrambling an array is sorting an array. Often, an array is already scrambled as it is entered, but needs to be sorted. Program QBME0806.BAS, Scramble and Sort an Array of Numbers, contains a simple FOR...NEXT loop that sorts an array of scrambled numbers. This program generates an array of consecutive numbers (1, 2, 3, and so on), scrambles and prints the array, sorts the array, and prints the sorted array. A REM outline of this program is shown next.

```
REM ** QBME0806.BAS ***
REM ** 1/1/90 **
REM ** Scramble and Sort an Array of Numbers **
' QuickBASIC Made Easy, Chapter 8
' Microsoft QuickBASIC 4.5

REM ** Set up **

REM ** Get number of array elements and
'        dimension array **

REM ** Generate the original (unscrambled) array **

REM ** Scramble the array **
```

```
Scramble and Sort an Array of Numbers

How many numbers shall I scramble?

Here are the original (unscrambled) numbers:

 1           2           3           4           5
 6           7

Here are the mixed-up numbers:

 5           3           6           4           2
 7           1

Here are the sorted number:

 1           2           3           4           5
 6           7
```

FIGURE 8-12   Sample run of Scramble and Sort an Array of Numbers program

```
REM ** Print the scrambled array **

REM ** Sort the array **

REM ** Print the sorted array **
```

A sample run of this program is shown in Figure 8-12. Study the REM outline and sample run, and then try to write the program. To make this task easier, begin with program QBME0805.BAS and edit it to make program QBME0806.BAS.

```
REM ** QBME0806.BAS **
REM ** 1/1/90 **
REM ** Scramble and Sort an Array of Numbers **
' QuickBASIC Made Easy, Chapter 8
' Microsoft QuickBASIC 4.5

REM ** Set up **
DEFINT A-Z      'Define all numeric variables as integers
RANDOMIZE TIMER

REM ** Get number of array elements and dim array **
```

```
CLS
PRINT "Scramble an Array of Numbers, then Sort It"
PRINT
INPUT "How many numbers shall I scramble"; NbrOfElements
PRINT
DIM array(1 TO NbrOfElements)

REM ** Generate the original (unscrambled) array **
FOR i = 1 TO NbrOfElements
  array(i) = i
NEXT i

REM ** Scramble the array **
FOR i = 1 TO NbrOfElements
  RandomSubscript = INT(NbrOfElements * RND) + 1
  SWAP array(i), array(RandomSubscript)
NEXT i

REM ** Print the scrambled array **
PRINT "Here are the mixed-up numbers:"
PRINT
FOR i = 1 TO NbrOfElements
  PRINT array(i),          'Comma prints 5 numbers/line
NEXT i

REM ** Sort the array **
FOR i = 1 TO NbrOfElements - 1
  FOR k = i + 1 TO NbrOfElements
    IF array(k) < array(i) THEN SWAP array(k), array(i)
  NEXT k
NEXT i

REM ** Print the sorted array **
PRINT "Here are the unscrambled numbers:"
PRINT
FOR i = 1 TO NbrOfElements
  PRINT array(i),          'Comma prints 5 numbers/line
NEXT i

END
```

Perhaps the most complex and important block in this program is the block that sorts the scrambled array. The sort used in this program is called a bubble sort because the smallest numbers "bubble up" to the top. This sort is shown following. It consists of a FOR...NEXT loop within a FOR...NEXT loop.

```
REM ** Sort the array **
FOR i = 1 TO NbrOfElements - 1
  FOR k = i + 1 TO NbrOfElements
    IF array(k) < array(i) THEN SWAP array(k), array(i)
  NEXT k
NEXT i
```

Suppose that the value of *NbrOf Elements* is 4 and the values of the scrambled array are as shown in Table 8-4. Assume that in this example, the value of *i* (in the outside FOR...NEXT loop) will run from 1 to 3. For each value of *i*, the value of *k* (in the inside FOR...NEXT loop) will run from *i* + 1 to 4. Together, *i* and *k* will take on the values shown next.

i	*k*
1	2
1	3
1	4
2	3
2	4
3	4

For each pair of values of *i* and *k,* the values of *array(k)* and *array(i)* are compared. If the value of *array(k)* is less than the value of *array(i)*, the two values are exchanged, thus putting the smaller value in *array(i)*. The following diagram shows what happens the first time through both FOR...NEXT

Array Element	Value
array(1)	2
array(2)	4
array(3)	1
array(4)	3

TABLE 8-4   Scrambled *array( )* Values

loops, when i is 1 and k is 2, 3, and 4. Arrows indicate any exchanges that are made.

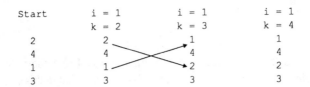

```
Start          i = 1          i = 1          i = 1
               k = 2          k = 3          k = 4
  2              2              1              1
  4              4              4              4
  1              1              2              2
  3              3              3              3
```

After the two FOR...NEXT loops have been executed once, *array(1)* contains the smallest number. The value of k has gone through all its values: 2, 3, and 4. The value of i then becomes 2 and k will now go through the values 3 and 4. The diagram that follows shows what happens the second time through; arrows indicate any exchanges that are made.

```
Start          i = 2          i = 2
               k = 3          k = 4
  1              1              1
  4              2              2
  2              4              4
  3              3              3
```

After the second pass ($i = 2$), the second smallest number is in *array(2)*. The third (and last for an array of four elements) pass completes the sort. The next diagram shows the results of the third pass; again, the arrows indicate any exchanges made in this pass.

```
Start          i = 3
               k = 4
  1              1
  2              2
  4              3
  3              4
```

After the third pass, the array is in sorted order. The final block in the program then prints the sorted array.

When an entire array is in reverse order, it requires the most swaps to sort since most numbers are out of order. The sorting process for an array of four elements in reverse order is shown in Figure 8-13.

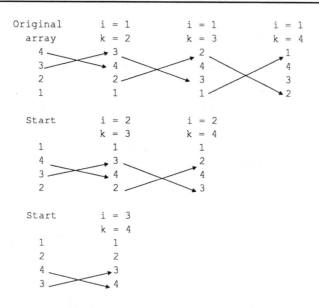

FIGURE 8-13   Reverse order sorting process

Sort a String Array

You will often need to sort string variable arrays as well as numeric arrays. You can use a FOR...NEXT loop to sort string arrays that is very similar to the FOR...NEXT loop you used to sort in program QBME0806.BAS, Scramble and Sort an Array of Numbers.

To a computer, each character has a number equivalent, or ASCII value. The ASCII values of the alphabet, for example, are 65 for the letter "A" through 90 for the letter "Z"; 97 for the letter "a" through 122 for the letter "z." Notice that the ASCII values for A-Z and a-z are in ascending order: A is less than B, B is less than C, and so on.

This means that you can compare two strings directly to determine which is "less" than the other. Program QBME0807.BAS, Sort a String Array, asks for *NbrOf Elements* names to sort, and then sorts and prints them.

```
REM ** QBME0807.BAS **
REM ** 1/1/90 **
REM ** Sort a String Array **
' QuickBASIC Made Easy, Chapter 8
' Microsoft QuickBASIC 4.5

REM ** Set up **
DEFINT A-Z      'Define all numeric variables as integers

REM ** Get number of array elements and dim array **
CLS
PRINT "Sort a String Array"
PRINT
INPUT "How many names shall I sort"; NbrOfElements
PRINT
DIM Names$(1 TO NbrOfElements)

REM ** Get names to sort **
PRINT : PRINT
FOR k = 1 to NbrOfElements
  LINE INPUT "Name to sort (Last, First)?"; Names$(k)
NEXT k

REM ** Print the unsorted array **
PRINT : PRINT
PRINT "Here are the names to sort:"
PRINT
FOR i = 1 TO NbrOfElements
  PRINT Names$(i)
NEXT i

REM ** Sort the array **
FOR i = 1 TO NbrOfElements - 1
  FOR k = i + 1 TO NbrOfElements
    IF Names$(k) < Names$(i) THEN SWAP Names$(k), Names$(i)
  NEXT k
NEXT i

REM ** Print the sorted array **
PRINT : PRINT
PRINT "Here are the sorted names:"
PRINT
FOR i = 1 TO NbrOfElements
  PRINT Names$(i)
NEXT i

END
```

Compare the sort block in this program with the sort block in QBME0806.BAS. Note that the logic is the same—the only difference is the type of array being sorted. String arrays are sorted according to their ASCII values; therefore, names beginning with "A" sort to the top of *Names$()*, names beginning with "B" sort below those that begin with "A," and so on.

An array is a set of related variables referenced by the same name and a subscript. Arrays, like simple variables, can be string or numeric. Numeric arrays can be integer, long integer, single precision, or double precision arrays. The size of an array defaults to 11 elements, 0 through 10, but can be set to any number of elements (dimensioned) with the DIM statement. An array subscript can be a number, a numeric variable, or a numeric expression. The LBOUND and UBOUND functions are used to determine the smallest subscript in an array (LBOUND) and the largest subscript in an array (UBOUND).

Arrays can be used in many ways to make programs more powerful; some useful examples are included in this chapter. Sorting is one of the most powerful uses of arrays. Many applications require sorting to be useful. Looking up a name, for example, would be very difficult in an unsorted list of several hundred or thousand names. The bubble sort can be used to sort either numeric arrays (as in QBME0806.BAS) or string arrays (as in QBME0807.BAS).

9

UNSTRUCTURED SEQUENTIAL FILES

Types of Data Files
Unstructured Sequential Files
Some Useful Suggestions About File Names

In this chapter you will learn about the different types of data files: sequential and random-access. You will learn about unstructured sequential files and structured sequential files. You will then learn how to create and access records from an unstructured sequential file. In particular you will

- Learn to use unstructured sequential files
- Learn to use the OPEN...FOR OUTPUT, LINE INPUT, WRITE #, and CLOSE statements to create a sequential file
- Learn to use the VIEW PRINT statement to display text in the Output screen
- Learn to use the LOCATE statement to control where text is printed in the Output screen

- Learn to use the OPEN...FOR INPUT, LINE INPUT #, and CLOSE statements to access records in a sequential file
- Learn how to change the name of a file by using the NAME statement

TYPES OF DATA FILES

A file is a collection of information; the information contained in a file can be on any topic and organized in any way you choose. Think of a computer file as a file in a file cabinet: it contains information and notes that you choose to save on one or more topics.

There are several different kinds of computer files, including program files and data files. You have used and created many different program files in previous chapters; each program you saved is a program file. In this chapter and in the next two chapters you will learn to create and use data files, which are used to store information. Data files are used, for example, to store the information for your telephone bill and bank statements. QuickBASIC has two types of data files: sequential files and random-access files.

Sequential Files

A data file is organized into records. A record in a bank statement file, for example, may contain the account number, the date, and the amount of the deposit or check. A *sequential file* is a file in which the records must be accessed sequentially: to read the fifth record in a sequential file, records one through four must be accessed first. You might think of a cassette tape as a kind of sequential file. To hear the third song on the tape, you have to play or fast-forward past the first and second songs on the tape. This sequential file structure is depicted in Figure 9-1.

Since each record in a sequential file must be accessed in order, using such files can be cumbersome—but they do have some advantages. A record in a sequential file can be any length, very short to very long, and uses only as much space as the data being stored. This means that sequential files store data efficiently, without wasting space: if a record is only 15 characters long, only 15 bytes (plus any end of record characters) are used to store it.

Sequential files also have some disadvantages. Although the data stored in a sequential file is stored in a minimum of space, searching for a given record, especially in a large file, can be slow. Modifying, inserting, and deleting records in a sequential file also can be very slow, usually requiring that

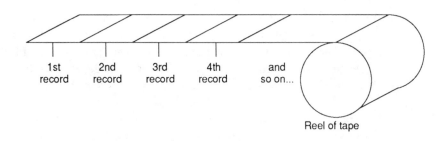

1st   2nd   3rd   4th   and
record   record   record   record   so on...

Reel of tape

FIGURE 9-1   Diagram of sequential file structure

the file be rewritten. In addition, sorting a large sequential file can be very awkward, often considerably more difficult than sorting a random-access file.

Imagine how difficult it would be to delete a song from a cassette tape, add one, or change the length of one—without leavings gaps or deleting parts of other songs. You would need to make an entirely new tape. Imagine trying to create a tape in which the songs appear in an entirely different order. This is the situation with sequential files.

A *random-access file* is a file in which the records can be accessed in any order. You can access record 17, then record 4, then record 235, then record 2, and so on. A record can be accessed whether or not the previous records have already been accessed. All records in a random-access file are the same length, which means that random-access files can be somewhat wasteful of storage space. Modifying a record in a random-access file, however, is much easier than modifying a record in a sequential file. Only the record being changed needs to be rewritten, rather than the entire file.

In this book, two types of sequential files are used: unstructured sequential files and structured sequential files. The rest of this chapter briefly describes unstructured sequential and structured sequential files, and then concentrates on how to use unstructured sequential files. In Chapter 10, "Structured Sequential Files," you will learn to use structured sequential files; and in Chapter 11, "Random-Access Files," you will learn to use random-access files.

UNSTRUCTURED SEQUENTIAL FILES

An *unstructured* sequential file consists of records that can contain any information of any length. It is a free-form file, in which one record is one string. A record can be any length; it can even be a null (or empty) record. For example, a file that contains a letter to a friend is an unstructured file. Each line in the letter, including any blank lines, is a record in the file.

In contrast, a *structured* sequential file consists of records that have two or more fields. Each record has the same fields. A record in a bank statement file that contains an account number, date, and amount of check or deposit is an example of a structured record with three fields. A field in a structured file can be either string or numeric. A string field can be any length a string variable can be, up to a maximum of 32,767 characters. Numeric fields are stored one byte per digit, and are limited in length by the numeric variables used to write them to the file. You will learn more about structured sequential files in Chapter 10.

Sequential files, whether unstructured or structured, are stored as ASCII text files. This means that they can be used by word processors and other application programs that accept ASCII text. You could use a word processor to create, view, or modify a sequential file.

An Example of an Unstructured Sequential File

You will now create and use an unstructured sequential file called Note-Pad.Txt. This file consists of free-form records that are notes. A record in this file can be anything you wish, as long as it is typed as a single string. This might contain, for example, notes on how to use QuickBASIC, or, as in Figure 9-2, notes on QuickBASIC as well as on any appointments you have.

Remember: In an unstructured sequential file, each record is one string. One record can be the empty string (""), a string with 32,767 characters, or anything in between.

NAMING A FILE   Data files must be named. As with programs you named in previous chapters, file names for data files must conform to MS-DOS file-naming conventions. File names are limited to eight characters plus a three-letter extension. The following example of a file name, used in a program later in this chapter, contains seven characters plus a three-letter extension:

NotePad.Txt

Record 1: This is the NotePad.Txt file

Record 2: NotePad.Txt is an unstructured sequential file

Record 3: Each record is one string, up to 32767 characters

Record 4: Use NotePad.Txt for notes of any kind

Record 5: Meeting 9/19 at 10 AM with Daniel

Record 6: Library books due 9/23

Record 7: CMC Meeting in Fresno, 10/28

FIGURE 9-2   Example of NotePad.Txt file

The three-letter extension (Txt) was chosen to indicate that this is a text file. QuickBASIC does not distinguish between uppercase and lowercase letters in file names. Therefore, NotePad.Txt, notepad.txt, and NOTEPAD.TXT are considered the same name. When naming files it is wise to choose names that reflect the contents of the file.

Creating the NotePad.Txt File

The notepad file, shown in Figure 9-2, is a good example of an unstructured sequential file. To create this file, you will

- Open the file so that information can be entered into it
- Enter records from the keyboard and write them to the file
- Close the file after all records have been entered

To do this, you will use statements containing the following QuickBASIC keywords:

OPEN   To open a file
LINE INPUT   To obtain a string from the keyboard
WRITE #   To write a record (string) to a file
CLOSE   To close a file

Each of these statements is described below, and is also used later in the program that creates NotePad.Txt.

THE OPEN STATEMENT   An OPEN statement is *required* before a file can be written to or read from. When a file is opened, it is assigned a file number. This file number is then used whenever the file is accessed or written to.

When a sequential file is opened, you must declare the kind of access for which it is to be opened: output, append, or input. A file opened for output can only be written to; if the file already exists, its contents are emptied automatically before any records are written to it. If you attempt to read from a file opened for output, you will see an error message.

The statement OPEN "NotePad.Txt" FOR OUPUT AS #1 assigns "NotePad.Txt" as file #1, and allows you to write records to file #1. If this file already exists, it is emptied immediately. Therefore, before you use an OPEN...FOR OUTPUT statement, check the directory of the disk you are using to be sure that you will not erase the contents of a file that you wish to save.

A file opened for appending, like a file opened for output, can only be written to. However, its contents are not erased before any records are written to it. Also, as the term "append" implies, any records written to a file opened for appending are added to the bottom of the file.

The statement OPEN "NotePad.Txt" FOR APPEND AS #1 assigns "NotePad.Txt" as file #1, and allows you to write records to the bottom of file #1. Unlike a file opened for output, if this file already exists, its contents remain untouched.

If a file is opened for input, it can only be read from. If you attempt to write to a file opened for input, you will see an error message.

The statement OPEN "NotePad.Txt" FOR INPUT AS #1 assigns "NotePad.Txt" as file #1, and allows you to read records from file #1. If a file opened for input does not already exist, an error message will be generated.

Unless specified otherwise, a file is opened on the default disk drive, assumed to be Drive A. In the following example, the file NotePad.Txt is opened for output on your QuickBASIC work disk.

```
OPEN "NotePad.Txt" FOR OUTPUT AS #1
```

File name———┘   File number———┘

If you want the file to be opened on another disk drive, such as Drive B, write the OPEN statement as follows:

Disk drive

If you wish, you can use NOTEPAD.TXT or notepad.txt as the file name, since QuickBASIC does not distinguish between lowercase and uppercase letters in a file name.

Remember: If there is already a file named NotePad.Txt on the disk, the OPEN...FOR OUTPUT statement will erase its contents before writing any new data to it.

THE CLOSE STATEMENT   When a file is no longer needed in a program, it should be closed. Any files still open at the end of a program should also be closed. In addition, to reuse a file number with a different file, the file previously assigned to it must be closed. The statement CLOSE #1 closes the file assigned as #1.

Once a file has been closed, you can no longer read from or write to that file, unless it is opened again. If a file has been closed, a new file can be opened and assigned to the closed file's number.

Sequential files may be opened for output (or append) or input, but not both at the same time. If you need to write to and read from a sequential file in a program, the file must be closed and then reopened with a new access mode. You can open and close a file as many times as you wish within a program.

THE LINE INPUT STATEMENT   The LINE INPUT statement is well suited for entering records in an unstructured sequential data file. Since each record in an unstructured file is a single string, each string entered when the LINE INPUT statement is executed is then written to the file as a single record.

The statement LINE INPUT ">"; *record$* assigns the characters entered to the variable *record$*. This string will then be written to the NotePad.Txt file as a single record.

THE WRITE # STATEMENT   The WRITE # statement is used to write information to a previously opened file. The statement WRITE #1, *record$* writes the string variable *record$* to the file previously opened as file #1.

The numeral following the number sign specifies which file is to be written to. If you were writing to a file opened as file #2, then the statement would look like this:

WRITE #2, *record$*

The WRITE statement encloses the contents of the variable written to the file in quotation marks. In the next chapter, you will learn another way to write information to a file, using the PRINT # statement.

A Program to Create the NotePad.Txt File

Program QBME0901.BAS, Create the NotePad.Txt File, creates an unstructured sequential file of records you enter from the keyboard. Each record can have up to 255 characters, the number of characters allowed by the LINE INPUT statement. A REM outline of program QBME0901.BAS is shown next.

```
REM ** QBME0901.BAS **
REM ** 1/1/90 **
REM ** Create the NotePad.Txt File **
' QuickBASIC Made Easy, Chapter 9
' Microsoft QuickBASIC 4.5

REM ** Set up **
' Assign instructions to string array Inst$()
' Put instructions in lines 21 - 25
' Define rows 1 to 20 as a view port for data entry
' Wait for a key press to begin

REM ** Open a new NotePad.Txt file for output as file #1
' File is opened on the default disk drive

REM ** Enter records from keyboard and write to file **

REM ** Close the file and end the program **
```

Study the REM outline of this program and think about how you might write a program to create the NotePad.Txt file, and then study the QBME0901.BAS program that follows.

```
REM ** QBME0901.BAS **
REM ** 1/1/90 **
REM ** Create the NotePad.Txt File **
' QuickBASIC Made Easy, Chapter 9
' Microsoft QuickBASIC 4.5

REM ** Set up **
DEFINT A-Z      'Define numeric variables as integers,
```

```
'                    unless specified otherwise

' Assign instructions to string array Inst$()
DIM Inst$(1 TO 5)
Inst$(1) = STRING$(74, "_")
Inst$(2) = "Create a new file called NotePad.Txt."
Inst$(3) = "NotePad.Txt will be on the default disk drive."
Inst$(4) = "At the > prompt, type a record and press ENTER."
Inst$(5) = "To quit, press ENTER without typing data."

' Write instructions in lines 21 - 25 of the output screen
CLS
FOR i = 1 TO 5
  LOCATE i + 20, 3: PRINT Inst$(i);
NEXT i

' Define rows 1 to 20 as a view port for data entry
VIEW PRINT 1 TO 20

' Wait for a key press to begin
LOCATE 10, 28: PRINT "Press a key to begin"
anykey$ = INPUT$(1)
CLS 2

REM ** Open a new NotePad.Txt file for output as file #1 **
' File is opened on the default disk drive
OPEN "NotePad.Txt" FOR OUTPUT AS #1

REM ** Enter records from keyboard and write to file **
DO
  LINE INPUT ">"; record$
  IF record$ = "" THEN EXIT DO
  WRITE #1, record$
LOOP

REM ** Close the file and end the program **
CLOSE #1
VIEW PRINT: CLS
END
```

Program QBME0901.BAS Explained

Program QBME0901.BAS begins by defining all numeric variables as integers, unless specified otherwise. Instructions on how to use the program are assigned to the string array *Inst$()*.

```
REM ** Set up **
DEFINT A-Z     'Define numeric variables as integers,
'                  unless specified otherwise
```

```
' Assign instructions to string array Inst$()
DIM Inst$(1 TO 5)
Inst$(1) = STRING$(74, "_")
Inst$(2) = "Create a new file called NotePad.Txt."
Inst$(3) = "NotePad.Txt will be on the default disk drive."
Inst$(4) = "At the > prompt, type a record and press ENTER."
Inst$(5) = "To quit, press ENTER without typing data."
```

QBME0901.BAS introduces a new function, the STRING$ function. The STRING$ function repeats the string specified in the second argument for the number of times specified in the first argument.

The statement Inst$(1) = STRING$(74, "_") assigns a string of 74 underline characters (_) to the first element of *Inst$()*. Thus, *Inst$(1)* is a string consisting of 74 characters, each of which is the underline character. When *Inst$(1)* is printed, it appears as a horizontal line 74 characters wide, which separates the view port in lines 1 to 20 from the instructions to be printed in lines 22 to 25. The instructions are printed to the screen by means of the FOR...NEXT loop shown next.

```
FOR i = 1 TO 5
  LOCATE i + 20, 3: PRINT Inst$(i);
NEXT i
```

This FOR...NEXT loop introduces a new statement, the LOCATE statement. You can use the LOCATE statement to position the cursor anywhere on the screen.

The statement LOCATE *row, column* places the cursor at line number *row*, and column number *column*. Line numbers begin at line number 1 and end at line number 25; columns begin at 1 and end at 80.

The statement LOCATE 10, 28 moves the cursor to line number 10, column number 28.

The statements LOCATE *i* + 20, 3: PRINT *Inst$(i)*; position the cursor at line *i* + 20, column 3, and then print *Inst$(i)* beginning at this position. This FOR...NEXT loop is equivalent to the following set of five statements:

```
LOCATE 21, 3: PRINT Inst$(1);
LOCATE 22, 3: PRINT Inst$(2);
LOCATE 23, 3: PRINT Inst$(3);
LOCATE 24, 3: PRINT Inst$(4);
LOCATE 25, 3: PRINT Inst$(5);
```

This program introduces another new statement, the VIEW PRINT statement. This statement defines a text *view port*, which restricts the screen area in which information can be printed.

The statement VIEW PRINT 1 TO 20 establishes lines 1 to 20 of the Output screen as a view port in which information is displayed. Any information previously written in lines 21 to 25 remains on the screen. Since the instructions to the user are printed in lines 21 to 25 before the VIEW PRINT 1 TO 20 statement is executed, the instructions remain on the screen and do not scroll off. The Output screen is thus divided into two areas, as shown in Figure 9-3.

The next program block prints the message "Press a key to begin" in the center of the view port, waits for a key press, and then clears the view port.

```
' Wait for a key press to begin
LOCATE 10, 28: PRINT "Press a key to begin"
anykey$ = INPUT$(1)
CLS 2
```

This block uses a new CLS statement. CLS clears the Output screen. CLS 2 clears the view port only, not the entire Output screen.

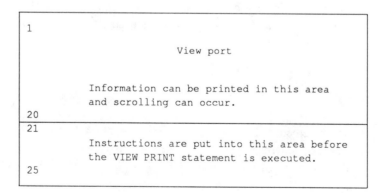

FIGURE 9-3　VIEW PRINT divides Output screen into two areas

The NotePad.Txt file is then opened on the default disk drive for output, as follows:

OPEN "NotePad.Txt" FOR OUTPUT AS #1

To open the file on a different disk drive, include the drive designation as part of the file name enclosed in quotation marks. For example, to open the file on Drive B, use the statement OPEN "B:NotePad.Txt" FOR OUTPUT AS #1. The records to be written to the NotePad.Txt file are then entered from the keyboard and written to the file by means of a DO...LOOP structure.

```
REM ** Enter records from keyboard and write to file **
DO
  LINE INPUT " > "; record$
  IF record$ = "" THEN EXIT DO
  PRINT #1, record$
LOOP
```

To terminate the DO...LOOP structure, simply press ENTER in response to the prompt (>). This exit from the loop precludes entering the empty string as a record. You can, however, type a single space and press ENTER as a record, thus creating a record consisting of one space.

When you terminate DO...LOOP, the program closes the file and returns the text-printing portion of the screen to its normal 25 lines. The entire Output screen is then cleared and the program ends.

```
REM ** Close the file and end the program **
CLOSE #1
VIEW PRINT: CLS
END
```

The statement VIEW PRINT is the same as VIEW PRINT 1 TO 25. This statement redefines the view port as the entire screen, instead of only part of the screen. In general, the VIEW PRINT statement can be written as follows:

VIEW PRINT *TopLine* TO *BottomLine*

This defines a view port beginning at *TopLine* and ending at *BottomLine*, as shown in Figure 9-4.

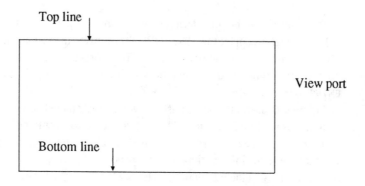

Top line

View port

Bottom line

FIGURE 9-4   View port defined by VIEW PRINT statement

Now run program QBME0901.BAS. It begins as shown in Figure 9-5. Line 21 is a horizontal line (*Inst$(1)*) separating the view port from the in-

```
                    Press a key to begin
```

```
Create a new file called NotePad.Txt.
NotePad.Txt will be on the default disk drive.
At the > prompt, type a record and press ENTER.
To quit, press ENTER without typing data.
```

FIGURE 9-5   Beginning of a run, program QBME0901.BAS

structions, which appear in lines 22 to 25 (*Inst$(2)* through *Inst$(5)*). The view port in lines 1 to 20 is empty, except for the message "Press a key to begin."

Press any key to begin entering notes for the notepad file. The view port will then clear except for the LINE INPUT prompt (>) in the upper left corner. The instructions remain in lines 21 to 25. The NotePad.Txt file has also been opened for output and the computer is waiting for a string to be typed and ENTER to be pressed.

Figure 9-6 shows the screen after seven records have been entered. The computer is waiting for the next (the eighth) record to be entered. If you continue entering notes, the view port in lines 1 to 20 will become full; new lines will then cause the information in the view port to scroll upward. This scrolling does not affect the instructions in lines 21 to 25, since they are outside of the view port.

To stop the program, simply press ENTER without typing any characters. The NotePad.Txt file is then closed, the Output screen cleared, and the program ended. You will then see the familiar "Press any key to continue" at the bottom of the screen.

```
>This is the NotePad.Txt file
>NotePad.Txt is an unstructured sequential file
>Each record is one string, up to 32767 characters
>Use NotePad.Txt for notes of any kind
>Meeting 9/19 at 10 AM with Daniel
>Library books due 9/23
>CMC meeting in Fresno, 10/28
>_
```

```
Create a new file called NotePad.Txt.
NotePad.Txt will be on the default disk drive.
At the > prompt, type a record and press ENTER.
To quit, press ENTER without typing data.
```

FIGURE 9-6   Output screen after entry of seven records

CONFIRMING THAT THE TEXT FILE HAS BEEN CREATED   The
NotePad.Txt file should now reside on the default disk drive. But is it really
there? Was it really created? To confirm that NotePad.Txt is on your disk,
select the Open Program option from the File menu. You will see the Open
Program... dialog box, like the one shown in Figure 9-7. The Files box shows
the names of all program files with the .BAS extension. File names with other
extensions are not shown.

As you learned in Chapter 3, "Introduction to Programming," you can display the names of all the files stored on the disk in the default disk drive. Do
the following in the File Name box.

Type:
.
and press ENTER

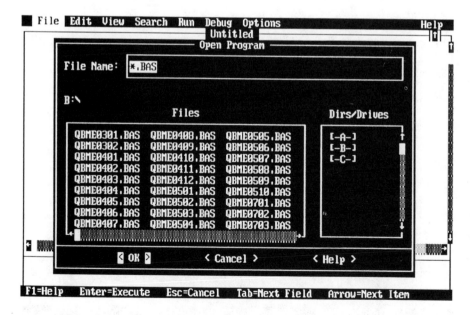

FIGURE 9-7   Open Program dialog box

The Files box will then show the names of all files on the default drive disk, perhaps as shown in Figure 9-8. The file names on your disk may be different from those shown in Figure 9- 8, but you should see NOTEPAD.TXT as one of the file names.

DISPLAYING THE TEXT FILE IN THE VIEW WINDOW   You can display any text file in the View window, even if it is not a QuickBASIC program. To display the NotePad.Txt file, select Open Program... from the File menu. Enter NOTEPAD.TXT in the File Name box or highlight NOTE-PAD.TXT in the Files box and press ENTER to open the file. The NotePad.Txt file will appear in the View window, as shown in Figure 9-9.

Scanning the NotePad.Txt File

You can use program QBME0902.BAS, Scan the NotePad.Txt File, to read each record in the NotePad.Txt file and print it to the Output screen, one record at a time. The program begins as shown in Figure 9-10. When you

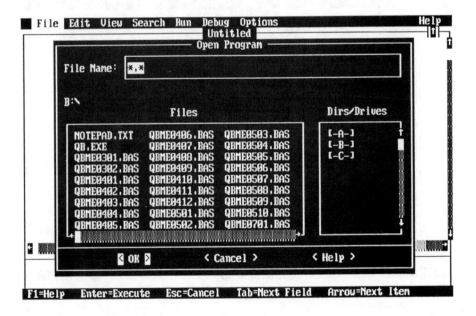

FIGURE 9-8   All files in Files box

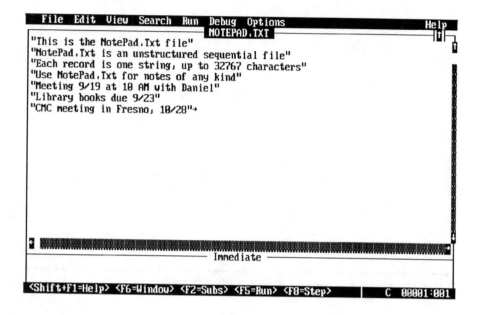

FIGURE 9-9   NotePad.Txt file displayed in the View window

```
                         Press a key to begin
```

```
Scan the NotePad.Txt file, one record at a time.
The file is read from the default disk drive.
Starts with the first record in the view port.
Press spacebar for next record, or Q to quit.
```

FIGURE 9-10   Beginning of a run, program QBME0902.BAS

```
This is the NotePad.Txt file
```

```
Scan the NotePad.Txt file, one record at a time.
The file is read from the default disk drive.
Starts with the first record in the view port.
Press spacebar for next record, or Q to quit.
```

FIGURE 9-11   First record from NotePad.Txt in the view port

press a key, the view port is cleared and the first record is read from the Note-Pad.Txt file and printed at the top of the view port, as shown in Figure 9-11.

Each time you press SPACEBAR, another record is read from the file and displayed in the view port. If all records in the file have been read and you press SPACEBAR, an end-of-file message will be printed, as shown in Figure 9-12. When the end of the file is reached, you will also hear a beep.

```
This is the NotePad.Txt file
NotePad.Txt is an unstructured sequential file
Each record is one string, up to 32767 characters
Use NotePad.Txt for notes of any kind
Meeting 9/19 at 10 AM with Daniel
Library books due 9/23
CMC meeting in Fresno, 10/28

*** End of file ***
Press a key to end program.
```

FIGURE 9-12   All lines in NotePad.Txt displayed in the view port

You can stop scanning the file at any time by pressing Q. In this case, the view port might look as shown in this illustration:

```
This is the NotePad.Txt file
NotePad.Txt is an unstructured sequential file
Each record is one string, up to 32767 characters
Press a key to end program
```

When you press a key, the NotePad.Txt file is closed, the screen is returned to normal and cleared, and the program ends.

```
REM ** QBME0902.BAS **
REM ** 1/1/90 **
REM ** Scan the NotePad.Txt File **
' QuickBASIC Made Easy, Chapter 9
' Micosoft QuickBASIC 4.5

REM ** Set up **
DEFINT A-Z        ' Define numeric variables as integers,
'                   unless specified otherwise

' Assign instructions to string array Inst$()
DIM Inst$(1 TO 5)
Inst$(1) = STRING$(74, 196)
Inst$(2) = "Scan the NotePad.Txt file, one record at a time."
Inst$(3) = "The file is read from the default disk drive."
Inst$(4) = "Starts with the first record in the view port."
Inst$(5) = "Press spacebar for next record, or Q to quit."

' Put instructions in lines 21 - 25
CLS
FOR i = 1 TO 5
  LOCATE i + 20, 3: PRINT Inst$(i);
NEXT i

' Define rows 1 to 20 as a view port for scanning records
VIEW PRINT 1 TO 20

' Wait for a key press to begin
LOCATE 10, 28: PRINT "Press a key to begin";
anykey$ = INPUT$(1)
CLS 2

REM ** Open the NotePad.Txt file for input as file #1 **
' File is opened on the default disk drive
OPEN "NotePad.Txt" FOR INPUT AS #1
```

```
REM ** DO...LOOP to scan the NotePad.Txt file **
' Exits at end of file (EOF) or when 'Q' key is pressed
DO UNTIL EOF(1)
  LINE INPUT #1, record$   'Read one record as record$
  PRINT record$            'Print record$ in the view port
  ' Wait for a key press, space or 'q' or 'Q'
  DO
    anykey$ = INPUT$(1)
  LOOP UNTIL anykey$ = " " OR UCASE$(anykey$) = "Q"
  IF UCASE$(anykey$) = "Q" THEN EXIT DO
LOOP

REM ** Check for DO...LOOP exit due to end of file **
IF EOF(1) THEN BEEP: PRINT "*** End of file ***"
PRINT "Press a key to end program"; : anykey$ = INPUT$(1)

REM ** Close the file and end the program **
CLOSE #1
VIEW PRINT: CLS
END
```

Program QBME0902.BAS Explained

The setup block in program QBME0902.BAS is the same as that in program QBME0901.BAS, except for the instructions assigned to the string array *Inst$()*. After the setup block, the program opens the file for input, as follows:

```
REM ** Open the NotePad.Txt file for input as file #1 **
' File is opened on the default disk drive
OPEN "NotePad.Txt" FOR INPUT AS #1
```

If you want to read the file from a specific disk drive, include the drive designation in the file name enclosed in quotation marks. For example, if the Note-Pad.Txt file is on a disk in Drive B, write the OPEN...FOR INPUT statement as follows:

```
OPEN "B:Notepad.Txt" FOR INPUT AS #1
```

The file is scanned by means of the DO...LOOP structure shown next.

```
REM ** DO...LOOP to scan the NotePad.Txt file **
' Exits at end of file (EOF) or when 'Q' key is pressed
```

```
DO UNTIL EOF(1)
   LINE INPUT #1, record$   'Read one record as record$
   PRINT record$            'Print record$ in the view port
   ' Wait for a key press, space or 'q' or 'Q'
   DO
      anykey$ = INPUT$(1)
   LOOP UNTIL anykey$ = " " OR UCASE$(anykey$) = "Q"
   IF UCASE$(anykey$) = "Q" THEN EXIT DO
LOOP
```

Note the new DO UNTIL statement used in this DO...LOOP structure:

DO UNTIL EOF(1)

This statement tells the computer to repeat the DO...LOOP structure until the end of file #1 (EOF(1)) is reached. When the end of file #1 is detected, DO...LOOP is exited and the program continues with the statement following the LOOP statement.

Also note the new LINE INPUT statement used in this DO...LOOP structure:

LINE INPUT #1, *record$*

This LINE INPUT statement works like previous LINE INPUT statements you have used, except that the characters are input from file #1, rather than from the keyboard. It reads one record from file #1 and assigns that as the value of the string variable *record$*.

The record just input from the file is then printed in the view port. The computer waits for you to press SPACEBAR to see the next record or Q to exit.

The statement LOOP UNTIL *anykey$* = " " OR UCASE$(*anykey$*) = "Q" tells the computer to loop until the value of *anykey$* is a space (" ") or the letter "Q." You can enter "q" or "Q," since the UCASE$ function converts the character to uppercase.

This DO...LOOP structure can be exited in two ways: by reaching the end of the file or by pressing Q before the end-of-file is reached. The following block prints an end-of-file message if all the lines in the file have been displayed. The program then waits for you to press a key to end the program.

```
REM ** Check for DO...LOOP exit due to end of file **
IF EOF(1) THEN BEEP: PRINT "*** End of file ***"
PRINT "Press a key to end program"; : anykey$ = INPUT$(1)
```

The statement IF EOF(1) THEN BEEP: PRINT "∗∗∗ End of file ∗∗∗" determines if the end of file #1 has been reached; if it has, the computer will beep and print the message "∗∗∗ End of file ∗∗∗". This statement is helpful because it tells you whether all the records in the file have been displayed. If you terminate the DO...LOOP structure by pressing Q, this statement will not be executed. In either case, press any key and the program will end, as directed by the following program block:

```
REM ** Close the file and end the program **
CLOSE #1
VIEW PRINT: CLS
END
```

SOME USEFUL SUGGESTIONS ABOUT FILE NAMES

It is helpful to keep a list of the files that you create with a description of each file. A list helps you to determine which file you need at a given time, or even which files you no longer need. This section describes ways of creating such lists, and also explains how to change the name of a file.

Creating a List of Your Files

Sometimes, especially when you have several different kinds of files on your disks, you might wish to create a text file that lists each file name and a brief description of the file's contents. You could use an unstructured sequential file for this purpose, perhaps called FileNote.Txt. For example, FileNote.Txt might include these records:

Record 1: This is the FileNote.Txt file
Record 2: NotePad.Txt contains notes of any type

Try writing a program to create and append to the FileNote.Txt file. Also, try writing a program to display this file in the Output screen or to print the contents of FileNote.Txt on paper.

There is another way to keep track of your file names and the contents of each file. You can write a QuickBASIC program that contains only REM statements and lines that begin with an apostrophe ('), as follows:

```
REM ** FILENOTE.BAS **
REM ** 1/1/90 **
REM ** This is the FILENOTE.BAS File **

' NotePad.Txt contains notes of any type
```

Name this "program" FILENOTE.BAS. You can then load it by using the
Open Program... option on the File menu. Since FILENOTE.BAS is a
program file with the .BAS extension, the name will automatically appear in
the Files box when you use the Open Program... option on the File menu. As
you create new text files, load FILENOTE.BAS and add these new files to
FILENOTE.BAS.

Changing a File Name

You can change the name of a file by using the MS-DOS RENAME command, or by using QuickBASIC's NAME statement. The NAME statement
has the form

NAME "*oldfilename*" AS "*newfilename*"

where *oldfilename* is the current name of the file and *newfilename* is the new
name to be given to the file. Note that both file names must be enclosed in
quotation marks. For example, to change the name of the Scratch.Pad file to
Doodle.Doo, use the following statement:

NAME "scratch.pad" AS "doodle.doo"

If Scratch.Pad is on Drive B, change its name as follows:

NAME "b:scratch.pad" AS "b:doodle.doo"

You can also change a file's name by using a NAME statement in which
the file names are the values of string variables:

NAME *oldname$* AS *newname$*

The current name of the file is *oldname$*, and the name to change it to is *newname$*.

After a file's name has been changed, the file still exists on the same disk drive and in the same place on the disk as before—the only difference is that it has a new name.

There are several different kinds of files on a computer, the most important of which are program files and data files. Each program you create and save is a program file. Data files are used to store information of all kinds. There are two types of data files: sequential files and random-access files.

The records in a sequential file must be accessed in order: record 1, record 2, record 3, and so on. The records in a random-access file can be accessed in any order: record 344, record 3, record 11, record 102, and so on. This book presents both unstructured sequential files and structured sequential files. An unstructured sequential file is one in which each record is a single string. A structured sequential file contains records that have two or more fields.

To create a sequential file, the file is opened, records are written to it, and, finally, it is closed. To access the records in a sequential file, the file is opened and the records are input from the file. When all the records have been accessed, the file is closed.

Keep a list of your files and a brief description of each. You will find such a list especially useful as you create more and more files. Use the NAME statement to change the name of a file.

10

STRUCTURED SEQUENTIAL FILES

Two Ways to Write to a Text File
Structured Sequential Files
Japanese Words and Phrases

In this chapter you will learn to use structured sequential files. You will also learn two ways to write information to files. In particular, you will

- Learn to use PRINT # to write information to a file

- Learn to use WRITE # to write information to a file

- Learn about the differences between the PRINT # and WRITE # statements

- Learn to create and use structured sequential files with at least two fields

- Learn to write string and numeric records to a structured sequential file

- Learn to use DATA and READ statements to assign information to variables

- Learn how to input information from a file and store it in arrays

TWO WAYS TO WRITE TO A TEXT FILE

You can use program QBME1001.BAS, "File Input/Output Experiments, Unstructured Files," to learn more about how information is stored in files. This program uses two unstructured sequential files called Doodle.One and Doodle.Two to illustrate the difference between the PRINT # statement and the WRITE # statement.

```
REM ** QBME1001.BAS **
REM ** 1/1/90 **
REM ** File Input/Output Experiments, Unstructured Files **
' QuickBASIC Made Easy, Chapter 10
' Microsoft QuickBASIC 4.5

REM ** I/O experiments using files Doodle.One & Doodle.Two **
DO
  CLS
  ' Open both files for output on default disk drive
  OPEN "Doodle.One" FOR OUTPUT AS #1
  OPEN "Doodle.Two" FOR OUTPUT AS #2

  ' Get one record, write to the files in two ways
  LINE INPUT "String, please: ", strng$
  PRINT #1, strng$      'Prints record to Doodle.One (File #1)
  WRITE #2, strng$      'Writes record to Doodle.Two (File #2)

  ' Print length of file (LOF) for both files
  ' and close both files
  PRINT
  PRINT "Doodle.One has"; LOF(1); "characters."
  PRINT "Doodle.Two has"; LOF(2); "characters."
  CLOSE #1, #2

  ' Open both files for input on default disk drive
  OPEN "Doodle.One" FOR INPUT AS #1
  OPEN "Doodle.Two" FOR INPUT AS #2

  ' Get one record from Doodle.One and print to screen
  LINE INPUT #1, record$
  PRINT : PRINT "Doodle.One record (written with PRINT #):"
  PRINT record$

  ' Get one record from Doodle.Two and print to screen
  LINE INPUT #2, record$
  PRINT : PRINT "Doodle.Two record (written with WRITE #):"
  PRINT record$
  CLOSE #1, #2 'Close both files
  ' Do again ?
  PRINT
```

```
PRINT "Press Q to quit or any other key to do another"
anykey$ = INPUT$(1)
IF UCASE$(anykey$) = "Q" THEN EXIT DO
LOOP

END
```

The program operates as follows:

1. Both files are opened for OUTPUT.

2. One record is entered as a single string from the keyboard with a LINE INPUT statement.

3. The record is written to Doodle.One with a PRINT # statement.

4. The record is written to Doodle.Two with a WRITE # statement.

5. The lengths of the files are printed.

6. Both files are closed.

7. Both files are reopened for INPUT.

8. The record in Doodle.One is read with a LINE INPUT # statement and printed to the screen.

9. The record in Doodle.Two is read with a LINE INPUT # statement and printed to the screen.

10. Both files are closed.

11. Another record may be entered or the program may be exited.

In the examples that follow, note similarities and differences in the way the same record is stored in the two files; also note the size of the two files. The differences between the two files are caused by differences between the PRINT # statement used to write to Doodle.One and the WRITE # statement used to write to Doodle.Two.

Run program QBME1001.BAS. Enter a single letter as the record to be written to both files, as shown in Figure 10-1. Look carefully at Figure 10-1 and at the results on your screen.

The one-letter string (a) was written to Doodle.One by the PRINT # statement exactly as it was entered. However, the Doodle.One file is three characters long. It contains the letter a and two invisible end-of-record characters, which are added automatically by the PRINT # statement: a return character

```
String, please: a

Doodle.One has 3 characters.
Doodle.Two has 5 characters.

Doodle.One record (written with PRINT #):
a

Doodle.Two record (written with WRITE #):
"a"

Press Q to quit or any other key to do another
```

FIGURE 10-1   A sample run of QBME1001.BAS

(ASCII 13) and a linefeed character (ASCII 10). Refer to Appendix A, "ASCII Codes for the PC" for other ASCII character equivalencies.

When the same record was written to Doodle.Two with the WRITE # statement, the record (a) was enclosed in quotation marks. This file is five characters long. It contains a quotation mark, the letter "a," a second quotation mark, and two end-of-record characters, which are added automatically by the WRITE # statement: a return character (ASCII 13) and a linefeed character (ASCII 10).

Enter another record using QBME1001.BAS; a second example is shown in Figure 10-2. In that example, a three-letter string (123) was entered. Therefore:

- Doodle.One contains one record with five characters: 1, 2, 3, a return character, and a linefeed character.

- Doodle.Two contains one record with seven characters: a quotation mark, 1, 2, 3, a second quotation mark, a return character, and a linefeed character.

Now enter another record, the null (or empty) string. To do so, press ENTER when asked to enter the next string. That run is shown in Figure 10-3.

When the null string is written to both files, Doodle.One contains only the two end-of-record characters: a return character and a linefeed character; Doodle.Two contains four characters: a quotation mark, a quotation mark, and the two end-of-record characters. You might think of these files as "empty" files, since each contains an "empty" record.

```
String, please : 123

Doodle.One has 5 characters.
Doodle.Two has 7 characters.

Doodle.One record (written with PRINT #):
123

Doodle.Two record (written with WRITE #):
"123"

Press Q to quit or any other key to do another
```

FIGURE 10-2   A second run of QBME1001.BAS

To see some other differences between the PRINT # and WRITE # statements, enter **a, b, c** as the string to be written to both files, as shown in Figure 10-4. How many characters will each file have? How will the record be written to each file? Again, the same string was written to both files. Both files contain the same information, stored in the same way, except for the quotation marks appended by the WRITE # statement in Doodle.Two.

Program QBME1001.BAS writes a string to two unstructured sequential files, Doodle.One and Doodle.Two. As you learned earlier, an unstructured

```
String, please:                ENTER was pressed

Doodle.One has 2 characters.
Doodle.Two has 4 characters.

Doodle.One record (written with PRINT #):

Doodle.Two record (written with WRITE #):
""

Press Q to quit or any other key to do another
```

FIGURE 10-3   A third run of QBME1001.BAS

```
String, please:  a, b, c

Doodle.One has 9 characters.
Doodle.Two has 11 characters.

Doodle.One record (written with PRINT #):
a, b, c

Doodle.Two record (written with WRITE #):
"a, b, c"

Press Q to quit or any other key to do another
```

FIGURE 10-4   A run of QBME1001.BAS with a, b, c

sequential file is a file in which one record is one string. In the sections that follow you will learn about structured sequential files, and change Doodle.One and Doodle.Two from unstructured to structured sequential files.

STRUCTURED SEQUENTIAL FILES

In a structured sequential file, each record consists of at least two fields. Each field in a record is a variable-length string: that is, a field can be any length.

For example, consider a file called Japanese.Txt. Japanese.Txt contains Japanese words and phrases and their English equivalents. Each record in this file has two fields: *Japanese$* and *English$*. Sample records from this file are shown in Table 10-1.

Another example of a structured sequential file is inspired by a catalog of camping equipment. In this file, each record has five fields, as follows:

```
Page%         Page number, a numeric field
CatNum$       Catalog number, a string field
Description$  Brief description of item, a string field
Price!        Price, a numeric field
Grams!        Weight in grams, a numeric field
```

Table 10-2 shows sample records from the Camping.Cat file.

Record Number	First Field (*Japanese$*)	Second Field (*English$*)
1	Nihongo	Japanese language
2	Ohayoo gozaimasu	Good morning
3	Konnichi wa	Hello, Good day
4	Konban wa	Good evening
5	Sayoonara	Goodbye

TABLE 10-1   Sample Records from Japanese.Txt, a Structured Sequential File

Suppose the entire catalog were in a file. It would then be easy to write a program to browse through and assemble various combinations of gear, complete with tota price and total weight. Since the catalog information usually changes only a few times a year, this would be an appropriate application for a sequential file.

In the next section, you will learn how to create and access a structured sequential file with two fields.

Using Structured Sequential Files

Modify program QBME1001.BAS to enter two strings, and then write them to Doodle.One and Doodle.Two as one record with two fields. To do this, you need only change the following portion of program QBME1001.BAS.

Page%	CatNum$	Description$	Price!	Grams!
5	33-972	Backpack	129.95	1824
10	47-865	Tent	199.95	3175
19	50-336	Sleeping bag	99.95	1653
25	40-027	Stove	41.95	375
27	40-115	Cooking kit	29.95	884
31	45-820	Compass	25.95	86
44	47-322	Swiss army knife	13.95	57

TABLE 10-2   Sample Records from Camping.Cat

```
' Get one record, write to files in two ways
LINE INPUT "String, please: ", strng$
PRINT #1, strng$      'Prints record to Doodle.One  (File #1)
WRITE #2, strng$      'Writes record to Doodle.Two  (File #2)
```

Change the preceding block in QBME1001.BAS to the following:

```
' Get one record, write to files in two ways
INPUT "First string "; Firststring$
INPUT "Second string"; Secondstring$
PRINT #1, Firststring$, Secondstring$ 'Write to Doodle.One
WRITE #2, Firststring$, Secondstring$ 'Write to Doodle.Two
```

Make any other changes you wish and then save the modified program as program QBME1002.BAS, "File Input/Output Experiments, Structured Files." This program writes the two fields *FirstString$* and *SecondString$* to each file as one record. The records are then read from the two files and displayed on the Output screen. Run program QBME1002.BAS with the example shown in Figure 10-5.

Firststring$* and *Secondstring$ were written to Doodle.One with the PRINT # statement just as they would have been printed on the Output screen. The comma separating the two strings caused *Firststring$* and *Secondstring$* to be printed every 14 spaces. Doodle.One therefore contains 17 characters: the letter "a," 13 spaces, the letter "b," and the two end-of-record characters.

```
First string ? a
Second string? b

Doodle.One has 17 characters.
Doodle.Two has 9 characters.

Doodle.One record (written with PRINT #):
a             b

Doodle.Two record (written with WRITE #):
"a","b"

Press Q to quit or any other key to do another
```

FIGURE 10-5   A sample run of QBME1002.BAS

Firststring$* and *Secondstring$ were both enclosed in quotation marks and were separated by a comma when they were written to Doodle.Two. Thus, Doodle.Two contains 9 characters: a quotation mark, the letter "a," a quotation mark, a comma, a quotation mark, the letter "b," another quotation mark, and the two end-of-record characters.

In the next example, shown in Figure 10-6, *Firststring$* has 13 characters, and *Secondstring$* has 3 characters. Since a comma was used to control the spacing of the two strings, and since *Firststring$* is 13 characters long, only one space separates *Firststring$* from *Secondstring$*. Doodle.One is therefore 19 characters long, including the two end-of-record characters.

Doodle.Two, on the other hand, is 23 characters long. It contains a quotation mark, *Firststring$* (13 characters), a quotation mark, a comma, a quotation mark, *Secondstring$* (3 characters), another quotation mark, and the two end-of-record characters.

Now see what happens when *Firststring$* has 14 characters. Look at the example shown in Figure 10-7, and note the spacing between the two strings in each file. Since strings separated by a comma are printed every 14 characters, and *Firststring$* is too long to print in only one print field, *Secondstring$* is printed in the third print field. Thus, the record in Doodle.One consists of a first field with 23 characters (including spaces) and a second field of three characters, plus the two end-of-record characters. Doodle.Two, however, looks as expected: each field enclosed in quotation marks and separated by a comma, plus the two end-of-record characters.

```
First string ? 1234567890123
Second string? abc

Doodle.One has 19 characters.
Doodle.Two has 23 characters.

Doodle.One record (written with Print #):
1234567890123 abc

Doodle.Two record (written with WRITE #):
"1234567890123","abc"

Press Q to quit or any other key to do another
```

FIGURE 10-6   A second run of QBME1002.BAS

```
First string ? 12345678901234
Second string? abc

Doodle.One has 33 characters.
Doodle.Two has 24 characters.

Doodle.One record (written with PRINT #):
12345678901234                  abc

Doodle.Two record (written with WRITE #):
"12345678901234","abc"

Press Q to quit or any other key to do another
```

FIGURE 10-7   A third run of QBME1002.BAS

Now try one last experiment on the differences between the PRINT # and WRITE # statements. Modify program QBME1002.BAS to change the PRINT # statement to the following:

```
PRINT #1, Firststring$; Secondstring$
```
                              ↑
                        Semicolon here

Notice that if you try to make a similar change to the WRITE # statement, QuickBASIC will automatically replace the semicolon with a comma. Now run the modified program with the example shown in Figure 10-8. Notice the difference that a semicolon between the two strings makes when the strings are printed to the file.

The statement PRINT #1, *Firststring$; Secondstring$* prints the values of *Firststring$* and *Secondstring$* in file #1, adjacent to one another, rather than in print fields. As a result, they appear in the record as a single string without any spaces. The record written to Doodle.Two with a WRITE # statement again looks as expected.

When you write records to a sequential file, use the statement PRINT # or WRITE #, whichever is appropriate for the task. If the amount of space used by each record is a concern, use the statement that uses the least characters.

```
First string ? a
Second string? b

Doodle.One has 4 characters.
Doodle.Two has 9 characters.

Doodle.One record (written with PRINT #):
ab

Doodle.Two record (written with WRITE #):
"a","b"

Press Q to quit or any other key to do another
```

FIGURE 10-8   A run of modified QBME1002.BAS

Using Numeric Fields in Structured Files

So far in this chapter you have experimented with various ways to print string variables to sequential files. In this section you will learn about the different ways to write numeric variables to structured sequential files. Modify either QBME1001.BAS or QBME1002.BAS to make program QBME1003.BAS, "File Input/Output Experiments, Numeric Fields." Most of the original program should remain unchanged; if you are modifying program QBME1001.BAS, you need only change the following lines:

```
' Get one record, write to files in two ways
LINE INPUT "String, please: ", strng$
PRINT #1, strng$      'Prints record to Doodle.One (File #1)
WRITE #2, strng$      'Writes record to Doodle.Two (File #2)
```

Change those lines from QBME1001.BAS to the following:

```
' Get one record, write to files in two ways
INPUT "First number "; Firstnumber
INPUT "Second number"; Secondnumber
PRINT #1, Firstnumber, Secondnumber   'Write to Doodle.One
WRITE #2, Firstnumber, Secondnumber   'Write to Doodle.Two
```

After making these changes, save the modified program as program QBME1003.BAS. The final program should look like the following.

```
REM ** QBME1003.BAS **
REM ** 1/1/90 **
REM ** File Input/Output Experiments, Numeric Fields **
' QuickBASIC Made Easy, Chapter 10
' Microsoft QuickBASIC 4.5

REM ** I/O experiments using files Doodle.One & Doodle.Two **
DO
  CLS
  ' Open both files for output on default disk drive
  OPEN "Doodle.One" FOR OUTPUT AS #1
  OPEN "Doodle.Two" FOR OUTPUT AS #2

  ' Get one record, write to files in two ways
  INPUT "First number "; Firstnumber
  INPUT "Second number"; Secondnumber
  PRINT #1, Firstnumber, Secondnumber  'Write to Doodle.One
  WRITE #2, Firstnumber, Secondnumber  'Write to Doodle.Two

  ' Print length of file (LOF) for both files
  ' and close both files
  PRINT
  PRINT "Doodle.One has"; LOF(1); "characters."
  PRINT "Doodle.Two has"; LOF(2); "characters."
  CLOSE #1, #2

  ' Open both files for input on default disk drive
  OPEN "Doodle.One" FOR INPUT AS #1
  OPEN "Doodle.Two" FOR INPUT AS #2

  ' Get one record from Doodle.One and print to screen
  LINE INPUT #1, record$
  PRINT : PRINT "Doodle.One record (written with PRINT #):"
  PRINT record$

  ' Get one record from Doodle.Two and print to screen
  LINE INPUT #2, record$
  PRINT : PRINT "Doodle.Two record (written with WRITE #):"
  PRINT record$

  CLOSE #1, #2 'Close both files

  ' Do again ?
  PRINT
  PRINT "Press Q to quit or any other key to do another"
  anykey$ = INPUT$(1)
  IF UCASE$(anykey$) = "Q" THEN EXIT DO
LOOP

END
```

Now run this program; try an example like that in Figure 10-9. Notice how each record was written to the files.

When the two numeric variables were written to Doodle.One, the PRINT # statement recorded the two numbers in two print fields: a space, the number 1, a space, and 11 spaces to move to the next print field; then a space, the number 2, and a space, plus the end-of-record characters. The two variables are printed with a leading space because they are numeric. As mentioned in a previous chapter, when a number is printed it is preceded by a space if the number is not negative, or by a minus sign if the number is negative, and is followed by a space. Thus, Doodle.One contains 19 characters.

The two fields written to Doodle.Two are not strings, so they are not enclosed in quotation marks. Doodle.Two contains 5 characters: the number 1, a comma, the number 2, and the end-of- record characters.

In both files, the numbers are stored as one ASCII character for each digit. Each digit therefore occupies one byte in the file.

Figure 10-10 shows some additional examples of printing and writing numeric fields. Experiment with several different numbers, both negative and positive, large and small. Try changing program QBME1003.BAS to use a semicolon between the two variables in the PRINT # statement, as you did earlier in this chapter. Try writing one string variable and one numeric variable to each file and see what happens.

```
First number ? 1
Second number? 2

Doodle.One has 19 characters.
Doodle.Two has 5 characters.

Doodle.One record (written with PRINT #):
 1             2

Doodle.Two record (written with WRITE #):
1,2

Press Q to quit or any other key to do another
```

FIGURE 10-9   An example of numeric fields, QBME1003.BAS

```
First number ? -1
Second number? -2

Doodle.One has 19 characters.
Doodle.Two has 7 characters.

Doodle.One record (written with PRINT #):
-1            -2

Doodle.Two record (written with WRITE #):
-1,-2

Press Q to quit or any other key to do another


First number ? 12345678
Second number? 123

Doodle.One has 35 characters.
Doodle.Two has 18 characters.

Doodle.One record (written with PRINT #):
 1.234568E+07                123

Doodle.Two record (written with WRITE #):
1.234568E+07,123

Press Q to quit or any other key to do another
```

FIGURE 10-10   More examples of numeric fields, QBME1003.BAS

For example:

```
' Get one record, write to files in two ways
INPUT "String"; Strng$
INPUT "Number"; Number
PRINT #1, Strng$, Number   'Record to Doodle.One
WRITE #2, Strng$, Number   'Record to Doodle.Two
```

Make this change and save the modified program as program
QBME1004.BAS, "File Input/Output Experiments, String and Number."
Experiment with records that have three or more fields and with files that
have more than one record. In the sections that follow you will learn how to
create and use a structured sequential file with two fields.

JAPANESE WORDS AND PHRASES

Program QBME1005.BAS, "Japanese Words and Phrases," creates a structured sequential file of Japanese words and phrases and their English equivalents. Each record in the file has two fields:

> *Japanese$*   A Japanese word or phrase. This is a variable
>   length field of up to 32,767 characters.
>   For practical purposes, it will be restricted
>   to 38 characters maximum
>
> *English$*   The English equivalent, or near-equivalent, of
>   the Japanese word or phrase. This variable
>   length field is restricted to 38 characters
>   maximum

If you enter a field with more than 38 characters, the first 38 characters will be stored in the file. Since both fields are restricted to 38 characters, they can be displayed on the same line on the Output screen.

```
REM ** QBME1005.BAS **
REM ** 1/1/90 **
REM ** Create Japanese.Txt File **
' QuickBASIC Made Easy, Chapter 10
' Microsoft QuickBASIC 4.5
' Structured sequential file with fields: Japanese$, English$

REM ** Open Japanese.Txt for output on default drive **
OPEN "Japanese.Txt" FOR OUTPUT AS #1

REM ** Read records from data statements & write to file **
' Terminates on reading end of data message
DO
  READ Japanese$, English$          'Read data for one record
  Japanese$ = LEFT$(Japanese$, 38)  'Limit to 38 characters
  English$ = LEFT$(English$, 38)    'Limit to 38 characters
  WRITE #1, Japanese$, English$     'Write the record to file
  IF LCASE$(Japanese$) = "data no owari" THEN EXIT DO
LOOP

CLOSE #1    'Close Japanese.Txt file
END

REM ** Data for Japanese.Txt File **
' Each DATA statement has one record: Japanese$, English$
DATA Nihon or Nippon, Japan
```

```
DATA Nihon'go, Japanese language
DATA Nihon'jin, Japanese person
DATA Ohayoo gozaimasu, Good morning
DATA Kon'nichi wa, Hello or Good day
DATA Sayoonara or Sayonara, Goodbye
DATA Oyasumi nasai, Good night
DATA Arigatoo gozaimasu, Thank you
DATA Doomo arigatoo gozaimasu, Thank you very much
DATA Hai, Yes
DATA Iie, No
DATA "Jaa, mata ashita", "Well, I'll see you again tomorrow"
DATA Data no owari, End of data
```

Program QBME1005.BAS creates a file called Japanese.Txt on the default disk drive with the following OPEN...FOR OUTPUT statement.

OPEN "Japanese.Txt" FOR OUTPUT AS #1

If this file should be created on Drive B, change the OPEN statement to the following:

OPEN "B:Japanese.Txt" FOR OUTPUT AS #1

This program introduces two new statements, a DATA statement and a READ statement. A DATA statement stores a number or string value to be assigned later to variables. A DATA statement can contain more than one value, separated by commas. A READ statement is used in conjunction with a DATA statement to read the information stored in DATA statements into variables.

The information to be stored in Japanese.Txt is stored in several DATA statements as part of the program, as follows:

```
REM ** Data for Japanese.Txt File **
' Each DATA statement has one record: Japanese$, English$
DATA Nihon or Nippon, Japan
DATA Nihon'go, Japanese language
DATA Nihon'jin, Japanese person
DATA Ohayoo gozaimasu, Good morning
DATA Kon'nichi wa, Hello or Good day
DATA Sayoonara or Sayonara, Goodbye
DATA Oyasumi nasai, Good night
DATA Arigatoo gozaimasu, Thank you
DATA Doomo arigatoo gozaimasu, Thank you very much
DATA Hai, Yes
```

```
DATA Iie, No
DATA "Jaa, mata ashita", "Well, I'll see you again tomorrow"
DATA Data no owari, End of data
```

The number of DATA statements in a program is up to the programmer. You can use only one, or even a hundred or more such statements. You can add DATA statements to this program if you wish, but be sure the final DATA statement is the last one shown in the preceding example; it signals the end of the data to be read.

Each DATA statement contains one record comprising two strings, *Japanese$* and *English$*. The two strings are separated by a comma, as shown next.

```
DATA Nihon or Nippon, Japan
```

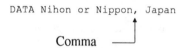

Comma

Since a comma is a separator between fields, if a string in a DATA statement contains a comma as part of the string, the entire string must be enclosed in quotation marks, as in the DATA statement that follows:

```
DATA "Jaa, mata ashita", "Well, I'll see you again tomorrow"
```

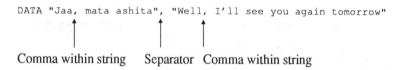

Comma within string   Separator Comma within string

The data is read from the DATA statements and written to the file by the following program block:

```
REM ** Read records from data statements & write to file **
' Terminates on reading end of data message
DO
  READ Japanese$, English$              'Read data for one record
  Japanese$ = LEFT$(Japanese$, 38)      'Limit to 38 characters
  English$ = LEFT$(English$, 38)        'Limit to 38 characters
  WRITE #1, Japanese$, English$         'Write the record to file
  IF LCASE$(Japanese$) = "data no owari" THEN EXIT DO
LOOP
```

The statement READ *Japanese$*, *English$* reads two strings from a DATA statement. The first string is the value of *Japanese$;* the second string is the value of *English$*.

Since this READ statement is in a DO...LOOP structure, the two strings in the first DATA statement are read the first time through the loop, the two strings in the second DATA statement are read the second time through the loop, and so on. Each pair of strings is a record, written to the file with a WRITE # statement. When the two strings in the last DATA statement are read, the IF...THEN statement will cause an exit from DO...LOOP. The file is then closed and the program ends.

The strings read from the DATA statements are each limited to 38 characters by the following two statements:

```
Japanese$ = LEFT$(Japanese$, 38)
English$ = LEFT$(English$, 38)
```

Run this program. To check the contents of Japanese.Txt, display it in the View window. You can display any text file in the View window, even if it is not a QuickBASIC program. To do so, select the Open Program... option from the File menu. Enter Japanese.Txt in the File Name box, and press ENTER. The Japanese.Txt file will appear in the View window, as shown in Figure 10-11. Japanese.Txt is a text file, not a QuickBASIC program, so you can view it but you cannot modify it in the View window.

FIGURE 10-11   Japanese.Txt in the View window

Scan the Japanese.Txt File

In this section you will learn now to access several records in a structured sequential file. You can use program QBME1006.BAS, "Scan the Japanese.Txt File," for some drill and practice on Japanese phrases.

```
REM ** QBME1006.BAS **
REM ** 1/1/90 **
REM ** Scan the Japanese.Txt File **
' QuickBASIC Made Easy, Chapter 10
' Microsoft QuickBASIC 4.5

REM ** Set up **
DEFINT A-Z   'Define all numeric variables as integers,
'              unless specified otherwise

' Put instructions in lines 21 to 25
CLS
LOCATE 21, 3: PRINT STRING$(74, "_")  'Draw line in row 21
FOR row = 22 TO 25
  READ Inst$                          'Read instruction from DATA
   LOCATE row, 3: PRINT Inst$;        'and print in proper place
NEXT row
' Here are the instructions for rows 22 to 25
DATA "Scan Japanese.Txt file, one record at a time."
DATA The file is read from the default disk drive.
DATA Press spacebar for next Japanese or English phrase.
DATA Press Q to quit.

' Define rows 1 to 20 as a view port for data viewing
VIEW PRINT 1 TO 20

' Wait for a key press to begin
LOCATE 10, 28: PRINT "Press a key to begin";
anykey$ = INPUT$(1)
CLS 2                                 'Clears only the viewport

REM ** Open Japanese.Txt for input on default disk drive **
OPEN "Japanese.Txt" FOR INPUT AS #1

REM ** DO...LOOP to scan the Japanese.Txt file **
' Exits at end of file (EOF) or when 'Q' key is pressed
DO UNTIL EOF(1)
  INPUT #1, Japanese$, English$
  ' Wait for a key press, space or 'q' or 'Q'
  DO
    BEEP: anykey$ = UCASE$(INPUT$(1))
  LOOP UNTIL anykey$ = " " OR anykey$ = "Q"
  IF anykey$ = " " THEN
    PRINT Japanese$;                  'Do this if key was a space
```

```
      ELSE EXIT DO                 'Do this if key was 'q' or 'Q'
      END IF
      ' Wait for a key press, space or 'q' or 'Q'
      DO
        BEEP: anykey$ = UCASE$(INPUT$(1))
      LOOP UNTIL anykey$ = " " OR anykey$ = "Q"
      IF anykey$ = " " THEN
        PRINT TAB(40); English$   'Do this if key was a space
      ELSE EXIT DO                 'Do this if key was 'q' or 'Q'
      END IF
      PRINT
LOOP

REM ** Check for DO...LOOP exit due to end of file **
IF EOF(1) THEN BEEP: PRINT "*** End of file ***"
PRINT : PRINT "Press a key to end program";
anykey$ = INPUT$(1)

REM ** Close the file and end the program **
CLOSE #1
VIEW PRINT: CLS
END
```

Run the program; it begins as shown in Figure 10-12. Press any key to begin scanning the file. The view port (lines 1 to 20) clears and the computer beeps. Press SPACEBAR; the first Japanese phrase is displayed in the left half of the screen. Press SPACEBAR again: the corresponding English phrase is displayed on the right. Continue pressing SPACEBAR to see the rest of the file. When the end-of file is reached, the screen appears as shown in Figure 10-13. You can exit the program before reaching the end of the file, by pressing Q. In this case, the view port might appear as shown here:

```
   Nihon or Nippon                    Japan

   Nihon'go                           Japanese language

   Press a key to end program
```

PROGRAM QBME1006.BAS EXPLAINED   Program QBME1006. BAS assigns the instructions on how to use the program to *Inst$()* from DATA statements, as shown in the following program block.

```
              Press a key to begin




Scan Japanese.Txt file, one record at a time.
The file is read from the default disk drive.
Press spacebar for next Japanese or English phrase.
Press Q to quit.
```

FIGURE 10-12   Beginning screen, QBME1006.BAS

```
    Sayoonara or Sayonara       Goodbye

    Oyasumi nasai               Good night

    Arigatoo gozaimasu          Thank you

    Doomo arigatoo gozaimasu    Thank you very much

    Hai                         Yes

    Iie                         No

    Jaa, mata ashita            Well, I'll see you again tomorrow

    Data no owari               End of data

    *** End of file ***

    Press a key to end program
```
```
Scan Japanese.Txt file, one record at a time.
The file is read from the default disk drive.
Press spacebar for next Japanese or English phrase.
Press Q to quit.
```

FIGURE 10-13   End of file reached, QBME1006.BAS

```
' Put instructions in lines 21 to 25
CLS
LOCATE 21, 3: PRINT STRING$(74, "_")   'Line in row 21
FOR row = 22 TO 25
   READ Inst$                          'Read instruction from DATA
   LOCATE row, 3: PRINT Inst$;         'and print in proper place
NEXT row

' Instructions for rows 22 to 25
DATA "Scan Japanese.Txt file, one record at a time."
DATA The file is read from the default disk drive.
DATA Press spacebar for next Japanese or English phrase.
DATA Press Q to quit.
```

The program then prints the instructions and defines lines 1 to 20 as a view port. New lines will now only be printed in lines 1 to 20. The program then shows "Press a key to begin," and waits for a key to be pressed. The Japanese.Txt file is then opened for input on the default disk drive, as in the following:

```
REM ** Open Japanese.Txt for input on default drive **
OPEN "Japanese.Txt" FOR INPUT AS #1
```

To read the file from Drive B, include the drive designation as part of the file name enclosed in quotation marks. For example:

```
OPEN "B:Japanese.Txt" FOR INPUT AS #1
```

The records in the file are read within the DO...LOOP structure. The loop is automatically exited when the end-of-file (EOF) is reached. Press Q to exit the program before reaching the end of the file. Each time SPACEBAR is pressed, the next Japanese or English phrase is printed on the screen.

The statement INPUT #1, *Japanese$, English$* reads both fields in file #1 into *Japanese$* and *English$*. The comma is a separator between fields, and thus indicates that there are two fields in this file.

Remember that the records in Japanese.Txt were written with a WRITE # statement. Each record therefore consists of a string enclosed in quotation marks, a comma, and another string enclosed in quotation marks. Commas within a string enclosed in quotation marks are not recognized as delimiters.

This program displays the Japanese word or phrase first, then the English equivalent. You can reverse this by changing only two lines of the program, as follows.

```
Change:    PRINT Japanese$;
To:        PRINT English$;

Change:    PRINT TAB(40); English$
To:        PRINT TAB(40); Japanese$
```

You can easily modify programs QBME1005.BAS and QBME1006.BAS to help you learn something other than Japanese. For example, you might want to use them to learn Spanish words and phrases, the states and capitals, or answers to trivia questions. In the next two sections you will learn how to use the Japanese.Txt file or a similar file for random drill and practice.

Read a File into Arrays

A small sequential file can be read into memory and stored in arrays. This can be very helpful when searching for names or sorting. Program QBME1007.BAS, "Read the Japanese.Txt File into Arrays," stores the information in the Japanese.Txt file in two string arrays, *Japanese$()* and *English$()*.

```
REM ** QBME1007.BAS **
REM ** 1/1/90 **
REM ** Read the Japanese.Txt File into Arrays **
' QuickBASIC Made Easy, Chapter 10
' Microsoft QuickBASIC 4.5

REM ** Set up **
DEFINT A-Z            'Define all numeric variables as integers,
'                      unless specified otherwise
CLS                   'Clear output screen

REM ** Open Japanese.Txt for input on default disk drive **
OPEN "Japanese.Txt" FOR INPUT AS #1

REM ** Dimension string arrays Japanese$() & English$() **
' Japanese$() & English$() can each hold 1000 phrases
DIM Japanese$(1 TO 1000), English$(1 TO 1000)
REM ** DO...LOOP to read Japanese.Txt file into the arrays **
' Exits at end of file (EOF)
RecordCount = 0                       'Use to count records
DO UNTIL EOF(1)
  RecordCount = RecordCount + 1
  INPUT #1, Japanese$(RecordCount), English$(RecordCount)
LOOP
```

```
REM ** Print first & last records to verify input **
PRINT Japanese$(1); TAB(40); English$(1)
PRINT Japanese$(RecordCount); TAB(40); English$(RecordCount)

REM ** Close the file and end the program **
CLOSE #1
END
```

The file is read into the arrays *Japanese$()* and *English$()* within the
DO...LOOP structure. This loop counts the number of records that have been
input from the file and uses this count (*RecordCount*) to store a phrase in
each of the two arrays. The first record is stored in *Japanese$(1)* and
English$(1);* the second record is stored in *Japanese$(2) and *English$(2);*
and so on, until the end of the file is reached. The number of items stored in
each array is *RecordCount.*

```
REM ** DO...LOOP to read Japanese.Txt file into the arrays **
' Exits at end of file (EOF)
RecordCount = 0                         'Use to count records
DO UNTIL EOF(1)
  RecordCount = RecordCount + 1
  INPUT #1, Japanese$(RecordCount), English$(RecordCount)
LOOP
```

After the file is loaded into *Japanese$()* and *English$()*, the contents of
the arrays are verified by printing the first and last items, as follows:

```
REM ** Print first & last records to verify input **
PRINT Japanese$(1); TAB(40); English$
PRINT Japanese$(RecordCount); TAB(40); English$(RecordCount)
```

The two records should appear like this:

```
Nihon or Nippon                        Japan
Data no owari                          End of data
```

The file is then closed and the program ends:

```
REM ** Close the file and end the program **
CLOSE #1
END
```

The bottom line contains the familiar message, "Press any key to continue."
    Now that *Japanese$()* and *English$()* have been loaded, they can be used
for random drill and practice.

Use the Japanese.Txt File to Study Japanese

Program QBME1006.BAS displayed the Japanese.Txt file sequentially, from the first record to the last. You can use the *Japanese$() and English$()* arrays to display the records in a random order. To do this, first read the file into the arrays, and then select a random element to print. Program QBME1008.BAS, "Use Japanese.Txt File for Random Drill & Practice," provides this capability.

```
REM ** QBME1008.BAS **
REM ** 1/1/90 **
REM ** Use Japanese.Txt File for Random Drill & Practice **
' QuickBASIC Made Easy, Chapter 10
' Microsoft QuickBASIC 4.5

REM ** Set up **
DEFINT A-Z              'Define all numeric variables as integers,
'                        unless specified otherwise
RANDOMIZE TIMER

' Put instructions in rows 21 to 25
CLS
LOCATE 21, 3: PRINT STRING$(74, "_")  'Line across row 21
FOR row = 22 TO 25
  READ Inst$                          'Read instruction from DATA
  LOCATE row, 3: PRINT Inst$;'and print in proper place
NEXT row
' Here are the instructions for rows 22 to 25
DATA Use the Japanese.Txt file for random drill & practice.
DATA The file is read from the default disk drive.
DATA Press spacebar for next Japanese or English phrase.
DATA Press Q to quit.

VIEW PRINT 1 TO 20                'View port in lines 1 to 20

' Wait for a key press to begin
LOCATE 10, 28: PRINT "Press a key to begin"
anykey$ = INPUT$(1): CLS 2
REM ** Open Japanese.Txt for input on default disk drive **
OPEN "Japanese.Txt" FOR INPUT AS #1

REM ** Dimension arrays Japanese$() & English$() **
DIM Japanese$(1 TO 1000), English$(1 TO 1000)
```

```
REM ** DO...LOOP to read Japanese.Txt file into the arrays **
RecordCount = 0
DO UNTIL EOF(1)
  RecordCount = RecordCount + 1
  INPUT #1, Japanese$(RecordCount), English$(RecordCount)
LOOP
CLOSE #1

REM ** DO...LOOP for random drill -- Press Q to quit **
DO
  RandomIndex = INT(RecordCount * RND) + 1
  Question$ = Japanese$(RandomIndex)
  Answer$ = English$(RandomIndex)
  ' Wait for a key press, space or 'q' or 'Q'
  DO
    BEEP: anykey$ = UCASE$(INPUT$(1))
  LOOP UNTIL anykey$ = " " OR anykey$ = "Q"
  IF anykey$ = " " THEN
    PRINT Question$;           'Do this if key was a space
    ELSE EXIT DO               'Do this if key was 'q' or 'Q'
  END IF
  ' Wait for a key press, space or 'q' or 'Q'
  DO
    BEEP: anykey$ = UCASE$(INPUT$(1))
  LOOP UNTIL anykey$ = " " OR anykey$ = "Q"
  IF anykey$ = " " THEN
    PRINT TAB(40); Answer$    'Do this if key was a space
    ELSE EXIT DO              'Do this if key was 'q' or 'Q'
  END IF
  PRINT
LOOP

REM ** clear entire screen and end program
VIEW PRINT: CLS : END
```

The program prints instructions in rows 21 to 25, creates a view port in lines 1 to 20, prints "Press a key to begin" in the view port, and waits for a key to be pressed. The program then reads the Japanese.Txt file from the default disk drive into *Japanese$()* and *English$()*. The arrays are dimensioned to store up to 1000 items each. The number of records actually input from the file is *RecordCount*.

Since the items printed are selected at random, it is possible to see a given item more than once. A sample run is shown in Figure 10-14. As before, the Japanese phrase is printed first on the left half of the screen and the English phrase is printed on the right. To print the English phrase first, make the following changes.

Nihon'go	Japanese language
Nihon or Nippon	Japan
Nihon'go	Japanese language
Doomo arigatoo gozaimasu	Thank you very much
Iie	No
Nihon'jin	Japanese person
Ohayoo gozaimasu	Good morning
Jaa, mata ashita	Well, I'll see you again tomorrow
Nihon'go	Japanese language
Ohayoo gozaimasu	

```
Use the Japanese.Txt file for random drill & practice.
The file is read from the default disk drive.
Press spacebar for next Japanese or English phrase.
Press Q to quit.
```

FIGURE 10-14   A sample run of QBME1008.BAS

```
Change:   Question$ = Japanese$(RandomIndex)
To:       Question$ = English$(RandomIndex)

Change:   Answer$ = English$(RandomIndex)
To:       Answer$ = Japanese$(RandomIndex)
```

Experiment with this program. For example, add more phrases in two languages (Spanish and English, for example) and combine them randomly to make complete sentences. Or, sort the arrays and print them sequentially. How would you sort the two arrays? (Hint: Sort *English$()*, and for every *English$()* element that is exchanged, also exchange that element in *Japanese$().*)

In the next chapter you will learn to use files that are even more structured than structured sequential files: random-access files.

A structured sequential file is a sequential file in which each record consists of at least two fields. A field can be numeric or string. You can use two statements to write records to a sequential file: PRINT # and WRITE #. Use the statement that is most appropriate or most efficient for your task.

Information can be stored in DATA statements within a program and then assigned to variables with a READ statement. Information can also be input from a file and stored in simple or array variables.

11

RANDOM-ACCESS FILES

Sequential and Random-Access File Storage
Create Japanese.Ran, a Random-Access File
Create Japanese.Ran, Input from the Keyboard
Scan the Japanese.Ran File
PUT or GET Individual Records
A Personal Camping Equipment Catalog
Get Individual Records from Camping.Cat

In this chapter you will learn about the differences between random-access and sequential files, as well as how to use random-access files. In particular, you will

- Learn how information is stored in sequential and random-access files

- Learn to create a random-access file from a sequential file

- Learn to use the TYPE...END TYPE structure to define a random-access file structure

- Learn to write (PUT) records to a random-access file

- Learn to access (GET) records from a random-access file

- Learn to access and modify individual records in a random-access file

SEQUENTIAL AND RANDOM-ACCESS FILE STORAGE

As you learned in the two previous chapters, a sequential file is one in which the records must be accessed in the order in which they occur in the file. To access record number 3, you must first access record number 1 and then record number 2. A random-access file, in contrast, is one in which the records can be accessed in a random order. You can access record 5, then record 72, then record 1, then record 11, and so on. Any record can be obtained directly and quickly without first reading any other record. If you wish to access record number 237, you can read it immediately, without first reading the previous 236 records in the file.

Random-access files are highly structured, fixed-length files. This means that all records in a random file are the same length, as are all the fields within a record. When you open a random-access file, you set the record length of that file; if you do not specify a record length, QuickBASIC assigns a default record length of 128 characters.

Random-access records are divided into fields. Each record in a random-access file has the same fields, in the same order; each field within a record has a fixed length. That is, corresponding fields in different records are the same length.

Random-access files have several advantages over sequential files: any record can be accessed very quickly; a record can be modified without having to rewrite the entire file; records can be inserted or deleted more easily than in sequential files; and they are easier to sort than sequential files.

Random-access files also have some disadvantages: data is often not stored efficiently; since random-access files have fixed-length fields and fixed-length records, the same number of bytes is used regardless of the number of characters being stored. In addition, a random-access file must be designed in advance. The length of each field must allow enough space for any data that might possibly be stored in that field.

Sequential and random-access files store information somewhat differently. While they both have fields, the fields in a sequential file may or may not be of fixed length while the fields in a random-access file must be of fixed length. Also, numbers are stored differently in the two types of files.

Sequential File Storage

Sequential files are stored as ASCII text files. In a sequential file, each character in a string is stored as 1 character and each digit in a number is stored as 1 character. For example: the string "abc" is stored as 3 characters; the number 123 is stored as 3 characters; −123456 is stored as 7 characters; 1.234 is stored as 5 characters; and the number 1.234567E+13 is stored as 12 characters.

Sequential files have variable-length records, and can be either unstructured or structured. An unstructured sequential file is one in which one string is one record. Structured sequential files have at least two variable-length fields. In Chapter 9, "Unstructured Sequential Files," and Chapter 10, "Structured Sequential Files," you created and used four sequential files, briefly described here:

- **NotePad.Txt**   This file is an unstructured sequential file. One record is one string of variable length; this is the simplest structure a file can have.

- **Doodle.One and Doodle.Two**   These files are sequential files that were used to demonstrate the different ways to write to and read from sequential files.

- **Japanese.Txt**   This is a structured sequential file with two fields, *Japanese$* and *English$*. Each field is of variable length, but is limited to 38 characters. This limit was imposed by the program that created the file.

Figure 11-1 shows the Japanese.Txt file as it would appear if displayed in the View window. Each character in this file appears in Figure 11-1, except the two end-of-record characters that follow each record. Notice that the fields in this file vary in length. Each field is enclosed in quotation marks and the fields are separated by commas. In this file, a record can vary from 7 to 83 characters in length, as follows:

```
First field enclosed in quotation marks:   2 to 40
Comma separating the two fields:           1    1
Second field enclosed in quotation marks:  2 to 40
End-of-record characters:                  2    2

                             Total:        7 to 83
```

```
"Nihon or Nippon","Japan"
"Nihon'go","Japanese language"
"Nihon'jin","Japanese person"
"Ohayoo gozaimasu","Good morning"
"Kon'nichi wa","Hello or Good day"
"Sayoonara or Sayonara","Goodbye"
"Oyasumi nasai","Good night"
"Arigatoo gozaimasu","Thank you"
"Doomo arigatoo gozaimasu","Thank you very much"
"Hai","Yes"
"Iie","No"
"Jaa, mata ashita","Well, I'll see you again tomorrow"
"Data no owari","End of data"
```

FIGURE 11-1   Japanese.Txt file

For example, the first record in Japanese.Txt is 27 bytes long: 25 visible characters plus the two end-of-record characters, as shown next.

```
"Nihon or Nippon","Japan"[Return][Linefeed]
```

End-of-record characters ⎤

The file shown in Figure 11-1 has 13 records. The shortest record is stored as 10 bytes, and the longest record is stored as 56 bytes. The average record length is 32 bytes (422 divided by 13, rounded to the nearest integer).

Random-Access File Storage

In a random-access file, all records are the same length; each record consists of the same fields, each of which is of fixed length. The first field is the same size in every record, the second field is the same size in every record, and so on. The record length and field lengths must be specified before any information is stored in the file.

There are two kinds of fields in a random-access file: string and numeric. Strings are stored in random-access files as they are in sequential files: one character in a string is stored as one character in a string field. However, unlike in sequential files, if a string in a random-access file is shorter than the field, spaces are added to fill out the field. If a string is longer than the field, it is truncated to fit into the field.

Numbers are stored differently in a random-access file than in a sequential file. They are not stored as strings in a random-access file. Instead, they are stored in a compact binary form just as they are stored in memory, as follows:

```
Short integers are stored in 2 bytes.
Long integers are stored in 4 bytes.
Single precision numbers are stored in 4 bytes.
Double precision numbers are stored in 8 bytes.
```

Random-access files, then, are not ASCII text files, as are sequential files. You cannot display a random-access file in the View window, as you can a sequential file.

In this chapter, you will create and use two random-access files. Japanese.Ran is a random-access version of the Japanese.Txt file used in Chapter 10; this file has two string fields. Camping.Cat is a random-access file containing camping equipment; it has three string fields and three numeric fields.

CREATE JAPANESE.RAN, A RANDOM-ACCESS FILE

You have previously written programs that create data files in the following two ways:

- Information is entered from the keyboard and then written to the file.

- Information is read from DATA statements and then written to the file.

Now you will create Japanese.Ran, a random-access file, in yet another way. Information is read from one file and then written to a second file. Program QBME1101.BAS, Create Japanese.Ran Random-access File, reads the records from Japanese.Txt and writes them to the random-access file Japanese.Ran.

```
REM ** QBME1101.BAS **
REM ** 1/1/90 **
REM ** Create Japanese.Ran Random-access File **
' QuickBASIC Made Easy, Chapter 11
' Microsoft QuickBASIC 4.5
```

```
REM ** Set up **
DEFINT A-Z          'Define all numeric variables as integers
CLS                 'Clear Output screen

REM ** Tell what to do **
PRINT "Use Japanese.Txt file to create Japanese.Ran file."
PRINT "Files read from and written to default disk drive."
PRINT
PRINT "Press a key to begin": anykey$ = INPUT$(1)

REM ** Define structure of random-access file record **
' Each record consists of two fixed-length string fields
TYPE RecordType
   Japanese AS STRING * 38      'String field with 38 characters
   English AS STRING * 38       'String field with 38 characters
END TYPE

REM ** Declare a variable of above type **
DIM PhraseRecord AS RecordType

REM ** Open Japanese.Txt file for input on default drive **
OPEN "Japanese.Txt" FOR INPUT AS #1

REM ** Open Japanese.Ran random-access file on default drive**
OPEN "Japanese.Ran" FOR RANDOM AS #2 LEN = LEN(PhraseRecord)

REM ** No records yet, so set record number to zero **
RecordNumber = 0
REM ** Read records from Japanese.Txt & write to
'        Japanese.Ran **
DO UNTIL EOF(1)
   INPUT #1, PhraseRecord.Japanese, PhraseRecord.English
   RecordNumber = RecordNumber + 1
   PUT #2, RecordNumber, PhraseRecord
LOOP

REM ** Print length of both files **
PRINT
PRINT "Japanese.Txt file has"; LOF(1); "bytes."
PRINT "Japanese.Ran file has"; LOF(2); "bytes."

CLOSE #1, #2          'Close both files

END
```

A run of the program begins as follows:

```
Use Japanese.Txt file to create Japanese.Ran file
Files read from and written to default disk drive

Press a key to begin
```

Press any key. The computer reads the records from Japanese.Txt and writes them to Japanese.Ran. When all the records have been read from Japanese.Txt, the length of each file is printed and the program stops, as shown here:

```
Use Japanese.Txt file to create Japanese.Ran file
Files read from and written to default disk drive

Press a key to begin

Japanese.Txt file has 422 bytes
Japanese.Ran file has 988 bytes
```

Note that although both files have 13 records, Japanese.Ran is more than twice the length of Japanese.Txt. This size difference results from their different file structures. Japanese.Txt is a sequential file with 13 variable-length records, and Japanese.Ran is a random-access file with 13 fixed-length records. Each record in Japanese.Ran is 76 bytes long. Figure 11-2 shows the two ways in which this record length can be calculated.

```
Length of field #1 (Japanese$)  = 38
Length of field #2 (English$)   = 38
                                  ----
                                  76 bytes per record

                        988 bytes
Length of record = ----------- = 76 bytes per record
                        13 records
```

FIGURE 11-2   Record length of Japanese.Ran

Program QBME1101.BAS Explained

When creating a random-access file, you must first define the record structure. This is done by the following program block:

```
REM ** Define structure of random-access file record **
' Each record consists of two fixed-length string fields
TYPE RecordType
   Japanese AS STRING * 38    'String field with 38 characters
   English AS STRING * 38     'String field with 38 characters
END TYPE
```

The TYPE...END TYPE structure defines *RecordType* as a kind of variable with two fields called *Japanese* and *English*. The names *RecordType*,
Japanese, and *English* were chosen to be descriptive of this file; all type
names must conform to the conventions for QuickBASIC variables. Once a
TYPE structure has been defined, you must declare a variable to be of this
type. This variable is then used whenever you assign data to this type. The
following block declares the variable *PhraseRecord* as type *RecordType*:

```
REM ** Declare a variable of above type **
DIM PhraseRecord AS RecordType
```

The variable *PhraseRecord* is now of the type defined by the TYPE...END
TYPE structure. You will use the variable *PhraseRecord* to write to or read
from the Japanese.Ran file. Associated with *PhraseRecord* are two string
field variables, as follows:

PhraseRecord.Japanese is a string field variable, with a
length of 38 characters

PhraseRecord.English is a string field variable, with a
length of 38 characters

These variables are then used to read the two strings constituting a record
from the Japanese.Txt file (*Japanese$* and *English$*). Since *PhraseRecord*
consists of these two string fields, its length is 38 + 38 = 76 characters.
Next, the Japanese.Txt and the Japanese.Ran files are opened, as follows:

```
REM ** Open Japanese.Txt file for input on default drive **
OPEN "Japanese.Txt" FOR INPUT AS #1

REM ** Open Japanese.Ran random-access file on
'      default drive **
OPEN "Japanese.Ran" FOR RANDOM AS #2 LEN = LEN(PhraseRecord)
```

When a random-access file is opened, it is opened for both input and output. Records can be read from and written to a random-access file without having to close and reopen it with a new access mode.

Notice that Japanese.Txt is file number 1, and Japanese.Ran is file number 2. These file numbers are used in the statements that read from or write to the files. When a random-access file is opened, you must specify its record length. The length (LEN) of Japanese.Ran is the length of *PhraseRecord*.

The statement OPEN "Japanese.Ran" FOR RANDOM AS #2 LEN = LEN(*PhraseRecord*) opens Japanese.Ran as a random-access file with a record length equal to the length of *PhraseRecord*.

Since *PhraseRecord* has a length of 76 characters, a record in Japanese.Ran also has a length of 76. Note that random-access files do not have the two extra end-of-record characters found in sequential files.

Records in a random-access file are numbered 1, 2, 3, and so on. Record number 1 is the first record in the file, record number 2 is the second record, and so on. When a record is accessed in a random-access file, it is accessed by its record number. The next program block sets the *RecordNumber* variable to zero (0). *RecordNumber* is then used within the DO...LOOP structure to count the number of records written to the random file.

```
REM ** No records yet, so set record number to zero **
RecordNumber = 0
```

The following DO...LOOP structure then reads the records from Japanese.Txt and writes them to Japanese.Ran.

```
REM ** Read records from Japanese.Txt & write to
'       Japanese.Ran **
DO UNTIL EOF(1)
  INPUT #1, PhraseRecord.Japanese, PhraseRecord.English
  RecordNumber = RecordNumber + 1
  PUT #2, RecordNumber, PhraseRecord
LOOP
```

The statement INPUT #1, *PhraseRecord.Japanese, PhraseRecord.English* reads two strings (*Japanese$* and *English$*) from file number 1 (Japanese.Txt) and assigns them as the values of the string field variables *PhraseRecord.Japanese* and *PhraseRecord.English*.

Regardless of the length of each string when it is input from Japanese.Txt, both are exactly 38 characters long when they are assigned as values of *PhraseRecord.Japanese* and *PhraseRecord.English*. If necessary, spaces are appended to make them 38 characters long. To verify this, add the following PRINT statements just after the INPUT #1 statement.

```
PRINT "Length of PhraseRecord.Japanese:";
LEN(PhraseRecord.Japanese)
PRINT "Length of PhraseRecord.English: ";
LEN(PhraseRecord.English)
PRINT
```

The statement *RecordNumber* = *RecordNumber* + 1 increases the value of *RecordNumber* by 1. The first time through the DO...LOOP structure, the value of *RecordNumber* is set to 1 and is used to write the first record to Japanese.Ran; the second time through the loop, *RecordNumber* is increased by 1 and is then used to write the second record to the file; and so on.

The statement PUT #2, *RecordNumber*, *PhraseRecord* writes (puts) the 76 character record, *PhraseRecord,* as record number *RecordNumber* to file number 2 (Japanese.Ran). You must use the PUT keyword when writing records to a random-access file.

When the end of the Japanese.Txt file is reached (EOF(1)), the DO...LOOP structure is exited. The length of both files is then printed, both files are closed, and the program ends.

```
REM ** Print length of both files **
PRINT
PRINT "Japanese.Txt file has"; LOF(1); "bytes"
PRINT "Japanese.Ran file has"; LOF(2); "bytes"

CLOSE #1, #2        'Close both files

END
```

Here again are the steps that were used to define the Japanese.Ran file structure:

- The structure of the random-access file is defined in a TYPE...END TYPE structure. *RecordType* is the name of the random-access record type defined by the TYPE...END TYPE structure. This name was chosen arbitrarily. You may use any name that conforms to the conventions for naming variables.

- *PhraseRecord* is declared as a variable of the type defined previously as *RecordType*. This is done with a DIM statement. The value of *PhraseRecord* is a complete record containing both fields defined in the TYPE...END TYPE structure. Therefore:

PhraseRecord.Japanese is a string field variable representing the first field of *PhraseRecord*. This field is defined as *Japanese* in the TYPE...END TYPE structure.

PhraseRecord.English is a string field variable representing the second field of *PhraseRecord*. This field is defined as *English* in the TYPE...END TYPE structure.

Thus *PhraseRecord* has the following values for the first record read from Japanese.Txt:

PhraseRecord

PhraseRecord.Japanese	PhraseRecord.English
Nihon or Nippon	Japan

CREATE JAPANESE.RAN, INPUT FROM THE KEYBOARD

You can quickly and easily modify program QBME1101.BAS to make program QBME1102.BAS, Create Japanese.Ran, Input from the Keyboard. Several program blocks are the same in both programs. Other blocks require only minor editing.

```
REM ** QBME1102.BAS **
REM ** 1/1/90 **
REM ** Create Japanese.Ran, Input from the Keyboard **
' QuickBASIC Made Easy, Chapter 11
' Microsoft QuickBASIC 4.5

REM ** Set up **
DEFINT A-Z        'Define all numeric variables as integers
CLS               'Clear Output screen

REM ** Define structure of random-access file record **
' Each record consists of two fixed-length string fields
TYPE RecordType
   Japanese AS STRING * 38     'String field with 38 characters
   English AS STRING * 38      'String field with 38 characters
END TYPE
```

```
REM ** Declare a variable of above type **
DIM PhraseRecord AS RecordType

REM ** Open Japanese.Ran random-access file on
'       default drive **
OPEN "Japanese.Ran" FOR RANDOM AS #2 LEN = LEN(PhraseRecord)

REM ** No records yet, so set record number to zero **
RecordNumber = 0

REM ** Enter records from keyboard, write to Japanese.Ran **
DO
  LINE INPUT "Japanese (Q to quit)? "; PhraseRecord.Japanese
  FirstCharacters$ = LEFT$(PhraseRecord.Japanese, 2)
  IF UCASE$(FirstCharacters$) = "Q " THEN EXIT DO
  LINE INPUT "English            ? "; PhraseRecord.English
  PRINT
  RecordNumber = RecordNumber + 1
  PUT #2, RecordNumber, PhraseRecord
LOOP

REM ** Print length of file, close file, and end program **
PRINT
PRINT "Japanese.Ran file has"; LOF(2); "bytes."
CLOSE #2

END
```

Figure 11-3 shows a sample run of program QBME1102.BAS. Two records were entered and then the run was terminated by pressing Q.

```
Japanese (Q to quit)? Nihon or Nippon
English            ? Japan

Japanese (Q to quit)? Nihon'go
English            ? Japanese language

Japanese (Q to quit)? q

Japanese.Ran file has 152 bytes.


Press any key to continue
```

FIGURE 11-3   Sample run, QBME1102.BAS

Records are entered from the keyboard and written to the file in the following DO...LOOP structure:

```
REM ** Enter records from keyboard, write to Japanese.Ran **
DO
  LINE INPUT "Japanese (Q to quit)? "; PhraseRecord.Japanese
  FirstCharacters$ = LEFT$(PhraseRecord.Japanese, 2)
  IF UCASE$(FirstCharacters$) = "Q " THEN EXIT DO
  LINE INPUT "English             ? "; PhraseRecord.English
  PRINT
  RecordNumber = RecordNumber + 1
  PUT #2, RecordNumber, PhraseRecord
LOOP
```

When a value for *PhraseRecord.Japanese* is entered, spaces are appended automatically if fewer than 38 characters were typed. If more than 38 characters were entered, only the first 38 are stored as the value of *Phrase-Record.Japanese*. If no characters were entered, *PhraseRecord.Japanese* consists of 38 spaces.

If Q is pressed to stop the program, 37 spaces are automatically appended and the result assigned as the value of *PhraseRecord.Japanese*. It is unlikely that a Japanese phrase will actually begin with a Q and a space. The first two characters of *PhraseRecord.Japanese* are therefore assigned to *First-Characters$*. If *FirstCharacters$* equals a Q and a space, the DO...LOOP structure is exited.

```
FirstCharacters$ = LEFT$(PhraseRecord.Japanese, 2)
IF UCASE$(FirstCharacters$) = "Q " THEN EXIT DO
```

Here is a sample run in which one complete record was entered and then the program was stopped by pressing Q.

```
Japanese (Q to quit)?  Nihon or Nippon
English            ?  Japan

Japanese (Q to quit)?  q

Japanese.Ran file has 988 bytes.
```

Note that the file still has 988 bytes, even though you have just written a new record to it. Japanese.Ran consists of 13 records from when it was created using program QBME1101.BAS. Record number 1 has been rewritten in this run of program QBME1102.BAS, but the rest of the file remains untouched.

This is an important feature of random-access files: any record can be replaced or modified without affecting the other records in the file.

SCAN THE JAPANESE.RAN FILE

After creating any new file, it is a good idea to proofread it. Sequential files can be displayed in the View window for this purpose, but random-access files cannot be displayed in the View window, because they are not ASCII text files.

Program QBME1103.BAS, Scan Japanese.Ran, A Random-access File, displays Japanese.Ran on the Output screen, thus allowing you to examine it. Several program blocks are the same as in program QBME1102.BAS; other blocks are very similar. You can modify QBME1102.BAS to make program QBME1103.BAS.

```
REM ** QBME1103.BAS **
REM ** 1/1/90 **
REM ** Scan Japanese.Ran, A Random-access File **
' QuickBASIC Made Easy, Chapter 11
' Microsoft QuickBASIC 4.5

REM ** Set up **
DEFINT A-Z          'Define all numeric variables as integers
CLS                 'Clear Output screen

REM ** Define structure of random-access file record **
' Each record consists of two fixed-length string fields
TYPE RecordType
   Japanese AS STRING * 38     'String field with 38 characters
   English AS STRING * 38      'String field with 38 characters
END TYPE

REM ** Declare a variable of above type **
DIM PhraseRecord AS RecordType

REM ** Open Japanese.Ran random-access file on
'      default drive **
OPEN "Japanese.Ran" FOR RANDOM AS #2 LEN = LEN(PhraseRecord)

REM ** Put instruction in line 25 & define view port **
LOCATE 25, 1: PRINT "Press a key for another record";
VIEW PRINT 1 TO 24: CLS 2

REM ** Start at first record in file **
RecordNumber = 1
```

```
REM ** Get records from file and print to screen **
DO UNTIL EOF(2)
  GET #2, RecordNumber, PhraseRecord
  PRINT PhraseRecord.Japanese; TAB(40); PhraseRecord.English
  PRINT
  RecordNumber = RecordNumber + 1
  anykey$ = INPUT$(1)
LOOP

REM ** Print length of file, close file, and end program **
PRINT "Japanese.Ran file has"; LOF(2); "bytes"
CLOSE #2
VIEW PRINT    'Return screen to full 25 lines
END
```

Run program QBME1103.BAS. It displays the first record and then prints the message "Press a key for another record" at the bottom of the screen. You can quickly scan the entire file simply by holding down a key. When the end of the file is reached, the run ends as shown in Figure 11-4.

```
Ohayoo gozaimasu              Good morning

Kon'nichi wa                  Hello or Good day

Sayoonara or Sayonara         Goodbye

Oyasumi nasai                 Good night

Arigatoo gozaimasu            Thank you very much

Hai                           Yes

Iie                           No

Jaa, mata ashita              Well, I'll see you again tomorrow

Data no owari                 End of data


Japanese.Ran file has 988 bytes.


Press any key to continue
```

FIGURE 11-4   End-of-file reached in QBME1103.BAS

In this program, records are read from the file in record number order: first record number 1, then record number 2, and so on. The records are read and printed to the screen by the following program block:

```
REM ** Get records from file and print to screen **
DO UNTIL EOF(2)
  GET #2, RecordNumber, PhraseRecord
  PRINT PhraseRecord.Japanese; TAB(40); PhraseRecord.English
  PRINT
  RecordNumber = RecordNumber + 1
  anykey$ = INPUT$(1)
LOOP
```

The statement GET #2, *RecordNumber, PhraseRecord* reads the record number *RecordNumber* and assigns it to *PhraseRecord.* Each record has two fields: the first field is *PhraseRecord.Japanese;* the second field is *Phrase-Record.English.* You must use the GET keyword to access records in a random-access file.

Each time a key is pressed, the next consecutive record is retrieved and printed. When the end-of-file number 2 is detected (EOF(2)), the DO...LOOP structure is exited.

PUT OR GET INDIVIDUAL RECORDS

Perhaps the main advantage of random-access files over sequential files is the ability to access and change any record directly by using its record number. Program QBME1104.BAS, PUT or GET Individual Records, Japanese.Ran File, allows you to PUT or GET any record in the file. You can use this program to PUT new information in any existing record, or you can use it to PUT a new record in the file, after the last existing record.

```
REM ** QBME1104.BAS **
REM ** 1/1/90 **
REM ** PUT or GET Individual Records, Japanese.Ran File **
' QuickBASIC Made Easy, Chapter 11
' Microsoft QuickBASIC 4.5

REM ** Set up **
DEFINT A-Z           'Define numeric variables as integers
CLS                  'Clear output screen

REM ** Define structure of random-access file record **
' Each record consists of two fixed-length string fields
```

```
TYPE RecordType
  Japanese AS STRING * 38     'String field with 38 characters
  English AS STRING * 38      'String field with 38 characters
END TYPE


REM ** Declare a variable of above type **
DIM PhraseRecord AS RecordType


REM ** Open Japanese.Ran random-access file on
'       default drive **
OPEN "Japanese.Ran" FOR RANDOM AS #2 LEN = LEN(PhraseRecord)


REM ** Compute & print number of records **
GET #2, 1, PhraseRecord
NumberOfRecords = LOF(2) / LEN(PhraseRecord)
PRINT "Put or Get individual records, Japanese.Ran File"
LOCATE 3, 1: PRINT "The file has"; NumberOfRecords; "records"


REM ** GET or PUT records **
DO UNTIL EOF(2)

  ' Find out what to do
  PRINT
  INPUT "Record number (0 to quit)"; RecordNumber
  IF RecordNumber <= 0 THEN EXIT DO
  PRINT "Press P to PUT or G to GET"
  DO
    BEEP: PutOrGet$ = UCASE$(INPUT$(1))
  LOOP UNTIL PutOrGet$ = "P" OR PutOrGet$ = "G"

  ' Perform requested operation, PUT or GET
  SELECT CASE PutOrGet$
    CASE "P"
      LINE INPUT "Japanese? "; PhraseRecord.Japanese
      LINE INPUT "English ? "; PhraseRecord.English
      PUT #2, RecordNumber, PhraseRecord
    CASE "G"
      ' Record number > number of records will cause EOF exit
      GET #2, RecordNumber, PhraseRecord
      PRINT PhraseRecord.Japanese; TAB(40);
      PRINT PhraseRecord.English
  END SELECT

LOOP


REM ** Print length of file, close file, and end program **
IF EOF(2) THEN PRINT "End of file"
PRINT "File has"; LOF(2); "bytes."
CLOSE #2
END
```

```
Put or Get Individual Records, Japanese.Ran File

The file has 13 records

Record number (0 to quit)? 1
Press P to PUT or G to GET
Nihon or Nippon                           Japan

Record number (0 to quit)? 13
Press P to PUT or G to GET
Data no owari                             End of data

Record number (0 to quit)? 7
Press P to PUT or G to GET
Oyasumi nasai                             Good night

Record number (0 to quit)? 0
File has 988 bytes.



Press any key to continue
```

FIGURE 11-5   Sample run of QBME1104.BAS

Figure 11-5 shows a sample run, which displays records 1, 13, and 7. Zero (0) was entered to end the run.

The program can also be stopped by trying to GET a nonexistent record, as shown in Figure 11-6.

You cannot GET a record whose record number is greater than the number of records in the file. You can, however, PUT a record beyond the end of the existing file, thus lengthening the file. This is shown in Figure 11-7.

Record number 13 is rewritten, replacing the previous record. This is verified by getting record number 13—the new data is in this record. Then a new record, record number 14, is PUT in the file. The file now has 14 records and is therefore 1064 bytes ($14 \times 76 = 1064$) long.

Program QBME1104.BAS computes and prints the number of records in the file, as follows:

```
REM ** Compute & print number of records **
GET #2, 1, PhraseRecord
NumberOfRecords = LOF(2) / LEN(PhraseRecord)
PRINT "Put or Get individual records, Japanese.Ran File"
LOCATE 3, 1: PRINT "The file has"; NumberOfRecords; "records"
```

```
Put or Get Individual Records, Japanese.Ran File

The file has 13 records

Record number (0 to quit)? 14
Press P to PUT or G to GET

End of file
File has 988 bytes.



Press any key to continue
```

FIGURE 11-6   Access past end, QBME1104.BAS

The number of records is calculated by dividing the length of the file (LOF) by the number of bytes in one record. Since all records are the same size, the length of record number 1 was used.

The DO...LOOP structure that accesses the file has two parts. In the first part, the record number to access is entered. Then the program loops until a P (to PUT) or G (to GET) is entered and assigned to *PutOrGet$;* any other character is ignored.

```
' Find out what to do
PRINT
INPUT "Record number (0 to quit)"; RecordNumber
IF RecordNumber <= 0 THEN EXIT DO
PRINT "Press P to PUT or G to GET"
DO
  BEEP: PutOrGet$ = UCASE$(INPUT$(1))
LOOP UNTIL PutOrGet$ = "P" OR PutOrGet$ = "G"
```

The second part of the DO...LOOP structure consists of a SELECT CASE structure, which executes one of the CASE blocks, depending on whether *PutOrGet$* is a P or a G.

```
' Perform requested operation, PUT or GET
SELECT CASE PutOrGet$
  CASE "P"
    LINE INPUT "Japanese? "; PhraseRecord.Japanese
```

```
      LINE INPUT "English ? "; PhraseRecord.English
      PUT #2, RecordNumber, PhraseRecord
   CASE "G"
      ' Record number > number of records will cause EOF exit
      GET #2, RecordNumber, PhraseRecord
      PRINT PhraseRecord.Japanese; TAB(40); PhraseRecord.English
   END SELECT
```

A PERSONAL CAMPING EQUIPMENT CATALOG

If you are a catalog browser, you might find the next two programs useful.
They are designed to store and retrieve information from various camping

```
Put or Get Individual Records, Japanese.Ran File

The file has 13 records

Record number (0 to quit)? 13
Press P to PUT or G to GET
Japanese? atarashii data
English ? new data

Record number (0 to quit)? 13
Press P to PUT or G to GET
atarashii data                              new data

Record number (0 to quit)? 14
Press P to PUT or G to GET
Japanese? Data no owari
English ? End of data

Record number (0 to quit)? 0
File has 1064 bytes.




    Press any key to continue
```

FIGURE 11-7   Old record modified, new record added (QBME1104.BAS)

equipment catalogs. If you aren't interested in camping, you can use these programs to store information on other topics, with only minor changes.

Use program QBME1105.BAS, Create the Camping.Cat File, to create a new random-access file of information from catalogs. It is likely that no such file exists. If the file does exist, you can use program QBME1105.BAS to write new information to the file, thus replacing any information already in the file. This program writes records to the file sequentially, beginning with record number 1.

```
REM ** QBME1105.BAS **
REM ** 1/1/90 **
REM ** Create the Camping.Cat File **
' QuickBASIC Made Easy, Chapter 11
' Microsoft QuickBASIC 4.5

REM ** Set up **
DEFINT A-Z    'Define numeric variables as integers
CLS

REM ** Define structure of random-access record **
' Each record has three string and three numeric fields
TYPE FileStructure
  Catalog AS STRING * 20      'String field, name of catalog
  Item AS STRING * 78         'String field, item description
  CatNum AS STRING * 12       'String field, catalog number
  Page AS INTEGER             'Numeric field, page number
  Price AS SINGLE             'Numeric field, price each
  Ounces AS SINGLE            'Numeric field, weight
END TYPE

REM ** Declare a record variable of above type **
DIM Camping AS FileStructure

REM ** Open Camping.Cat file on default drive **
OPEN "Camping.Cat" FOR RANDOM AS #1 LEN = LEN(Camping)

REM ** No records yet, so set record number to zero **
RecordNumber = 0

REM ** Enter records from keyboard and put in Camping.Cat **
DO

  ' User can choose what to do
  CLS : PRINT "Camping.Cat file has"; LOF(1); "bytes."
  PRINT : PRINT "Press space to enter a record, or Q to quit"
  anykey$ = UCASE$(INPUT$(1)): IF anykey$ = "Q" THEN EXIT DO

  ' Enter a record in response to questions
```

```
CLS : LINE INPUT "Name of catalog? "; Camping.Catalog
PRINT : INPUT "Page number"; Camping.Page
PRINT : PRINT "Description of item:"
LINE INPUT "? "; Camping.Item
PRINT : LINE INPUT "Catalog number? "; Camping.CatNum
PRINT : INPUT "Price each "; Camping.Price
PRINT : INPUT "Weight in ounces "; Camping.Ounces

' User decides whether to put record in file
PRINT : PRINT "Should this record be saved (y/n)?"
DO
   BEEP: YesOrNo$ = UCASE$(INPUT$(1))
LOOP UNTIL YesOrNo$ = "Y" OR YesOrNo$ = "N"
IF YesOrNo$ = "Y" THEN
   RecordNumber = RecordNumber + 1
   PUT #1, RecordNumber, Camping
ELSE
END IF
LOOP

REM ** Print length of file, close it, end program **
CLS : PRINT "Camping.Cat file has"; LOF(1); "bytes."
CLOSE #1: END
```

The record structure is defined by the following program block. The record type name *FileStructure* was intentionally chosen to be different from the record type name *RecordType* used in other programs in this chapter. This was done to remind you that you can use any record type name you want, as long as it conforms to the conventions for naming QuickBASIC variables.

```
REM ** Define structure of random-access record **
' Each record has three string and three numeric fields
TYPE FileStructure
   Catalog AS STRING * 20      'String field, name of catalog
   Item AS STRING * 78         'String field, item description
   CatNum AS STRING * 12       'String field, catalog number
   Page AS INTEGER             'Numeric field, page number
   Price AS SINGLE             'Numeric field, price each
   Ounces AS SINGLE            'Numeric field, weight
END TYPE
```

This TYPE...END TYPE structure defines a record that has three string fields and three numeric fields. The storage requirements for these fields and the total for the entire record are shown in Table 11-1.

The structure of the records in the Camping.Cat file has now been defined. Now a variable is declared that represents the entire record. Again, any name

Name of Field	Type of Field	Bytes Required
Catalog	string	20
Item	string	78
CatNum	string	12
Page	numeric, integer	2
Price	numeric, single precision	4
Ounces	numeric, single precision	4
	Total bytes required	120

TABLE 11-1   Camping.Cat Record Storage Requirements

that conforms to QuickBASIC's naming conventions is fine. *Camping* is declared a *FileStructure* type by the following program block:

```
REM ** Declare a record variable of above type **
DIM Camping AS FileStructure
```

Camping has now been defined as the name of an entire record, 120 bytes long. Associated with the record name are three string variables and three numeric variables shown in Table 11-2.

Variable Name	Variable Type
Camping.Catalog	string
Camping.Item	string
Camping.CatNum	string
Camping.Page	numeric, short integer
Camping.Price	numeric, single precision
Camping.Ounces	numeric, single precision

TABLE 11-2   Field Variables in *Camping* Record

Once the file has been defined, it can be opened. Since a new file is being created, the record number is set to zero. This record number will be increased by 1 each time a record is written to the file.

```
REM ** Open Camping.Cat file on default drive **
OPEN "Camping.Cat" FOR RANDOM AS #1 LEN = LEN(Camping)

REM ** No records yet, so set record number to zero **
RecordNumber = 0
```

Next, records are entered from the keyboard and written to the file. Before examining the program block that does this, run this program. A sample run begins as follows:

```
Camping.Cat file has 0 bytes.
Press space to enter a record, or Q to quit
```

You can see that Camping.Cat is now empty since it has zero bytes. Press SPACEBAR to enter a record. Figure 11-8 shows a sample record selected from the Fall 1988 catalog of Recreational Equipment, Inc., Seattle, Washington.

Notice that you are asked if this record should be saved. If you made a mistake while entering the record, answer N and you can enter the record

---

```
Name of catalog? REI Fall '88

Page number? 39

Description of item:
? REI Peregrine internal frame backpack

Catalog number? C331-091 760

Price each? 160

Weight in ounces? 96

Should this record be saved (y/n)?
```

FIGURE 11-8   Sample entry of Camping.Cat record (QBME1105.BAS)

again. The information entered here is correct, so press Y and the record will be written to the file. You will then see the following message:

```
Camping.Cat file has 120 bytes.
Press spacebar to enter a record, or Q to quit
```

The file is no longer empty. It now contains one record, and is 120 bytes long. Press SPACEBAR and enter another record. The sample record shown in Figure 11-9 is from the Fall 1988 catalog of Campmor, Paramus, New Jersey.

Press Y to enter the record and you will see this message:

```
Camping.Cat file has 240 bytes.
Press spacebar to enter a record, or Q to quit.
```

Since the file now contains two records, it is 240 bytes long. Press Q to quit or SPACEBAR to enter another record of your choice.

The DO...LOOP structure within which records are entered and written to the file consists of three parts. The first part, shown next, clears the screen, prints the number of bytes already in the file, and waits for a key to be pressed. Press Q to quit or SPACEBAR to enter a record.

```
Name of catalog? Campmor  Fall '88

Page number? 51

Description of item:
? Slumberjack Deelite Regular sleeping bag

Catalog number? 41001-F

Price each? 75.99

Weight in ounces? 56

Should this record be saved (y/n)?
```

FIGURE 11-9   Second record in Camping.Cat (QBME1105.BAS)

```
' User can choose what to do
CLS : PRINT "Camping.Cat file has"; LOF(1); "bytes."
PRINT : PRINT "Press spacebar to enter a record, or Q to quit"
anykey$ = UCASE$(INPUT$(1)): IF anykey$ = "Q" THEN EXIT DO
```

To enter a record, enter information in response to each question. LINE INPUT statements are used to enter strings. INPUT statements are used to enter numbers.

```
' Enter a record in response to questions
CLS : LINE INPUT "Name of catalog? "; Camping.Catalog
PRINT : INPUT "Page number"; Camping.Page
PRINT : PRINT "Description of item:"
LINE INPUT "? "; Camping.Item
PRINT : LINE INPUT "Catalog number? "; Camping.CatNum
PRINT : INPUT "Price each"; Camping.Price
PRINT : INPUT "Weight in ounces"; Camping.Ounces
```

It is easy to make a mistake when entering so much information, so the third block asks whether the record should be saved or not. Note the use of the Block IF structure here:

```
' User decides whether to put record in file
PRINT : PRINT "Should this record be saved (y/n)?"
DO
  BEEP: YesOrNo$ = UCASE$(INPUT$(1))
  LOOP UNTIL YesOrNo$ = "Y" OR YesOrNo$ = "N"
IF YesOrNo$ = "Y" THEN
  RecordNumber = RecordNumber + 1
  PUT #1, RecordNumber, Camping
ELSE
END IF
```

GET INDIVIDUAL RECORDS FROM CAMPING.CAT

Now that you have created Camping.Cat, you can use program QBME1106.BAS, Get Individual Records from Camping.Cat, to browse through the file. Camping.Cat has only two records, those entered with QBME1105.BAS in the previous section of this chapter. A run of program QBME1106.BAS begins as follows:

```
The Camping.Cat file has 2 records
Record number (0 to quit)?
```

Since the file has only 2 records, there are only three valid record numbers: 1, 2, or 0 to quit. Enter **2** to display record number 2, as shown in Figure 11-10.

Press a key and you will again see this message:

```
The Camping.Cat file has 2 records
Record number (0 to quit)?
```

What will happen if you enter a nonexistent record such as record number 5? Enter **5** and you will see the following:

```
The Camping.Cat file has 2 records

Record number (0 to quit)? 5
There is no record number 5

Record number (0 to quit)?
```

```
The Camping.Cat file has 2 records

Record number (0 to quit)? 2

Name of catalog: Campmor  Fall '88

Page number: 51

Description of item:
Slumberjack Deelite Regular sleeping bag

Catalog number: 41001-F

Price each: 75.99

Weight in ounces: 56

Press a key to get another record
```

FIGURE 11-10   Sample run of program QBME1106.BAS (record 2)

```
Record number (0 to quit)? 1

Name of catalog: REI Fall '88

Page number: 39

Description of item:
REI Peregrine internal frame backpack

Catalog number: C331-091 760

Price each: 160

Weight in ounces: 96

Press a key to get another record
```

FIGURE 11-11   Sample run of program QBME1106.BAS (record 1)

Figure 11-11 shows a run with record number 1.

The program is similar to several other programs you have seen before. Experiment with programs QBME1105.BAS and QBME1106.BAS. For example, try modifying QBME1106.BAS to PUT or GET individual records. Or, write a program to sort the items in Camping.Cat and then display them in sorted order. Try including the option of which field to sort on, catalog or description.

Random-access files are files in which any record can be accessed at any time. They store information less efficiently than sequential files, but, unlike sequential files, any record can be accessed and modified without having to rewrite the entire file.

The TYPE...END TYPE structure is used to define the structure of a random-access file. A TYPE...END TYPE structure is given a name, and is declared as a variable. That variable name is then used when assigning or accessing the fields defined in the TYPE...END TYPE structure.

The records in a random-access file are accessed by record number. Use the GET keyword to read a record from a random-access file; use the PUT keyword to write a record to a random-access file.

12

FUNCTION AND SUB PROCEDURES

Accessing Full Menus
QuickBASIC Procedures

In this chapter, you will learn how to write programs in modular form using QuickBASIC's FUNCTION and SUB procedures. You will learn how to switch back and forth between Easy Menus and Full Menus. In particular you will

- Learn how to change from Easy Menus to Full Menus
- Learn how to return from Full Menus to Easy Menus
- Learn what a FUNCTION procedure is and how and when to use one
- Learn how to place either the main program or the procedure in the View window
- Learn what a SUB procedure is and how and when to use one
- Learn how to use more than one SUB procedure in the same program

In previous chapters you have used the QuickBASIC Easy Menus environment. Easy Menus contains all the commands you need to use for many programs. However, FUNCTION and SUB procedures are not available from Easy Menus.

The Edit menu is used when you want to create a FUNCTION or SUB procedure. If you are using Easy Menus, the Edit menu contains only the commands shown here.

Cut	Shift+Del
Cop	Ctrl+Ins
Paste	Shift+Ins

In order to expand the Edit menu to include the New FUNCTION... and New SUB... commands necessary to create a FUNCTION or SUB procedure, you must activate Full Menus. Full Menus is activated from the Options menu when you are in the Easy Menus environment. In Easy Menus, the Options menu contains only those items shown below.

Display...
Set Paths...
Full Menus

ACCESSING FULL MENUS

To access Full Menus, first press ALT to highlight the File menu. Then press RIGHT ARROW several times to move the highlight to the Options menu. Press ENTER to open the Options menu. When the Options menu is open, press DOWN ARROW until Full Menus is selected, as shown in Figure 12-1.

When the Full Menus command is highlighted, press ENTER. This activates Full Menus and returns you to the View window. To assure yourself that Full Menus has been activated, return to the Options menu. You will see a small colored circle (called a bullet) displayed in front of the Full Menus command. This bullet indicates that Full Menus is ready for use.

You will also notice that two new commands, Right Mouse and Syntax Checking, have been added to the Options menu. Syntax Checking will be explained later in this chapter; Right Mouse will not be covered in this book. Press ESC to return to the View window.

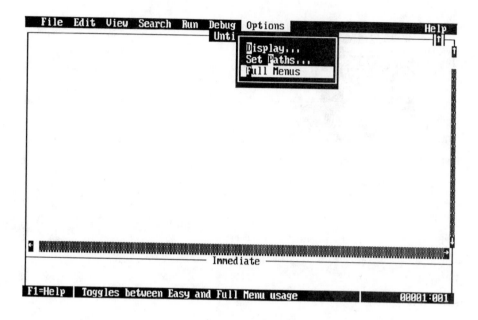

FIGURE 12-1   Options menu—Easy Menus

Press ALT + RIGHT ARROW to highlight the Edit menu. Then press ENTER to open the Edit menu. You will see the full Edit menu shown in Figure 12-2. The last two items on the Edit menu, New SUB... and New FUNCTION..., are used to create a FUNCTION or SUB procedure. You will use both of these commands later in this chapter.

QuickBASIC PROCEDURES

The two QuickBASIC procedures FUNCTION...END FUNCTION and SUB...END SUB are useful for creating routines that can be used to perform often-repeated tasks. These procedures allow you to break up long programs into small functional units. You can test and correct these small units more easily than you can a complete program that does not contain procedures. Once the procedures are working satisfactorily, they can be used as building blocks in other programs.

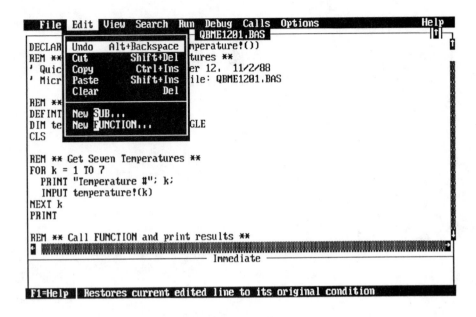

FIGURE 12-2   Edit menu—Full Menus

FUNCTION Procedures

The FUNCTION...END FUNCTION procedure has several advantages over the DEF FN function used earlier in this book. Probably the most important advantage of a FUNCTION procedure over a DEF FN is that a complete array, or any number of elements of an array, may be passed from a main program to a FUNCTION. The use of the elements of an array by a FUNCTION procedure will be demonstrated shortly.

Variables used in a DEF FN function are global by default to the QuickBASIC program in use. When the value of a global variable used within the DEF FN function is changed, its value is changed throughout the program. In contrast, variables within a FUNCTION procedure are local by default. When the value of a local variable is changed within a FUNCTION procedure, the value of the variable remains unchanged outside the FUNCTION procedure.

A FUNCTION procedure begins with the keyword FUNCTION followed by its name and an optional parameter list containing the variables being passed from the main program to the FUNCTION. The FUNCTION is then defined by a block of statements that describe the steps to be performed. The result is then assigned to the name of the FUNCTION so that it can be passed back to the main program. A FUNCTION ends with the keywords END FUNCTION. An example of a FUNCTION procedure is shown in the following listing:

```
FUNCTION SumArray! (temperature!())
  Total! = 0
  FOR day = 1 TO 7
    Total! = Total! + temperature!(day)
  NEXT day
  SumArray! = Total!
END FUNCTION
```

The name of this FUNCTION is SumArray!. The exclamation point defines the type of data being passed as single precision. The complete array (*temperature!*) is passed to the function, as indicated in parentheses following the function name in the opening line.

```
FUNCTION SumArray! (temperature!())
```

The body of the FUNCTION procedure defines the steps used in adding up the temperatures for seven days (the elements of the *temperature!* array). The sum is then assigned to the name of the FUNCTION so that it can be passed back to the main program.

```
SumArray! = Total!
```

Every FUNCTION procedure ends with a line composed of the keywords END FUNCTION.

The FUNCTION...END FUNCTION procedure will perform one of the tasks that appeared in the program High, Low, and Average Temperature in Chapter 8.

You access a FUNCTION procedure just as you access a built-in (intrinsic) QuickBASIC function such as INT or ABS. That is, you use the name of the FUNCTION in an expression. Two examples are shown here:

```
PRINT SumArray!(temperature!())

Sum! = SumArray!(temperature!())
```

When the first statement is executed, the FUNCTION is called and the sum is printed. The call to the FUNCTION is made directly by the PRINT statement.

The second statement calls the FUNCTION and assigns the result to a variable (*Sum!*). The variable may then be used in any other QuickBASIC statement you desire.

THE MAIN PROGRAM OF QBME1201.BAS   The program QBME-1201.BAS, Sum and Average Temperatures, uses SumArray! FUNCTION to add seven temperatures that you enter from the keyboard. The result is assigned to the *Sum!* variable. The value of *Sum!* is printed. Then the variable is used to find the average of the seven temperatures. This result is printed and the program ends.

```
DECLARE FUNCTION SumArray! (temperature!())
REM ** Sum and Average Temperatures **
' QuickBASIC Made Easy.  Chapter 12.  1/1/90
' Microsoft QuickBASIC 4.5.  File: QBME1201.BAS

REM ** Set up **
DEFINT A-Z
DIM temperature(1 TO 7) AS SINGLE
CLS

REM ** Get Seven Temperatures **
FOR k = 1 TO 7
  PRINT "Temperature #"; k;
  INPUT temperature!(k)
NEXT k
PRINT

REM ** Call FUNCTION and print results **
Sum! = SumArray!(temperature!())
PRINT "Total of temperatures"; Sum!
PRINT "Average temperature  "; Sum! / 7

END

FUNCTION SumArray! (temperature!())
  Total! = 0
  FOR day = 1 TO 7
    Total! = Total! + temperature!(day)
  NEXT day
  SumArray! = Total!
END FUNCTION
```

Enter the main program. It consists of all the statements following the
DECLARE statement through the END statement. Do not enter the
DECLARE statement or the FUNCTION procedure yet. Instructions for
those parts of the program will be given in the next section.

ADDING THE FUNCTION...END FUNCTION   When you have entered the main program, press ALT + RIGHT ARROW, and then ENTER to access
the Edit menu. Then press DOWN ARROW so that the highlight moves down
to the New FUNCTION... command at the bottom of the menu, as shown in
Figure 12-3.

When this command is highlighted, press ENTER. QuickBASIC opens the
dialog box shown in Figure 12-4 to ask you for the name of the FUNCTION.
Type in the name of the FUNCTION, **SumArray!**. Then press ENTER.

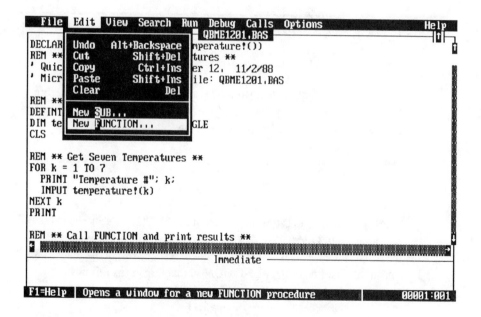

FIGURE 12-3   Edit menu—New FUNCTION... selected

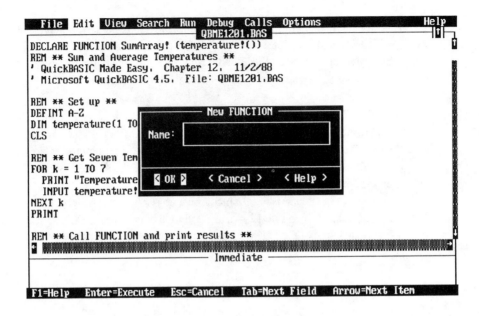

```
File  Edit  View  Search  Run  Debug  Calls  Options              Help
                        QBME1201.BAS
DECLARE FUNCTION SumArray! (temperature!())
REM ** Sum and Average Temperatures **
' QuickBASIC Made Easy, Chapter 12, 11/2/88
' Microsoft QuickBASIC 4.5, File: QBME1201.BAS

REM ** Set up **
DEFINT A-Z
DIM temperature(1 TO┌──────── New FUNCTION ────────┐
CLS                 │  Name: ┌─────────────────────┐ │
                    │        └─────────────────────┘ │
REM ** Get Seven Tem│                                 │
FOR k = 1 TO 7      │  ◄ OK ►    < Cancel >   < Help >│
  PRINT "Temperature└─────────────────────────────────┘
  INPUT temperature!
NEXT k
PRINT

REM ** Call FUNCTION and print results **
──────────────────────── Immediate ────────────────────────

F1=Help   Enter=Execute   Esc=Cancel   Tab=Next Field   Arrow=Next Item
```

FIGURE 12-4   New FUNCTION dialog box

QuickBASIC automatically provides a DEFINT A-Z statement before the
FUNCTION. It also provides part of the first line of the FUNCTION procedure, and all of the last line, as shown in the following listing:

```
DEFINT A-Z
FUNCTION SumArray!_
END FUNCTION
```

All you have to do is type in the rest of the FUNCTION shown in the listing of program QBME1201.BAS. Notice the cursor following the name of
the FUNCTION. This is where you begin to type the rest of the FUNCTION.
Finish the first line of the FUNCTION so that it reads as follows:

```
FUNCTION SumArray! (temperature!())
```

Press ENTER after finishing the first line and type in the rest of the FUNC-
TION procedure. Remember, QuickBASIC has already provided the final
line. When you have finished entering the FUNCTION, press ALT and move
the highlight to File on the menu bar. Press ENTER to access the File menu.

Then move the highlight to the SAVE command and press ENTER. Save the program with the name QBME1201.BAS.

After the program has been saved, use ALT to access the menu bar and RIGHT ARROW to highlight View on the menu bar. Then press ENTER to access the View menu. You will see that the View menu has been expanded and lists the commands shown here.

SUBs...	F2
Next SUB	Shift + F2
Split	
Next Statement	
Output Screen	F4
Included File	
Included Lines	

Press ENTER while the SUBs... command is highlighted. A dialog box appears, as shown in Figure 12-5. You have the choice of viewing the main program, QBME1201.BAS, or the FUNCTION, SumArray!.

The FUNCTION is not displayed in the View window at the same time as the main program. You can move the highlight to one of the two portions of the program: main program or FUNCTION. When you press ENTER, the selected portion will appear in the View window. Try each selection.

First, move the highlight to QBME1201.BAS and press ENTER. The main program will appear in the View window. Notice that QuickBASIC automatically added a DECLARE statement at the beginning of the main program. This was done when you saved the program. The DECLARE statement gives the type of procedure (FUNCTION or SUB), the name of the procedure, and a list of parameters that were passed. The DECLARE statement for program QBME1201.BAS is shown here:

```
DECLARE FUNCTION SumArray! (temperature!())
```

The parameter list uses the same format as the list in the first line of the FUNCTION procedure. Whenever the procedure is called, the variables in the parameter list of the FUNCTION are checked to be sure they agree with the number and type of parameters in the DECLARE statement.

The DECLARE statement is placed at the beginning of the program so that the program can call procedures that are defined later in the program. QuickBASIC places FUNCTION and SUB procedure definitions at the end of a program when the program is saved.

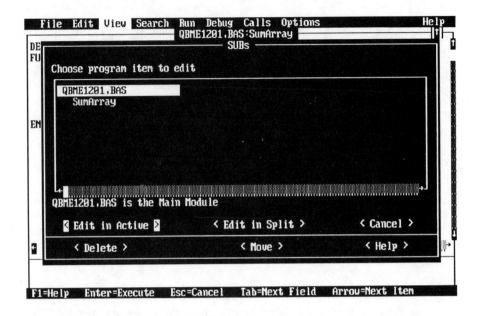

FIGURE 12-5   SUBs dialog box

Access the View menu again, select the SUBs... command, and press ENTER. When the dialog box displays the two choices again, move the highlight to the SumArray! FUNCTION and press ENTER. This time the FUNCTION appears in the View window.

You can edit the part of the program displayed in the View window. Use the SUBs... command of the View menu to place either part of the program in the View window.

RUNNING THE PROGRAM   You have now entered the main program, added the FUNCTION, and saved the combination as one program under the file name QBME1201.BAS. Run the program now.

The program begins by asking you to enter the temperatures, one at a time. The cursor indicates where to enter a temperature. The computer displays a text prompt to inform you of the number of the entry, as shown in this listing:

```
Temperature # 1 ? _
```

When you have entered all seven temperatures, the total of the temperatures is printed on one line and the average temperature is printed on the next line. A typical run with entries and results is shown in Figure 12-6.

Run the program several times, entering different temperatures. If you wish, change the number of temperatures entered. If you change this number, be sure to change the number divided by in the final PRINT statement of the program to correspond to your change. You will also need to alter the upper limit of the FOR...NEXT loop in the FUNCTION and in the DIM statement in the setup block of the program.

ANOTHER FUNCTION PROCEDURE   More than one array can be passed to a FUNCTION procedure. The parentheses following the name of the FUNCTION can include a long list of arrays, variables, or constants to be passed. Program QBME0803.BAS from Chapter 8 calculated the dot

```
Temperature # 1 ? 73.2
Temperature # 2 ? 68.8
Temperature # 3 ? 62.3
Temperature # 4 ? 70.5
Temperature # 5 ? 80.1
Temperature # 6 ? 65.8
Temperature # 7 ? 60.2

Total of temperatures 480.9
Average temperature   68.7




Press any key to continue
```

FIGURE 12-6   Typical input/output of program QBME1201.BAS

product of two arrays. This program will now be modified to use a FUNC-
TION procedure to perform the calculation of the dot product. The FUNC-
TION procedure will replace one block of program QBME0803.BAS, as
shown here:

```
Block from QBME0803

REM ** Compute dot product of Quantity&() and PriceEach#() **
DotProduct# = 0
FOR k = 1 TO Number
  DotProduct# = DotProduct# + Quantity&(k) * PriceEach#(k)
NEXT k


FUNCTION Replacement

FUNCTION DotProduct# (Quantity&(), PriceEach#(), Number)
  Total# = 0
  FOR k = 1 TO Number
    Total# = Total# + Quantity&(k) * PriceEach#(k)
  NEXT k
  DotProduct# = Total#
END FUNCTION
```

Program QBME1202.BAS, Dot Product of Two Arrays with a FUNC-
TION, passes the two arrays *Quantity#* and *PriceEach#* to the DotProduct#
FUNCTION along with the variable *Number*.

```
DECLARE FUNCTION DotProduct#(Quantity&(),PriceEach#(),Number)
REM ** Dot Product of Two Arrays with a FUNCTION **
' QuickBASIC Made Easy, Chapter 12.  1/1/90
' Microsoft QuickBASIC 4.5.  File: QBME1202.BAS

REM ** Define all variables as short integers **
' Use &, !, #, $ to designate other variable types
DEFINT A-Z

REM ** Get number of array elements **
CLS
PRINT"Dot Product of Two Arrays, Quantity&() and PriceEach#()"
PRINT
INPUT "How many items (quantity and price)"; Number
PRINT

REM ** Dimension arrays Quantity&() and PriceEach#() **
DIM Quantity&(1 TO Number)
DIM PriceEach#(1 TO Number)

REM ** Get data for arrays Quantity&() and PriceEach#() **
PRINT "Enter data as requested."
```

```
PRINT "Enter data as requested."
PRINT
FOR k = 1 TO Number
  PRINT "Quantity   #"; k; : INPUT Quantity&(k)
  PRINT "Price each #"; k; : INPUT PriceEach#(k)
  PRINT
NEXT k

REM ** Call FUNCTION and print dot product of arrays **
PRINT "The Dot Product is";
PRINT DotProduct#(Quantity&(), PriceEach#(), Number)
END

DEFINT A-Z
  FUNCTION DotProduct# (Quantity&(), PriceEach#(), Number)
  Total# = 0
  FOR k = 1 TO Number
    Total# = Total# + Quantity&(k) * PriceEach#(k)
  NEXT k
  DotProduct# = Total#
END FUNCTION
```

The FUNCTION is called and the dot product printed by the PRINT statement at the end of the main program, as follows:

```
    .
    .
    .
PRINT "The Dot Product is";
PRINT DotProduct#(Quantity&(), PriceEach#(), Number)
END
```

Enter the main program first. Then use ALT and RIGHT ARROW to access the Edit menu. Press DOWN ARROW until New FUNCTION... is highlighted. Then press ENTER. The New FUNCTION dialog box will be displayed as shown previously in Figure 12-4.

Type **DotProduct#** in the Name box and press ENTER. The following lines of the FUNCTION will be automatically provided:

```
DEFINT A-Z
FUNCTION DotProduct#_
END FUNCTION
```

Enter the complete parameter list at the cursor and the balance of the FUNCTION as shown in the listing of program QBME1202.BAS.

When you have finished entering the FUNCTION procedure, access the File menu and save the program with the name QBME1202.BAS. You are now ready to try out the program. A typical run is shown in Figure 12-7.

See if you can duplicate the run in the figure. Then enter different data for another run. Check the program with different sets of data until you are sure the program is executing successfully.

MORE ADVANCED USES OF A FUNCTION PROCEDURE   When you write more advanced programs, you may want to use the *recursive* capabilities of a FUNCTION. Recursion is a process by which a procedure can call itself within its own definition. This is another advantage that a FUNCTION procedure has over a DEF FN function.

When you begin to write multi-module programs, you will find in them another capability of FUNCTION procedures that DEF FN functions lack. A *module* is a file that contains either a complete program or one or more executable parts of a program.

```
Dot Product of Two Arrays, Quantity&() and PriceEach#()

How many items (quantity and price)? 3

Enter data as requested.

Quantity   # 1 ? 1250
Price each # 1 ? 14.95

Quantity   # 2 ? 258
Price each # 2 ? 30.15

Quantity   # 3 ? 792
Price each # 3 ? 15.75

The Dot Product is 38940.2




Press any key to continue
```

FIGURE 12-7   Output of program QBME1202.BAS

All of the programs in this book are written as single modules. That is, each is saved in its own file. However, a program can be divided into two or more modules. Modules are often stored in a library where they can be accessed quickly by any QuickBASIC program. Program modules and their advantages over single-module programs are discussed in Chapter 7 of the Microsoft *Programming in BASIC* manual.

SUB Procedures

A SUB procedure, like a FUNCTION procedure, is used as a building block to break long programs into smaller functional units. SUB procedures are a part of the program in which they are used but are stored as separate units at the end of the program.

A SUB procedure's variables are local by default. If the same variable is used inside and outside the SUB procedure, changes to the value of the variable inside the SUB procedure do not affect the value of the variable outside. Therefore, the SUB procedure can be used as a building block in many different programs with little or no change.

In contrast, a global variable is shared by all units in a program. When using SUB procedures, you have the option of making variables within the procedure global.

A SUB procedure can be called many times from the main program, passing different variables each time. This is done by calling the SUB with an argument list. The following listing shows how two calls may be made to the same SUB procedure, passing different variables in the argument list in each call.

```
NumOne = 7: NumTwo = 8
CALL SumNums (NumOne, NumTwo)

NumThree = 9: NumFour = 10
CALL SumNums (NumThree, NumFour)
```

The SUB procedure would contain a parameter list that matches the argument list of the two calls in number and type, but the variables in the parameter list do not have to be the same as those used in the argument list of the call statement.In other words the values of the variables of the previous examples could be received with the following parameter list in the SUB procedure:

```
SUB SumNums (Rnum1, Rnum2)
```

The parameters used in the SUB procedure are placeholders for the arguments passed in the CALL statements. When a procedure is called, the arguments in the CALL statement are assigned to the corresponding parameter in the parameter list for the SUB.

Thus on the first CALL in the example, 7 (the value of *NumOne*) is assigned to *Rnum1*, and 8 (the value of *NumTwo*) is assigned to *Rnum2* in the SUB procedure.

When the second CALL in the example is made, 9 (the value of *NumThree*) is assigned to *Rnum1*, and 10 (the value of *NumFour*) is assigned to *Rnum2* in the SUB procedure.

A SUB procedure is similar to a FUNCTION procedure in that it has an opening line, a block of executable statements, and a closing line. The SUB procedure does not return a value in its name as the FUNCTION procedure does. In addition, a SUB is called in a different way, as you will soon see.

USING A SUB PROCEDURE TO CREATE A FILE   In Chapter 10 you used a structured sequential file (program QBME1005.BAS) of Japanese words and phrases and their English equivalents. Each record in the file had two fields. One field was Japanese words or phrases. The other was the English equivalent of the Japanese words or phrases. Each field was restricted to 38 characters so that the Japanese and English equivalents could be placed side by side on the screen. Program QBME1203.BAS, Create Japanese.Txt File with SUB Procedure, modifies that program to demonstrate the use of a SUB procedure.

```
DECLARE SUB WriteFile (J$(), E$())
REM ** Create Japanese.Txt File with SUB Procedure **
' QuickBASIC Made Easy, Chapter 12.  1/1/90
' Microsoft QuickBASIC 4.5.  File: QBME1203.BAS

REM ** Assign Data for Japanese.Txt File to Strings **
DIM J$(1 TO 13), E$(1 TO 13)
J$(1) = "Nihon or Nipopon": E$(1) = "Japan"
J$(2) = "Nihon'go": E$(2) = "Japanese language"
J$(3) = "Nihon'jin": E$(3) = "Japanese person"
J$(4) = "Ohayoo gozaimasu": E$(4) = "Good morning"
J$(5) = "Kon'nichi wa": E$(5) = "Hello or Good day"
J$(6) = "Sayoonara or Sayonara": E$(6) = "Goodbye"
J$(7) = "Oyasumi nasai": E$(7) = "Good night"
J$(8) = "Arigatoo gozaimasu": E$(8) = "Thank you"
J$(9) = "Doomo arigatoo gozaimasu":
E$(9)="Thank you very much"
J$(10) = "Hai": E$(10) = "Yes"
J$(11) = "Iie": E$(11) = "No"
J$(12) = "Jaa, mata ashita":
```

```
E$(12) = "Well, I'll see you again tomorrow"
J$(13) = "Data no owari": E$(13) = "End of data"

CALL WriteFile(J$(), E$())
END

SUB WriteFile (J$(), E$())
  REM ** Select disk drive and Open Japanese.Txt file **
  INPUT "Which drive (A, B, C, etc.) for file "; drive$
  CLS
  drive$ = LEFT$(drive$, 1)
  Filename$ = drive$ + ":Japanese.Txt"
  OPEN Filename$ FOR OUTPUT AS #1

  REM ** Read records from strings & write to file **
  ' Terminates on reading end of data messagae
  k = 1                             'initialize element number
  DO
    Japanese$ = LEFT$(J$(k), 38)    'Limit to 38 characters
    English$ = LEFT$(E$(k), 38)     'Limit to 38 characters
    WRITE #1, Japanese$, English$   'Write the record to file
    IF LCASE$(Japanese$) = "data no owari" THEN EXIT DO
    k = k + 1
  LOOP

  CLOSE #1      ' Close Japanese.Txt file

END SUB
```

All file operations of the program in Chapter 10 formed a logical, or one-function, unit. The sections that open the file, read data, write records to the file, and close the file are therefore written in the revised program as a SUB procedure.

The format for the data used in the file has been changed from DATA statements to elements in two string arrays. This is done to demonstrate that string arrays can be passed from the main program to the SUB procedure easily. The data is assigned to elements of the string arrays as follows:

```
REM ** Assign Data for Japanese.Txt File to Strings **
DIM J$(1 TO 13), E$(1 TO 13)
J$(1) = "Nihon or Nipopon": E$(1) = "Japan"
J$(2) = "Nihon'go": E$(2) = "Japanese language"
J$(3) = "Nihon'jin": E$(3) = "Japanese person"
J$(4) = "Ohayoo gozaimasu": E$(4) = "Good morning"
        .                          .
        .                          .
        .                          .
```

The Japanese words or phrases are stored as elements of the *J$* array, and the English equivalents are stored in the corresponding elements of the *E$* array. Both arrays are passed to the SUB procedure by one statement in the main program.

```
CALL WriteFlile(J$(), E$())
   .
   .
   .
SUB WriteFile (J$(), E$())
```

The file is opened in the SUB procedure in a general way to allow you to enter the disk drive you wish to use to create the file. The program then adds the designated drive to the file name as follows:

```
REM ** Select disk drive and Open Japanexe.Txt File **
INPUT "Which drive (A, B, C, etc.) for file "; drive$
CLS 2                            'Clear view port only
drive$ = LEFT$(drive$, 1)
Filename$ = drive$ + ":Japanese.Txt"
OPEN Filename$ FOR INPUT AS #1
```

An element of each array, *J$(k)* and *E$(k)* is accessed and assigned to the variables *Japanese$* and *English$,* respectively. Each of these variables is written to the file as a field of one record. A check for end-of-data is then made. If more data is available, the program increases the subscript (*k*) of the arrays and loops back for another pair of array elements, as shown here:

```
k = 1
DO
  Japanese$ = LEFT$(J$(k), 38)     'Limit to 38 characters
  English$ = LEFT$(E$(k), 38)      'Limit to 38 characters
  WRITE #1, Japanese$, English$    'Write the record to file
  IF LCASE$(Japanese$) = "data no owari" THEN EXIT DO
  k = k + 1
LOOP
```

If there is no more data, the file is closed and the program ends.

Enter the main program before you enter the SUB procedure. When you have entered the main program, access the Edit menu. Press DOWN ARROW until the New SUB... command is highlighted, as shown in Figure 12-8.

While the New SUB... command is highlighted, press ENTER. This opens up the New SUB dialog box. It is very similar to that of the New FUNCTION dialog box shown previously in Figure 12-4, but it has a different title: New

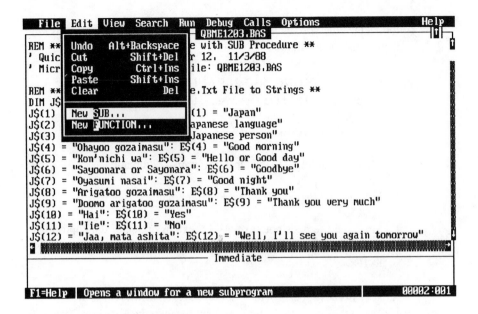

FIGURE 12-8   Edit menu—New SUB . . . selected

SUB. Type in the name **WriteFile**. Then press ENTER. The opening and closing lines of the WriteFile FUNCTION will be displayed, as shown here:

```
SUB WriteFile_
END SUB
```

Finish the line where the cursor is by typing the variables being passed,
as shown in program QBME1203.BAS. Complete the SUB procedure as
shown in that program. Then save the completed program with the name
QBME1203.BAS. When the program has been entered and saved, execute
it from the Run menu.

The prompt for the disk drive appears at the top of the screen, as shown
here:

```
Which drive (A, B, C, etc.) for file ? _
```

When you respond with a disk drive designation, the screen will go blank;
you should hear some noise in the disk drive as it stores the file. When the
file is closed, the usual message, "Press any key to continue," appears at the

bottom of the otherwise blank screen. The program has ended. Press any key to display the View window.

VIEWING AND EDITING THE JAPANESE.TXT FILE   Use the following steps to verify that the Japanese.Txt file has been created:

1. Access the File menu.

2. Move the highlight to the Open Program... command.

3. Press ENTER to open the Open Program dialog box.

4. Since the file does not have a BAS extension, enter the appropriate disk drive designation followed by *.* (for example, A:*.*) and press ENTER.

A list of all files appears in the Files box. JAPANESE.TXT is there. Press TAB to move the cursor to the first program listed in the Files box. Then use the arrow keys to move the highlight to the file name JAPANESE.TXT. Press ENTER and the Japanese.Txt file appears in the View window as shown in Figure 12-9.

Since you are now using Full Menus, you can turn off QuickBASIC's Syntax Checking feature and edit the file. Use the following steps to turn off Syntax Checking:

1. With the Japanese.Txt file in the View window, access the Options menu.

2. Notice the "bullet" in front of the Syntax Checking item. The bullet indicates that Syntax Checking is active. Move the highlight down to Syntax Checking.

3. Press ENTER. This turns Syntax Checking off and returns you to the Japanese.Txt file in the View window.

After performing these steps, you can move the cursor around the file and make any editing changes desired. When you finish editing, save the file from the File menu.

When you have edited and saved the file, go back to the Options menu. Notice that the bullet that was previously in front of Syntax Checking is gone. This indicates that Syntax Checking is *not* active. It has been turned off. Move the highlight down to Syntax Checking and press ENTER. This turns Syntax

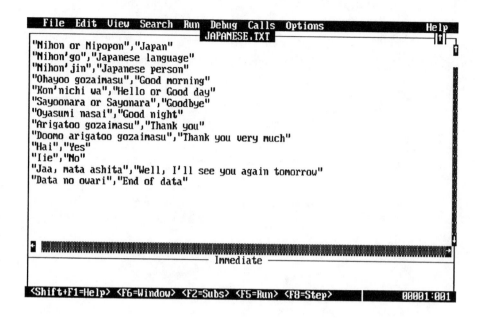

```
 File  Edit  View  Search  Run  Debug  Calls  Options                    Help
                           JAPANESE.TXT
"Nihon or Nipopon","Japan"
"Nihon'go","Japanese language"
"Nihon'jin","Japanese person"
"Ohayoo gozaimasu","Good morning"
"Kon'nichi wa","Hello or Good day"
"Sayoonara or Sayonara","Goodbye"
"Oyasumi nasai","Good night"
"Arigatoo gozaimasu","Thank you"
"Doomo arigatoo gozaimasu","Thank you very much"
"Hai","Yes"
"Iie","No"
"Jaa, mata ashita","Well, I'll see you again tomorrow"
"Data no owari","End of data"




                                   Immediate

<Shift+F1=Help> <F6=Window> <F2=Subs> <F5=Run> <F8=Step>          00001:001
```

FIGURE 12-9   Japanese.Txt file in View window

Checking back on and returns you to the View window. Your QuickBASIC programs will now be checked for syntax again.

Remember: To edit a text file, turn Syntax Checking off. If Syntax Checking is off, turn it back on before working with QuickBASIC programs.

USING A SUB PROCEDURE TO SCAN A FILE   A program that creates a data file is of little use unless you have another program that allows you to use the data in the data file. In Chapter 10, you used program QBME1006.BAS to scan the Japanese.Txt file. It provided instructions at the bottom of the screen. A view port was created to alternately display Japanese words or phrases on the left side and their English equivalents on the right side.

Program QBME1204.BAS, Scan Japanese.Txt File with SUB Procedure, is a modification of the scan file program of Chapter 10.

```
DECLARE SUB ScanFile ()
REM ** Scan Japanese.Txt File with SUB Procedure **
' QuickBASIC Made Easy, Chapter 12.  1/1/90
' Microsoft QuickBASIC 4.5.  File: QBME1204.BAS
```

```
REM ** Set up **
DEFINT A-Z           'All non-designated variables are integer

'Put instructions in lines 21 to 25
CLS
LOCATE 21, 3: PRINT STRING$(74, 196)  'Draw line in row 21
FOR row = 22 TO 25
   READ Inst$                          'Read instructions from DATA
   LOCATE row, 3: PRINT Inst$;         'and print in proper place
NEXT row
'Here are the instructions for rows 22 to 25
DATA "Scan Japanese.Txt file, one record at a time."
DATA "The file is read from the disk drive you specify."
DATA Press spacebar for next Japanese or English phrase.
DATA Press Q to quit.

' Define rows 1 to 20 as a view port for data viewing
VIEW PRINT 1 TO 20

' Wait for a key press to begin
LOCATE 10, 26: PRINT "Press a key to begin";
anykey$ = INPUT$(1)
CLS 2                                  'Clears only the view port

REM ** Call the SUB procedure to scan the file **
CALL ScanFile

REM ** Clear the screen and end the program **
VIEW PRINT: CLS
END

DEFINT A-Z
SUB ScanFile
   REM ** Select disk drive and Open Japanese.Txt File **
   INPUT "Which drive (A, B, C, etc.) for file "; drive$
   CLS 2                       'Clear view port only
   drive$ = LEFT$(drive$, 1)
   Filename$ = drive$ + ":Japanese.Txt"
   OPEN Filename$ FOR INPUT AS #1

   REM ** DO...LOOP to scan the Japanese.Txt file **
   ' Exits at end of file (EOF) or when 'Q' key is pressed
   DO UNTIL EOF(1)
      INPUT #1, Japanese$, English$
      ' Wait for a key press, space or 'q' or 'Q'
      DO
         BEEP: anykey$ = UCASE$(INPUT$(1))
      LOOP UNTIL anykey$ = " " OR anykey$ = "Q"
      IF anykey$ = " " THEN
         PRINT Japanese$;          'Do this if key was a space
      ELSE EXIT DO                  'Do this if key was 'q' or 'Q'
```

```
      END IF
      ' Wait for a key press, space or 'q' or 'Q'
      DO
         BEEP: anykey$ = UCASE$(INPUT$(1))
      LOOP UNTIL anykey$ = " " OR anykey$ = "Q"
      IF anykey$ = " " THEN
         PRINT TAB(40); English$    'Do this if key was a space
      ELSE EXIT DO                  'Do this if key was 'q' or 'Q'
      END IF
      PRINT
   LOOP

   REM ** Check for DO...LOOP exit due to end of file **
   IF EOF(1) THEN BEEP: PRINT "*** End of file ***"
   PRINT : PRINT "Press a key to end program";
   anykey$ = INPUT$(1)

   REM ** Close the file and end the subprogram **
   CLOSE #1
END SUB
```

The blocks of statements dealing with the file have been moved to a SUB procedure. Opening the file has been modified to allow you to enter the disk drive in which your Japanese.Txt file is located. A related change has been made in the instructions.

The SUB procedure that handles the text file is named ScanFile. No variables or arrays need to be passed when the SUB procedure is called. The balance of the program is the same as the scan file program in Chapter 10.

Enter the main program first. Then add the SUB procedure by accessing the New SUB... command from the Edit menu as you did with the previous program. When the main program and the SUB procedure have been entered, save the program as QBME1204.BAS.

When you run the new program, you will see the same prompts and displays as were shown in the scan program in Chapter 10. Figure 12-10 shows several records displayed in the view port and the instructions at the bottom of the screen.

You can scan the complete file by pressing SPACEBAR until you come to the end of the file, or you can exit at any time by pressing Q. You can modify the new program in any of the ways suggested in Chapter 10.

COMBINING THE CREATE AND SCAN FILES   From your introduction to SUB procedures, you can see that they allow you to break up a program into discrete functional blocks. Several short blocks are much easier to test and correct than one long program. In addition, the SUB procedures allow you to modify a program easily.

Nihon or Nipopon	Japan
Nihon'go	Japanese language
Nihon'jin	Japanese person
Ohayoo gozaimasu	Good morning
Kon'nichi wa	Hello or Good day
Sayoonara or Sayonara	Goodbye
Oyasumi nasai	

```
Scan Japanese.Txt file, one record at a time.
The file is read from the disk drive you specify.
Press space bar for next Japanese or English phrase.
Press Q to quit.
```

FIGURE 12-10   Japanese.Txt file records

You can use more than one SUB procedure in a program, and you can have one SUB procedure call another SUB procedure. These techniques are demonstrated in the next program.

Program QBME1205.BAS, Create or Scan Japanese.Txt File, the final program in this chapter, combines the Create Japanese.Txt and Scan Japanese.Txt files into one program.

```
DECLARE SUB UseFile ()
DECLARE SUB ScanFile ()
DECLARE SUB MakeFile ()
DECLARE SUB WriteFile (J$(), E$())
REM ** Create or Scan Japanese.Txt File **
' QuickBASIC Made Easy, Chapter 12  11/4/88
' Microsoft QuickBASIC 4.5.  File: QBME1205.BAS

REM ** Set up **
DEFINT A-Z: CLS
DIM SHARED J$(1 TO 13), E$(1 TO 13), S$(1 TO 4)
REM ** Make Selection **
DO
   CLS
   LOCATE 2, 2: PRINT "Enter your selection (1, 2, or 3)."
```

```
      LOCATE 6, 20: PRINT "1. Create a Japanese.Txt File"
      LOCATE 8, 20: PRINT "2. Scan the Japanese.Txt File"
      LOCATE 10, 20: PRINT "3. Quit"
      DO
         BEEP: kee$ = INPUT$(1)
      LOOP WHILE INSTR("123", kee$) = 0
      SELECT CASE kee$
         CASE "1"
            CALL MakeFile
         CASE "2"
            CALL UseFile
         CASE "3"
            EXIT DO
      END SELECT
   LOOP
   CLS
   END

   DEFINT A-Z
   SUB MakeFile
      ' Assign Data for Japanese.Txt File to Strings
      J$(1) = "Nihon or Nipopon": E$(1) = "Japan"
      J$(2) = "Nihon'go": E$(2) = "Japanese language"
      J$(3) = "Nihon'jin": E$(3) = "Japanese person"
      J$(4) = "Ohayoo gozaimasu": E$(4) = "Good morning"
      J$(5) = "Kon'nichi wa": E$(5) = "Hello or Good day"
      J$(6) = "Sayoonara or Sayonara": E$(6) = "Goodbye"
      J$(7) = "Oyasumi nasai": E$(7) = "Good night"
      J$(8) = "Arigatoo gozaimasu": E$(8) = "Thank you"
      J$(9) = "Doomo arigatoo gozaimasu"
      E$(9) = "Thank you very much"
      J$(10) = "Hai": E$(10) = "Yes"
      J$(11) = "Iie": E$(11) = "No"
      J$(12) = "Jaa, mata ashita"
      E$(12) = "Well, I'll see you again tomorrow"
      J$(13) = "Data no owari": E$(13) = "End of data"

      CALL WriteFile(J$(), E$())
   END SUB

   DEFINT A-Z
   SUB ScanFile
      REM ** Select disk drive and Open Japanese.Txt File **
      INPUT "Which drive (A, B, C, etc.) for file "; drive$
      CLS 2                              'Clear view port only
      drive$ = LEFT$(drive$, 1)
      Filename$ = drive$ + ":Japanese.Txt"
      OPEN Filename$ FOR INPUT AS #1
```

```
REM ** DO...LOOP to scan the Japanese.Txt file **
' Exits at end of file (EOF) or when 'Q' key is pressed
DO UNTIL EOF(1)
  INPUT #1, Japanese$, English$
  ' Wait for a key press, space or 'q' or 'Q'
  DO
    BEEP: anykey$ = UCASE$(INPUT$(1))
  LOOP UNTIL anykey$ = " " OR anykey$ = "Q"
  IF anykey$ = " " THEN
    PRINT Japanese$;             'Do this if key was a space
  ELSE EXIT DO                   'Do this if key was 'q' or 'Q'
  END IF
  ' Wait for a key press, space or 'q' or 'Q'
  DO
    BEEP: anykey$ = UCASE$(INPUT$(1))
  LOOP UNTIL anykey$ = " " OR anykey$ = "Q"
  IF anykey$ = " " THEN
    PRINT TAB(40); English$   'Do this if key was a space
  ELSE EXIT DO                   'Do this if key was 'q' or 'Q'
  END IF
  PRINT
LOOP

REM ** Check for DO...LOOP exit due to end of file **
IF EOF(1) THEN BEEP: PRINT "*** End of file ***"

REM ** Close the file and end the subprogram **
  CLOSE #1
END SUB

DEFINT A-Z
SUB UseFile
  'Put instructions in lines 21 to 25
  S$(1)="Scan Japanese.Txt file, one record at a time."
  S$(2)="The file is read from the disk drive you specify."
  S$(3)="Press spacebar for next Japanese or English phrase."
  S$(4)="Press Q to return to menu."
  CLS
  LOCATE 21, 3: PRINT STRING$(74, 196)     'Draw line in row 21
  FOR row = 22 TO 25
    LOCATE row, 3: PRINT S$(row - 21);     'print instructions
  NEXT row

  ' Define rows 1 to 20 as a view port for data viewing
  VIEW PRINT 1 TO 20

  ' Wait for a key press to begin
  LOCATE 10, 26: PRINT "Press a key to begin";
  anykey$ = INPUT$(1)
  CLS 2                                 'Clears only the view port
```

```
REM ** Call the SUB procedure to scan the file **
CALL ScanFile

REM ** Clear the screen and end the subprogram **
VIEW PRINT: CLS
END SUB

DEFINT A-Z
SUB WriteFile (J$(), E$())
  REM ** Select disk drive and Open Japanese.Txt file **
  LOCATE 14, 2
  INPUT "Which drive (A, B, C, etc.) for file "; drive$
  CLS
  drive$ = LEFT$(drive$, 1)
  Filename$ = drive$ + ":Japanese.Txt"
  OPEN Filename$ FOR OUTPUT AS #1

  REM ** Read records from strings & write to file **
  ' Terminates on reading end of data message
  k = 1                               'initialize element number
  DO
    Japanese$ = LEFT$(J$(k), 38)   'Limit to 38 characters
    English$ = LEFT$(E$(k), 38)    'Limit to 38 characters
    WRITE #1, Japanese$, English$  'Write the record to file
    IF LCASE$(Japanese$) = "data no owari" THEN EXIT DO
    k = k + 1
  LOOP

  REM ** Close the file and end the subprogram **
  CLOSE #1      ' Close Japanese.Txt file
END SUB
```

A new main program is written so that you can select from the following three-item menu:

1. Create a Japanese.Txt File

2. Scan the Japanese.Txt File

3. Quit

Statements from programs QBME1203.BAS and QBME1204.BAS are used as SUB procedures called when you select item 1 or item 2 from the menu of the main program. These SUB procedures then call the same SUB procedures they called before. The following SELECT CASE structure is used to make the selection:

```
SELECT CASE kee$
  CASE "1"
    CALL MakeFile
  CASE "2"
    CALL UseFile
  CASE "3"
    EXIT DO
END SELECT
```

If you select item 1, the CASE "1" block of SELECT CASE calls the MakeFile SUB, which contains the Japanese and English words and phrases. This SUB procedure then calls the WriteFile SUB procedure, which writes the data to the file. When this task is completed, the file is closed. You are then returned to the menu of the main program.

If you select item 2, the CASE "2" block of SELECT CASE calls the Use-File SUB procedure, which displays the instructions and the initial scan screen. When you press a key to begin, the ScanFile SUB procedure is called to display the Japanese and English text.

If you select item 3, the CASE "3" block of SELECT CASE causes an exit from the DO...LOOP structure. The screen is then cleared and the program ends.

The data for the records in the Japanese.Txt file and the instructions used in the scan portion of the program are written as string arrays. QuickBASIC will not let you use DATA statements in SUB procedures. The modifications for the instructions follow.

```
'Put instructions in lines 21 to 25
S$(1) = "Scan Japanese.Txt file, one record at a time."
S$(2) = "The file is read from the disk drive you specify."
S$(3) = "Press spacebar for next Japanese or English phrase."
S$(4) = "Press Q to return to menu."
LOCATE 21, 3: PRINT STRING$(74, 196)   'Draw line in row 21
FOR row = 22 TO 25
  LOCATE row, 3: PRINT S$(row - 21)    'print instructions
NEXT row
```

The MakeFile SUB procedure now contains the data for the Japanese and English words and phrases. The *J$* array contains the Japanese, and the *E$* array contains the English.

If you are entering the program from the keyboard, type in the main program first. Then access the New Sub... command from the Edit menu to enter each of the SUB procedures. The SUB procedures may be entered in any order. QuickBASIC will arrange them in alphabetical order by name.

```
Enter your selection (1, 2, or 3).



          1, Create a Japanese.Txt File

          2, Scan the Japanese.Txt File

          3, Quit
```

FIGURE 12-11   Menu of QBME1205.BAS

When you run the program, you are greeted by the menu shown in Figure 12-11. If you select item 1 from the menu, the WriteFile SUB procedure is called. It adds the prompt shown here:

```
Which drive (A, B, C, etc.) for file ? _
```

When you enter a disk drive designation, the screen is cleared and the file is written to the disk. Then the file is closed and the menu is displayed again.

If you select item 2 from the menu, the UseFile SUB procedure is called. It writes the instructions at the bottom of the screen, and creates a view port so that the records from the file will appear in a scrolling view port area. The ScanFile SUB procedure is then called to display file records as you press SPACEBAR. Figure 12-12 shows the display when ScanFile is first called.

Press SPACEBAR to see Japanese words or phrases. Press SPACEBAR again to see the English equivalent. If you press Q, the file will be closed. The program will return from ScanFile to UseFile, which clears the screen and returns to the menu of the main program.

```
Press a key to begin
```

```
Scan Japanese.Txt file, one record at a time.
The file is read from the disk drive you specify.
Press space bar for next Japanese or English phrase.
Press Q to return to menu.
```

FIGURE 12-12   Opening display of ScanFile

Selecting item 3 from the menu activates CASE "3" of SELECT CASE. An exit is made from the DO...LOOP structure, the screen is cleared, and the program ends.

Run program QBME1205 and test all items on the menu. Change the data in the Japanese.Txt file by changing the data in the string arrays *J$* and *E$*. Perform other modifications as desired. By all means, experiment with all the demonstration programs.

This chapter has merely scratched the surface of the uses of procedures, but it gives you a foundation on which to begin your own exploration. Try writing SUB and FUNCTION procedures for your own programs. You have QuickBASIC's Help features to guide you. More complete information on procedures may be found in Chapter 2, "SUB and FUNCTION Procedures," of the Microsoft *Programming in BASIC* manual.

ASCII CODES
FOR THE PC

Table A-1 lists the ASCII codes for characters.

Decimal Value	Hexadecimal Value	Control Character	Character
0	00	NUL	Null
1	01	SOH	☺
2	02	STX	●
3	03	ETX	♥
4	04	EOT	♦
5	05	ENQ	♣
6	06	ACK	♠
7	07	BEL	Beep
8	08	BS	◘
9	09	HT	Tab
10	0A	LF	Line-feed

TABLE A-1　ASCII Codes for the PC

Decimal Value	Hexadecimal Value	Control Character	Character
11	0B	VT	Cursor home
12	0C	FF	Form-feed
13	0D	CR	Enter
14	0E	SO	
15	0F	SI	
16	10	DLE	
17	11	DC1	
18	12	DC2	
19	13	DC3	
20	14	DC4	
21	15	NAK	
22	16	SYN	
23	17	ETB	
24	18	CAN	↑
25	19	EM	↓
26	1A	SUB	→
27	1B	ESC	←
28	1C	FS	Cursor right
29	1D	GS	Cursor left
30	1E	RS	Cursor up
31	1F	US	Cursor down
32	20	SP	Space
33	21		!
34	22		"
35	23		#
36	24		$
37	25		%
38	26		&
39	27		'
40	28		(
41	29		)
42	2A		*
43	2B		+
44	2C		,
45	2D		-
46	2E		.
47	2F		/

TABLE A-1   ASCII Codes for the PC (*continued*)

Decimal Value	Hexadecimal Value	Control Character	Character
48	30		0
49	31		1
50	32		2
51	33		3
52	34		4
53	35		5
54	36		6
55	37		7
56	38		8
57	39		9
58	3A		:
59	3B		;
60	3C		<
61	3D		=
62	3E		>
63	3F		?
64	40		@
65	41		A
66	42		B
67	43		C
68	44		D
69	45		E
70	46		F
71	47		G
72	48		H
73	49		I
74	4A		J
75	4B		K
76	4C		L
77	4D		M
78	4E		N
79	4F		O
80	50		P
81	51		Q
82	52		R
83	53		S
84	54		T

TABLE A-1   ASCII Codes for the PC (*continued*)

Decimal Value	Hexadecimal Value	Control Character	Character
85	55		U
86	56		V
87	57		W
88	58		X
89	59		Y
90	5A		Z
91	5B		[
92	5C		\
93	5D		]
94	5E		^
95	5F		–
96	60		`
97	61		a
98	62		b
99	63		c
100	64		d
101	65		e
102	66		f
103	67		g
104	68		h
105	69		i
106	6A		j
107	6B		k
108	6C		l
109	6D		m
110	6E		n
111	6F		o
112	70		p
113	71		q
114	72		r
115	73		s
116	74		t
117	75		u
118	76		v
119	77		w
120	78		x
121	79		y

TABLE A-1   ASCII Codes for the PC (*continued*)

Decimal Value	Hexadecimal Value	Control Character	Character
122	7A		z
123	7B		{
124	7C		¦
125	7D		}
126	7E		~
127	7F	DEL	⌂
128	80		Ç
129	81		ü
130	82		é
131	83		â
132	84		ä
133	85		à
134	86		å
135	87		ç
136	88		ê
137	89		ë
138	8A		è
139	8B		ï
140	8C		î
141	8D		ì
142	8E		Ä
143	8F		Å
144	90		É
145	91		æ
146	92		Æ
147	93		ô
148	94		ö
149	95		ó
150	96		û
151	97		ù
152	98		ÿ
153	99		Ö
154	9A		Ü
155	9B		¢
156	9C		£
157	9D		¥
158	9E		Pt

TABLE A-1   ASCII Codes for the PC (*continued*)

Decimal Value	Hexadecimal Value	Control Character	Character
159	9F		ƒ
160	A0		á
161	A1		í
162	A2		ó
163	A3		ú
164	A4		ñ
165	A5		Ñ
166	A6		ª
167	A7		º
168	A8		¿
169	A9		⌐
170	AA		¬
171	AB		½
172	AC		¼
173	AD		¡
174	AE		«
175	AF		»
176	B0		░
177	B1		▒
178	B2		▓
179	B3		│
180	B4		┤
181	B5		╡
182	B6		╢
183	B7		╖
184	B8		╕
185	B9		╣
186	BA		║
187	BB		╗
188	BC		╝
189	BD		╜
190	BE		╛
191	BF		┐
192	C0		└
193	C1		┴
194	C2		┬
195	C3		├

TABLE A-1   ASCII Codes for the PC (*continued*)

Decimal Value	Hexadecimal Value	Control Character	Character
196	C4		
197	C5		+
198	C6		╞
199	C7		╟
200	C8		╚
201	C9		╔
202	CA		╩
203	CB		╦
204	CC		╠
205	CD		═
206	CE		╬
207	CF		╧
208	D0		╨
209	D1		╤
210	D2		╥
211	D3		╙
212	D4		╘
213	D5		╒
214	D6		╓
215	D7		╫
216	D8		╪
217	D9		┘
218	DA		┌
219	DB		■
220	DC		▬
221	DD		▮
222	DE		▮
223	DF		▬
224	E0		α
225	E1		β
226	E2		Γ
227	E3		π
228	E4		Σ
229	E5		σ
230	E6		μ
231	E7		τ
232	E8		φ

TABLE A-1   ASCII Codes for the PC (*continued*)

Decimal Value	Hexadecimal Value	Control Character	Character
233	E9		θ
234	EA		Ω
235	EB		δ
236	EC		∞
237	ED		∅
238	EE		ε
239	EF		∩
240	F0		≡
241	F1		±
242	F2		≥
243	F3		≤
244	F4		⌠
245	F5		⌡
246	F6		÷
247	F7		≈
248	F8		°
249	F9		•
250	FA		·
251	FB		√
252	FC		^{n}
253	FD		^{2}
254	FE		■
255	FF		(blank)

TABLE A-1   ASCII Codes for the PC (*continued*)

QuickBASIC
RESERVED WORDS

The following words are reserved in QuickBASIC. They may not be used as labels or as names of variables or procedures.

ABS	CDBL	CSRLIN
ACCESS	CDECL	CVD
ALIAS	CHAIN	CVDMBF
AND	CHDIR	CVI
ANY	CHR$	CVL
APPEND	CINT	CVS
AS	CIRCLE	CVSMBF
ASC	CLEAR	DATA
ATN	CLNG	DATE$
BASE	CLOSE	DECLARE
BEEP	CLS	DEF
BINARY	COLOR	DEFDBL
BLOAD	COM	DEFINT
BSAVE	COMMAND$	DEFLNG
BYVAL	COMMON	DEFSNG
CALL	CONST	DEFSTR
CALLS	COS	DIM
CASE	CSNG	DO

DOUBLE	IS	OUTPUT
DRAW	KEY	PAINT
ELSE	KILL	PALETTE
ELSEIF	LBOUND	PCOPY
END	LCASE$	PEEK
ENDIF	LEFT$	PEN
ENVIRON	LEN	PLAY
ENVIRON$	LET	PMAP
EOF	LINE	POINT
EQV	LIST	POKE
ERASE	LOC	POS
ERDEV	LOCAL	PRESET
ERDEV$	LOCATE	PRINT
ERL	LOCK	PSET
ERR	LOF	PUT
ERROR	LOG	RANDOM
EXIT	LONG	RANDOMIZE
EXP	LOOP	READ
FIELD	LPOS	REDIM
FILEATTR	LPRINT	REM
FILES	LSET	RESET
FIX	LTRIM$	RESTORE
FOR	MID$	RESUME
FRE	MKD$	RETURN
FREEFILE	MKDIR	RIGHT$
FUNCTION	MKDMBF$	RMDIR
GET	MKI$	RND
GOSUB	MKL$	RSET
GOTO	MKS$	RTRIM$
HEX$	MKSMBF$	RUN
IF	MOD	SADD
IMP	NAME	SCREEN
INKEY$	NEXT	SEEK
INP	NOT	SEG
INPUT	OCT$	SELECT
INPUT$	OFF	SETMEM
INSTR	ON	SGN
INT	OPEN	SHARED
INTEGER	OPTION	SHELL
IOCTL	OR	SIGNAL
IOCTL$	OUT	SIN

SINGLE	SWAP	UNTIL
SLEEP	SYSTEM	USING
SOUND	TAB	VAL
SPACE$	TAN	VARPTR
SPC	THEN	VARPTR$
SQR	TIME$	VARSEG
STATIC	TIMER	VIEW
STEP	TO	WAIT
STICK	TROFF	WEND
STOP	TRON	WHILE
STR$	TYPE	WIDTH
STRIG	UBOUND	WINDOW
STRING	UCASE$	WRITE
STRING$	UEVENT	XOR
SUB	UNLOCK	

ERROR
MESSAGES[*]

Selected Error Messages

You might encounter the following four types of errors while using Quick-BASIC:

Invocation errors
Compile-time errors
Run-time errors
Link-time errors

Invocation errors can occur when you invoke QuickBASIC from theMS-DOS command line. That is, when you type **QB** and press ENTER at the MS-DOS prompt (A>, for example).

---

[*]This appendix is adapted with permission from Appendix I, Programming in BASIC (Redmond, Washington: Microsoft Corporation, 1988).

Compile-time errors can occur while you are writing a program. In most cases, QuickBASIC's extensive on-line help system will be all you need to understand and fix the error.

Run-time errors can occur when you run a program. Here again, Quick-BASIC's on-line help will be very useful. When a run-time error occurs, the error message appears in a dialog box and the cursor is placed on the line in the program where the error occurred.

Link-time errors can occur when you link files created with other languages. These procedures are not covered in this book.

An ERR code is shown for some error messages. This code can be used in error-trapping procedures, not covered in this book. For information, consult Chapter 6, "Error and Event Trapping," in *Microsoft Quick-BASIC: Programming in BASIC,* which is included in the QuickBASIC package.

SELECTED ERROR MESSAGES

The following error messages, presented in alphabetical order, are selected from the comprehensive list of error messages in Appendix I of *Microsoft QuickBASIC: Programming in BASIC.* That book contains more than 40 pages describing error messages. Most of those are not likely to occur at the level of QuickBASIC usage covered in this book.

Advanced feature unavailable   Compile-time or run-time error. Attempt made to use a feature of QuickBASIC that is not available. May also occur if DOS version 2.1 is in use and use of a feature supported only in later versions is attempted. ERR code 73.

Argument-count mismatch   Compile-time error. Incorrect number of arguments used with a subprogram or function.

Array already dimensioned   Compile-time or run-run error. (1) More than one DIM statement for the same static array. (2) A DIM statement after initial use of array; static arrays must be deallocated with an ERASE statement before they can be redimensioned; dynamic arrays are redimensioned with the REDIM statement. (3) An OPTION BASE statement occurs after an array is dimensioned.

Array not defined   Compile-time error. An array that is referenced has not been defined.

Array not dimensioned Compile-time warning. An array that is referenced has not been dimensioned.

Array too big Compile-time error. Not enough user data space to accommodate the array declaration.

AS clause required Compile-time error. A variable declared with an AS clause is referenced without one. If the first declaration of a variable has an AS clause, every subsequent DIM, REDIM, SHARED, and COMMON statement that references that variable must have an AS clause.

AS clause required on first declaration Compile-time error. A variable that has not been declared using an AS clause is referenced with an AS clause.

AS missing Compile-time error. The compiler expects an AS keyword, as in OPEN "FILENAME" FOR INPUT AS #1.

Asterisk missing Compile-time error. Asterisk is missing from a string definition in a user type.

Bad file mode Run-time error. (1) The program is trying to use PUT or GET with a sequential file or to execute an OPEN statement with a file mode other than I, O, or R; or (2) the program is trying to read from a file open for OUTPUT or APPEND; or (3) other possibilities not covered in this book. ERR code 54.

Bad file name Run-time error. An illegal form is used for the file name with LOAD, SAVE, KILL, or OPEN, for example, a file name with too many characters. ERR code 64.

Bad file name or number Run-time error. A statement or command references a file with a file name or number that is not specified in the OPEN statement or is out of the range of file numbers specified at initialization. ERR code 52.

Bad record length Run-time error. A GET or PUT statement is executed that specifies a record variable whose length does not match the record length specified in the corresponding OPEN statement. ERR code 59.

Bad record number Run-time error. In a PUT or GET statement, the record number is less than or equal to zero. ERR code 63.

Block IF without END IF   Compile-time error. No corresponding END IF in a Block IF structure.

Cannot continue   Compile-time error. While debugging, a change is made that will prevent execution from continuing.

Cannot find file (filename) Input Path: QB invocation error. Quick-BASIC cannot find a Quick library or stand-alone library required by the program. Enter the correct pathname or press CTRL + C to return to the DOS prompt.

Cannot start with 'FN'   Compile-time error. FN used as the first two letters of a subprogram or variable name. FN can only be used as the first two letters when calling a DEF FN function.

CASE ELSE expected   Run-time error. No matching case found for an expression in a SELECT CASE statement. ERR code 39.

CASE without SELECT   Compile-time error. The first part of a SELECT CASE statement is missing or misspelled.

Comma missing   Compile-time error. The compiler expects a comma.

COMMON and DECLARE must precede executable statements   Compile-time error. A COMMON statement or a DECLARE statement is misplaced. COMMON and DECLARE statements must appear before any executable statements. All BASIC statements are executable except COMMON DEF*type*, DIM (for static arrays), OPTION BASE, REM, TYPE.

Control structure in IF...THEN...ELSE incomplete   Compile-time error. An unmatched NEXT, WEND, END IF, END SELECT, or LOOP statement appears in a single-line IF...THEN...ELSE statement.

Data-memory overflow   Compile-time error. The program data is too big to fit in memory. Often caused by too many constants or too much static array data.

DECLARE required   Compile-time error. An implicit SUB or FUNCTION procedure call appears before the procedure definition. (An implicit call does not use the CALL statement.) All procedures must be defined or declared before they are called implicitly.

DEF FN not allowed in control statements   Compile-time error. DEF FN function definitions are not permitted inside control constructs such as IF...THEN...ELSE and SELECT CASE.

DEF without END DEF   Compile-time error. No corresponding END DEF in a multi-line function definition.

DEFtype character specification illegal   Compile- time error. A DEF*type* statement is entered incorrectly. DEF can only be followed by LNG, DBL, INT, SNG, STR, or, for user-defined functions, a blank space.

Device unavailable   Run-time error. Attempt made to access a device that is not on line or does not exist. ERR code 68.

Disk full   Run-time error. Not enough room on the disk for completion of a PRINT, WRITE, or CLOSE operation. ERR code 61.

Disk-media error   Run-time error. Disk-drive hardware detects a physical flaw on the disk. ERR code 72.

Disk not ready   Run-time error. Disk-drive door is open or no disk is in drive. ERR code 71.

Division by zero   Compile-time or run-time error. A division by zero is encountered in a numeric expression, or an exponentiation operation results in zero being raised to a negative power. ERR code 11.

DO without LOOP   Compile-time error. The terminating LOOP clause is missing from a DO...LOOP statement.

Duplicate definition   Compile-time or run-time error. An identifier that has already been defined is being used. For example, the same name is being used for a variable and for a SUB or FUNCTION procedure. This error can also occur if attempt is made to redimension an array. ERR code 10.

Element not defined   Compile-time error. A user-defined type element is referenced but not defined.

ELSE without IF   Compile-time error. An ELSE clause appears without a corresponding IF. Sometimes this is caused by incorrectly nested IF statements.

ELSEIF without IF   Compile-time error. An ELSEIF statement appears without a corresponding IF. Sometimes this error is caused by incorrectly nested IF statements.

END DEF without DEF   Compile-time error. An END DEF statement has no corresponding DEF statement.

END IF without Block IF   Compile-time error. The beginning of an IF block is missing.

END SELECT without SELECT   Compile-time error. The end of a SELECT CASE statement appears without a beginning SELECT CASE. The beginning of the SELECT CASE statement may be missing or misspelled.

END SUB or END FUNCTION must be last line in window   Compile-time error. Attempt made to add a code after a procedure. Either return to the main module or open another module.

END SUB/FUNCTION without SUB/FUNCTION   Compile- time error. SUB or FUNCTION statement deleted.

END TYPE without TYPE   Compile-time error. An END TYPE statement is used outside a TYPE declaration.

Equal sign missing   Compile-time error. The compiler expects an equal sign.

Error during QuickBASIC initialization   QB invocation error. Several conditions can cause this error. Most commonly occurs when there is not enough memory in the machine to load QuickBASIC.

Error in loading file (file)—Cannot find file   QB invocation error. Occurs when redirecting input to QuickBASIC from a file. The input file is not at the location specified on the command line.

Error in loading file (file)—Disk I/O error   QB invocation error. Physical problems in accessing the disk; for example, the drive door containing the file is open.

EXIT DO not within DO...LOOP   Compile-time error. An EXIT DO statement is used outside of a DO...LOOP statement.

EXIT not within FOR...NEXT   Compile-time error. An EXIT FOR statement is used outside of a FOR...NEXT statement.

Expected: item   Compile-time error. A syntax error. The cursor is positioned at the unexpected item.

Expression too complex   Compile-time error. Certain internal limitations are exceeded. For example, during expression evaluation, strings not associated with variables are assigned temporary locations by the compiler. A large number of such strings can cause this error to occur. Try simplifying expressions and assigning strings to variables.

File already exists   Run-time error. The file name specified in a NAME statement is identical to a file name already in use on the disk. ERR code 58.

File already open   Run-time error. The sequential output mode OPEN is issued for a file that is already open, or a KILL is given for a file that is open. ERR code 55.

File not found   Run-time error. A KILL, NAME, FILES, or OPEN statement references a file that does not exist at the specified location. ERR code 53.

File previously loaded   Compile-time error. Attempt made to load a file already in memory.

Fixed-length string illegal   Compile-time error. Attempt made to use a fixed-length string as a formal parameter.

FOR index variable already in use   Compile-time error. An index variable is used more than once in nested FOR loops.

FOR index variable illegal   Compile-time error. Usually occurs when an incorrect variable type is used in a FOR- loop index. A FOR-loop index variable must be a simple numeric variable.

FOR without NEXT   Compile-time error. Each FOR statement must have a matching NEXT statement.

Formal parameter specification illegal   Compile-time error. Error in a function or subprogram parameter list.

Formal parameters not unique   Compile-time error. A function or subprogram declaration contains duplicate parameters, as in SUB (A, B, C, A) STATIC.

Function already defined   Compile-time error. Previously defined FUNCTION is redefined.

Function name illegal   Compile-time error. A BASIC reserved word is used as a user-defined FUNCTION name.

Function not defined   Compile-time error. FUNCTION must be declared or defined before being used.

Identifier cannot end with %, & !, #, or $ Compile-time error. Suffixes listed are not allowed in type identifiers or named COMMON names.

Identifier cannot include period   Compile-time error. Scalar variable, array, user-type identifier, and record-element names cannot contain periods. The period may only be used as a record-variable separator.

Identifier expected   Compile-time error. Attempt made to use a number or a BASIC reserved word where an identifier is expected.

Identifier too long   Compile-time error. Identifiers may not be longer than 40 characters.

Illegal function call   Run-time error. A parameter that is out of range is passed to an arithmetic or string function. A function call error can also occur for these reasons: (1) negative or unreasonably large subscript; (2) negative number raised to a noninteger power; (3) negative record number with GET or PUT; (4) an I/O function or statement (LOF, for example) is performed on a device that does not support it; or (5) strings are catenated to create a string that is longer than 32,767 characters. ERR code 5.

Illegal in direct mode   Compile-time error. Statement is only valid within a program and cannot be used in the Immediate window.

Illegal in procedure or DEF FN   Compile-time error. Statement is not allowed inside a procedure.

Illegal number   Compile-time error. The format of the number does not correspond to a valid number format. Probably a typographical error. For example, the number 2p3 will produce this error message.

Illegal outside of SUB, FUNCTION, or DEF FN   Compile-time error. Statement is not allowed in module-level code. For example, STATIC.

Illegal outside of SUB/FUNCTION   Compile-time error. Statement is not allowed outside of SUB or FUNCTION procedures. For example, EXIT SUB or EXIT FUNCTION.

Illegal outside of TYPE block   Compile-time error. The *element* AS *type* clause is permitted only within a TYPE...END TYPE block.

Illegal type character in numeric constant   Compile-time error. A numeric constant contains an inappropriate type-declaration character.

INPUT missing   Compile-time error. The compiler expects the keyword INPUT.

Input past end of file   Run-time error. An INPUT statement reads from a null (empty) file or from a file in which all data has already been read. To avoid this error, use the EOF function to detect the end-of-file character. ERR code 62.

Integer between 1 and 32767 required   Compile-time error. Statement requires an integer argument.

Internal error   Run-time error. An internal malfunction occurred in the QuickBASIC compiler. ERR code 51.

Invalid character   Compile-time error. The compiler finds an invalid character, such as a control character, in the source file.

Invalid constant   Compile-time error. An invalid expression is used to assign a value to a constant.

Left parenthesis missing   Compile-time error. The compiler expects a left (opening) parenthesis.

Line too long   Compile-time error. Lines are limited to 255 characters.

LOOP without DO   Compile-time error. The DO starting a DO...LOOP statement is missing or misspelled.

Lower bound exceeds upper bound   Compile-time error. The lower bound exceeds the upper bound defined in a DIM statement.

Math overflow   Compile-time error. The result of a calculation is too large to be represented in BASIC number format.

Minus sign missing   Compile-time error. QuickBASIC expects a minus sign.

Module level code too large   Compile-time error. Module-level code exceeds QuickBASIC's internal limit. Try moving some of the code into SUB or FUNCTION procedures.

Module not found. Unload module from memory?   When loading the program, QuickBASIC created an empty module. Empty module must be deleted before the program can be run.

Must be first statement on the line   Compile-time error. In block IF...THEN...ELSE constructs, ELSE, ELSEIF, and END IF can only be preceded by a line number or label.

Name of subprogram illegal   Compile-time error. A subprogram name is a BASIC reserved word or a subprogram name is used twice.

Nested function definition   Compile-time error. A FUNCTION definition appears inside another FUNCTION definition or inside an IF...THEN...ELSE clause.

NEXT missing for variable   Compile-time error. A FOR statement appears without a corresponding NEXT statement. The *variable* is the FOR-loop index variable.

NEXT without FOR   Compile-time error. A NEXT statement appears without a corresponding FOR statement.

No main module. Choose Set Main Module from the Run menu to select one   Compile-time error. Attempt made to run the program after the main module has been unloaded. Every program must have a main module.

Not watchable   Run-time error. This error occurs when you are specifying a variable in a watch expression. The module or procedure in the active window must have access to the variable user wants to watch. For example, module-level code cannot access variables that are local to a SUB or FUNCTION procedure.

Only simple variables allowed   Compile-time error. User-defined types and arrays are not permitted in READ and INPUT statements. (Array elements that are not a user-defined type are permitted.)

Operation requires disk   Compile-time error. Attempt made to load from or save to a nondisk device such as the printer or keyboard.

Out of DATA   Run-time error. A READ statement is executed when there are no DATA statements with unread data remaining in the program. ERR code 4.

Out of memory   Compile-time or run-time error. More memory is required than is available. For example, there may not be enough memory to allocate a file buffer. ERR code 7.

Out of paper   Run-time error. The printer is out of paper or is not turned on. ERR code 27.

Out of string space   Run-time error. String variables exceed the allocated amount of string space. ERR code 14.

Overflow   Run-time error. The result of a calculation is too large to be represented within the range allowed for the type of number being used. ERR code 6.

Overflow in numeric constant   Compile-time error. The numeric constant is too large.

Parameter type mismatch   Compile-time error. A subprogram parameter type does not match the DECLARE statement argument or the calling argument.

Path not found   Run-time error. During an OPEN, MKDIR, CHDIR, or RMDIR operation DOS is unable to find the path specified. The operation is not completed. ERR code 76.

Path/File access error   Compile-time or run-time error. During an OPEN, MKDIR, CHDIR, or RMDIR operation the operating system is unable to make a correct path-to-filename connection. The operation is not completed. ERR code 75.

Permission denied   Run-time error. Attempt made to write to a write-protected disk. ERR code 70.

Procedure too large   Compile-time error. The procedure has exceeded QuickBASIC's internal limit. Make the procedure smaller by dividing it into two or more procedures.

Program-memory overflow   Compile-time error. Attempt made to compile a program whose code segment is larger than 64K. Try splitting the program into separate modules and placing them in the Quick library, or use the CHAIN statement.

Redo from start   Run-time error. Response to an INPUT prompt with the wrong number or type of items.

Rename across disks   Run-time error. Attempt made to rename a file with a new drive designation. This is not allowed. ERR code 74.

Requires DOS 2.10 or later   QB invocation error or run-time error. Attempt made to use QuickBASIC with an incorrect version of DOS.

Right parenthesis missing   Compile-time error. The compiler expects a right (closing) parenthesis.

SELECT without END SELECT   Compile-time error. The end of a SELECT CASE statement is missing or misspelled.

Semicolon missing   Compile-time error. The compiler expects a semicolon.

Separator illegal   Compile-time error. Illegal delimiting character in a PRINT USING or WRITE statement. Use a semicolon or a comma as a delimiter.

Simple or array variable expected   Compile-time error. The compiler is expecting a variable argument.

Skipping forward to END TYPE statement   Compile-time error. An error in the TYPE statement causes QuickBASIC to ignore everything between the TYPE and END TYPE statements.

Statement cannot precede SUB/FUNCTION definition   Compile-time error. The only statements allowed before a procedure definition are REM and DEF*type*.

Statement illegal in TYPE block   Compile-time error. The only statements allowed between the TYPE and END TYPE statements are REM and *element* AS *typename*.

Statement unrecognizable   Compile-time error. BASIC statement probably mistyped.

Statements/labels illegal between SELECT CASE and CASE   Compile-time error. Statements and line labels are not permitted between SELECT CASE and the first CASE statement. (Note: line labels are not used in this book.)

String expression required   Compile-time error. Statement requires a string expression argument.

String formula too complex   Run-time error. Either a string formula is too long or an INPUT statement requests more than 15 string variables. Break the string expression into two or more parts; use two or more INPUT statements. ERR code 16.

String variable required   Compile-time error. Statement requires a string variable argument.

SUB or FUNCTION missing   Compile-time error. A DECLARE statement has no corresponding procedure.

SUB/FUNCTION without END SUB/FUNCTION   Compile-time error. The terminating statement is missing from a procedure.

Subprogram error   Compile-time error. A subprogram definition error usually caused by one of the following: (1) the subprogram is already defined; (2) the program contains incorrectly nested SUB...END SUB statements; (3) the subprogram or function does not end with an END SUB or END FUNCTION statement.

Subprogram not defined   Compile-time error. A subprogram is called but never defined.

Subprograms not allowed in control statements   Compile-time error. Subprogram definitions are not permitted inside control constructs such as IF...THEN...ELSE and SELECT CASE.

Subscript out of range   Run-time error. An array element is referenced with a subscript that is outside the dimensions of the array or an element of an undimensioned dynamic array is accessed. ERR code 9.

Subscript syntax illegal   Compile-time error. An array subscript contains a syntax error, for example, a string data type.

Syntax error   Compile-time or run-time error. Several conditions can cause this error. The most common cause is a mistyped BASIC keyword or argument. ERR code 2.

Syntax error in numeric constant   Compile-time error. A numeric constant is not properly formed.

THEN missing   Compile-time error. The compiler expects a THEN keyword.

TO missing   Compile-time error. The compiler expects a TO keyword.

Too many arguments in function call   Compile-time error. Function calls are limited to 60 arguments.

Too many dimensions   Compile-time error. Arrays are limited to 60 dimensions.

Too many TYPE definitions   Compile-time error. The maximum number of user-defined types permitted is 240.

Too many variables for INPUT   Compile-time error. An INPUT statement is limited to 60 variables.

Too many variables for LINE INPUT   Compile-time error. Only one variable is allowed in a LINE INPUT statement.

Type mismatch   Compile-time or run-time error. The variable is not the required type. For example, user is trying to use the SWAP statement with a string variable and a numeric variable. ERR code 13.

TYPE missing   Compile-time error. The TYPE keyword is missing from an END TYPE statement.

Type more than 65535 bytes   Compile-time error. A user-defined type cannot exceed 64K.

Type not defined   Compile-time error. The *usertype* argument to the TYPE statement is not defined.

TYPE statement improperly nested   Compile-time error. User-defined type definitions are not allowed in subprograms.

TYPE without END TYPE   Compile-time error. An END TYPE statement appears without a corresponding TYPE statement.

Typed variable not allowed in expression   Compile-time error. Variables that are user-defined types are not permitted in expressions such as CALL Alpha, $((x))$, where x is a user-defined type.

Unprintable error   Run-time error. An error message is not available for the error condition that exists. This may be caused by an ERROR statement that doesn't have a defined error code.

Variable name not unique   Compile-time error. Attempt made to define x as a user-defined type after $x.y$ has been used.

Variable required   Compile-time error. The compiler encounters an INPUT, LET, READ, or SHARED statement without a variable argument.

WEND without WHILE   Compile-time error. A WEND statement has no corresponding WHILE statement.

WHILE without WEND   Compile-time error. A WHILE statement has no corresponding WEND statement.

Wrong number of dimensions   Compile-time error. An array reference contains the wrong number of dimensions.

TRADEMARKS

InSet™	Inset Systems, Inc.
MS-DOS®	Microsoft Corporation
Microsoft®	Microsoft Corporation
Tandy®	Tandy Corporation

INDEX

! (exclamation point) single precision
    designator, 96
" (double quotes), used to enclose
    string, 59, 106, 274, 287
""(null string), 144, 153, 191, 250
(number symbol), double precision
    designator, 96
$ (dollar sign), string designator, 124
% (percent sign), short integer
    designator, 96
& (ampersand), long integer
    designator, 96
' (apostrophe), as REM, 112
( ) (left and right parentheses), 86,
    187, 216, 217, 218, 331
+ (plus sign), arithmetic operator, 79,
    80, 81
+ (plus sign), string concatenation
    operator, 200
, (comma), in PRINT statement, 83, 84
, (comma), as string or field separator,
    278, 287, 292
– (minus sign), arithmetic operator,
    79, 80, 82
/ (slash), arithmetic operator, 79, 80,
    83
; (semicolon), in PRINT statement,
    83, 84
? (question mark), INPUT prompt,
    103, 106

* (asterisk), arithmetic operator, 79,
    80, 82
., 77, 261
*.BAS, 69, 71
^ (caret), arithmetic operator, 79, 86

A

Add Watch dialog box, 171, 172
Add Watch... command, 157, 171
ALT key, 23, 29
ALT + a key shortcuts, 39
Ampersand (&), long integer
    designator, 96
Apostrophe (') as shorthand for REM,
    112
Argument of a function, 184, 187, 194
Arithmetic, 79, 80
Array, 215
    dimension, 216
    element, 216
    numeric, 216
    passing, to FUNCTION, 330, 331
    passing, to SUB, 342, 344
    string, 217, 293
    variable, 216
Arrow keys (cursor control keys), 23
AS keyword, 252, 269, 306, 320
ASCII codes, 357-364
ASCII text file, 250, 301
Asterisk (*), 79, 80, 82

B

Background colors, 148
BACKSPACE key, 55, 106, 161
Backup copies, 6
.BAS extension, 69, 71
BASIC, 1
BASIC, Dartmouth, 2
BASIC history, 2
BEEP statement, 49
Block IF structure, 324
Block IF...END IF structure, 196
BREAK key, 127
Breakpoint, 158
    removing, 180
    toggling, 180
Bubble sort, 215, 240
Built-in functions, 184

C

CALL statement, 342, 354
Calling a FUNCTION procedure, 331
Calling a SUB procedure, 342, 354
Camping.Cat random-access file, 319
Cancel option, 68, 70
CASE clause, 206
CASE ELSE clause, 206
Catenate. See Concatenate
Changing file name, 269
Clear All Breakpoints command, 158,
    181
Clipboard, 163, 164, 165, 168
CLOSE statement, 247, 251, 253
CLS statement, 55, 81
Coin Flipping (QBME0707), 195
COLOR Demonstrator (QBME0507),
    148
COLOR statement, 124, 146, 148
Colors, background, 148
Colors, foreground, 147
Commas, in PRINT statement, 84

Compound interest. See Future Value
    of Money—Compound Interest
Concatenate strings, 200
Contents command, 39, 41
Control Center, QuickBASIC, 25, 27
Control structures, 183
COPY command (MS-DOS), 18, 19
Copy command, 157, 163
Copying a disk, 6, 10, 16
Copying a file, 18, 19
Copying text, 164, 166
Correcting typing mistakes, 55
Create Japanese.Ran, Input from the
    Keyboard (QBME1102), 309
Create Japanese.Ran Random-access
    File (QBME1101), 303, 306
Create Japanese.Txt File with SUB
    Procedure (QBME1203), 342
Create or Scan Japanese.Txt File
    (QBME1205), 350
Create the Camping.Cat File
    (QBME1105.BAS), 319
Create the NotePad.Txt File
    (QBME0901), 254
CTRL + a key, 159
CTRL + BREAK, to stop program, 124,
    127
CTRL+Y, to delete line of text, 162
Current module command, 119
Cursor, 25
Cursor control keys, 159
Cursor movement
    beginning of line, 159, 161
    beginning of program, 159, 160
    down one line, 159, 160
    down one page, 159
    end of line, 159, 161
    end of program, 159
    left one character, 159, 160
    left one word, 159, 160
    right one character, 159

Cursor movement, *continued*
    right one word, 159, 160
    up one line, 159
    up one page, 159
Cut command, 33, 34, 157, 163
Cutting text, 163

D

D in double precision floating point
    number, 95
Dartmouth BASIC, 2
Data file, 247
DATA statement, 271, 286
DATE$ function, 57, 183, 186
DATE$ statement, 60, 186
Date, setting, 24
Debug (menu bar option), 30
Debug menu, 34, 36, 157, 171
    Add Watch dialog box, 172
    Add Watch... command, 171
    Clear All Breakpoints command,
       181
    Delete Watch dialog box, 175
    Delete Watch... command, 174
    Instant Watch dialog box, 179
    Instant Watch... command, 178
    Toggle Breakpoints command,
       180
Debugging
    Add Watch dialog box, 172
    Add Watch... command, 171
    breakpoints, 180
    removing breakpoints, 181
    single stepping (F8 function key),
       176, 178
    watch expressions and variables,
       171, 173
    Watch window, 172
DECLARE statement, 333, 335
DEF FN statement, 193, 202
DEFINT A-Z, 334

DEFINT statement, 215, 222, 223, 334
DEL key, 55, 161
Deleting text
    block, 162
    character at cursor, 55, 161
    character to left of cursor, 55, 161
    entire line, 162
Delete Watch dialog box, 175
Delete Watch... command, 158, 174
Demonstrate FIX and INT Numeric
    Functions (QBME0702), 188
Demonstrate INPUT$ String Function
    (QBME0703), 190
Demonstrate LCASE$ and UCASE$
    String Functions (QBME0704), 190
Demonstrate TIMER Numeric
    Function (QBME0701), 184
DIM statement, 215, 216, 217, 306,
    320
Dimensioning an array, 216
Dirs/Drives box, 67, 68, 70, 71, 75
Disk drive, logical, 10, 18
Disk drive, physical, 10, 18
DISKCOPY command (MS-DOS), 12
Disks
    backup copies, 6
    copying, 6, 10, 16
    formatting, 6, 15
    labeling, 10, 15, 21
    write-protecting, 6, 7
Displaying all files, 76
Displaying text file in View Window,
    262
DO statement, 129
DO UNTIL statement, 143, 267
DO WHILE statement, 145
DO...LOOP, exit from, 137
DO...LOOP structure, 124, 127
Dollar sign ($), string designator, 124
Doodle.One sequential file, 272, 274,
    278, 301

Doodle.Two sequential file, 272, 274, 279, 301

Dot Product of Two Arrays (QBME0803), 229

Dot Product of Two Arrays with a FUNCTION (QBME1202), 338

Dot Product with Line Item Printout (QBME0804), 231

Double precision numbers, 79, 93, 96

Double precision variable, 112

DOWN ARROW key, 23

Drive A, 25

Duration, in SOUND statement, 150

Dynamic debugging, 170

E

E in floating point number, 88

Easy menus, 327

Edit (menu bar option), 30

Edit menu, 163, 330, 333, 345

    Copy command, 163, 165

    Cut command, 163, 164

    Paste command, 166

    New FUNCTION dialog box, 334

    New FUNCTION... command, 333

    New SUB dialog box, 344

    New SUB... command, 344

Editing, 157

Editing keys, 158

Element of array, 216

ELSE keyword, 204, 206, 290

Empty string (""). *See* ""(null string)

END DEF statement, 202

END FUNCTION statement, 331

END IF statement, 196

END key, 158

End of file, 267

END SELECT statement, 206

END SUB statement, 345

END TYPE statement, 306, 320

ENTER key, 24

Entering a program, 62

EOF function, 267

Erosion Savings and Loan, 141

Error messages, 369-383

ESC key, 23, 26, 29

Exclamation point (!), single precision designator, 96

Exit from DO...LOOP, 137, 142

EXIT statement, 139

EXIT DO statement, 139

Exiting QuickBASIC, 43

Exponation operator (^), 86, 88

Expression box in Instant Watch dialog box, 179

F

F6 function key, 49, 62, 80

F8 function key, 176

Field

    fixed-length, 300, 302

    in random-access file, 300

    in sequential file, 300

    variable-length, 276, 301

File

    ASCII text, 250, 301

    Camping.Cat, random-access, 319

    data, 247

    End of, 267

    field, 276, 300, 301, 302

    Japanese.Txt sequential, 276, 285, 288, 301, 342, 347

    Japanese.Ran random-access, 301

    length of, 317

    menu. *See* File menu

    names, 250, 268

    Notepad.Txt sequential, 251, 301

    random-access, 249, 299, 302

    sequential, 248, 249, 250, 271, 300

File, *continued*
    structured, 271, 276
    structured sequential, 249, 250,
        271, 276
    unstructured, 250, 272
File (menu bar option), 30
File Input/Output Experiments,
    Numeric Fields (QBME1003), 282
File Input/Output Experiments, String
    and Number (QBME1004), 284
File Input/Output Experiments,
    Structured Files (QBME1002), 278
File Input/Output Experiments,
    Unstructured Files, 272
File menu, 33, 64, 67, 70
    Exit command, 43, 44
    New Program command, 63
    Open Program dialog box, 71
    Open Program... command, 70
    Print dialog box, 119
    Print... command, 119
    Save As dialog box, 67, 68, 75
    Save As... command, 67, 75
File name, changing, 269
File Name box, 67, 68, 70, 71, 75
File names, 250, 268
File number, 252
FileNote.Txt sequential file, 268
Files, data (by name)
    Camping.Cat random-access, 319
    Doodle.One sequential, 272, 274,
        278, 301
    Doodle.Two sequential, 272, 274,
        278, 301
    Japanese.Ran random-access, 301
    Japanese.Txt sequential, 276, 285,
        288, 301, 342, 347
    NotePad.Txt sequential, 251, 301
Files, displaying all, 76
Files box, 70, 71
Find... command, 34, 35

FIX function, 183, 188
Fixed-length field, 300, 302
Fixed-length record, 249, 300, 302
Floating point numbers, 70, 86, 88, 93
FNDaysInMonth% function, 204, 207,
    208
FNflip$ function, 202
FNrndchr$ function, 200
FNrndint% function, 195
FNrndword$ function, 209
FNroll2D6% function, 194
FNroll3D6% function, 194
FNrollD6% function, 193
FOR statement, 209
FOR...NEXT loop structure, 183, 209
Foreground colors, 147
Format box, 67, 68, 75
FORMAT command (MS-DOS), 9, 15
Format string in PRINT USING, 114
Formatting a disk, 6, 8, 15
Freezing the screen, 131
Frequencies for musical notes, 151
Frequency, in SOUND statement, 150,
    155
Full menus, 327
Function
    argument, 184, 187, 194
    built-in, 184
    defined, 183, 193, 202, 204
    multi-line, 202, 204
    numeric, 184, 187, 192
    simple, 184
    single-line, 184
    string, 184, 187, 192
    user-defined, 183, 193, 202, 204
FUNCTION procedures (by name)
    DotProduct#, 338
    SumArray!, 331
FUNCTION...END FUNCTION
    procedure, 327, 330, 333
FUNCTION statement, 331

Future Value—Compound Interest
with DO...LOOP (QBME0506), 140
Future Value of Money—Compound
Interest (QBME0410), 115
Future Value of Money—Compound
Interest (QBME0411), 116
Future Value of Money—Compound
Interest (QBME0412), 118

G

GET # statement, 299, 314, 316
Global variable, 330, 341

H

Help (menu bar option), 30
Help dialog box, syntax error, 53
Help disk, 1, 14, 52
Help menu, 38, 39
    Contents command, 39, 41
    Contents dialog box, 42
    Help on Help command, 39, 43
    Index command, 39
    Index dialog box, 40, 41
    Help on Help command, 39, 43
    Help on Help dialog box, 43
    Topics command, 39, 42
Help option, 51, 68, 70
Hertz, 151
High, Low, and Average Temperature
(QBME0801), 220
High, Low, and Average Temperature
(QBME0802), 225
History of BASIC, 2
HOLD key (Tandy 1000 computers),
127, 131
HOME key, 62, 158
Hz, 151

I

IF statement, 137, 142, 196
IF...END IF structure, 196

IF...THEN statement, 137, 142, 196
IF...THEN...ELSE statement, 204
Immediate window, 28, 47
Index command, 39
Index dialog box, 40
INKEY$ function, 123, 142
INPUT statement, 79, 101, 102, 106
INPUT # statement, 292, 307
Input String Variables Program
(QBME0501), 126
INPUT$ function, 153, 183, 189
Insert line of text, 161, 162
Instant Watch dialog box, 179
Instant Watch... command, 158, 178
INT function, 149, 183, 188
Integers, 79, 90, 96

J

Japanese Words and Phrases
(QBME1005), 285
Japanese.Ran random-access file, 301
Japanese.Txt sequential file, 276, 285,
288, 301, 342, 347

K

K bytes, 87
Kemeny, John G., 2
Keywords, 47, 365-367
Kurtz, Thomas E., 2

L

Labeling a disk, 10, 15, 21
LBOUND function, 215, 219
LCASE$ function, 183, 190
*Learning to Use Microsoft
QuickBASIC*, 5
Learning to Use QuickBASIC, 159
LEFT ARROW key, 23, 32
LEFT$ function, 183, 208
LEN = clause, 307, 322
LEN function, 202, 307

Length of file, 317
LINE INPUT # statement, 191, 267
LINE INPUT statement, 247, 251, 253
Loading QuickBASIC from MS-DOS, 24, 26
Local variable, 195, 330, 341
LOCATE statement, 247, 256
LOF function, 317
Logical disk drive, 10, 18
Long integers, 79, 91, 96
LOOP statement, 129
LOOP UNTIL statement, 143
LOOP WHILE statement, 145
LPRINT statement, 124

M

MakeFile SUB procedure, 350
Mantissa, 88
Menu bar, 28, 29
Menus
    Debug, 34, 36, 157, 171
    easy, 327
    Edit, 163, 330, 333, 345
    File, 33, 64, 67, 70
    full, 327
    Help, 38, 39
    Options, 34, 37, 328, 329
    Run, 34, 36, 65, 66
    Search, 34, 35
    View, 34, 35, 335
Microsoft Disk Operating System, 1
Microsoft QuickBASIC, 4
MID$ function, 183, 197
Mistakes, correcting, 55
Mouse, 32
MOUSE.COM file, 5, 6
MS-DOS, 1
MS-DOS COPY command, 18, 19
MS-DOS DISKCOPY command, 12
MS-DOS prompt (>), 25
MS-DOS RENAME command, 269

Multi-line user-defined function, 202, 204

N

NAME statement, 269
Naming a file, 250, 268
New FUNCTION command, 333
New FUNCTION dialog box, 334
New Program command, 32, 33, 63, 64
New SUB... command, 345
NEXT statement, 209
NotePad.Txt sequential file, 251, 301
Null string. *See* "" (empty string)
Number of Days in a Month (QBME0711), 204
Number of Days in a Month (SELECT CASE) (QBME0712), 207
Number of Days in a Month with Alpha Input (QBME0713), 208
Numbers
    double precision, 79, 93, 96
    floating point, 86, 88, 93
    integer, 79, 90, 96
    long integer, 79, 91, 96
    single precision, 79, 93, 96
Numeric
    array, 216
    expression, 83
    field, in sequential file, 281
    function, 184, 187, 192
    variables, 70, 96

O

OK option, 51, 68, 70
Open Program dialog box, 70, 71, 261
Open Program... command, 69, 70
OPEN statement
    AS clause, 252
    FOR APPEND statement, 252
    FOR INPUT statement, 252

OPEN statement, *continued*
    FOR OUTPUT statement, 247,
      251, 252
    FOR RANDOM statement, 307
Options (menu bar option), 30
Options menu, 34, 37, 328, 329
OR operator, 267
Output screen, 55, 65, 81
Overflow dialog box, 91, 92

P

Parentheses in numerical expressions,
    86
Passing an array
    to FUNCTION procedure, 330,
      331
    to SUB procedure, 342, 344
Paste command, 157, 163
Pasting text, 164, 166
Percent sign (%), short integer
    designator, 96
PGDN key, 23, 158
PGUP key, 23, 158
Physical disk drive, 10, 18
Pitch, in SOUND statement, 150
PRINT # statement, 271, 278, 280,
    283
Print dialog box, 119
Print... command, 119
Print positions, 83
PRINT statement, 56, 58, 81
PRINT USING format string, 114
PRINT USING statement, 79, 108,
    110
Printing a message, 59
Printing a program, 119
Program
    entering, 62
    printing, 119
    REM outline, 135, 138
    saving, 66, 74, 75

Programming in BASIC, 5
Programs (by file name). *See* QBME...
Prompt string, 192
Pseudo-random numbers, 185
PUT # statement, 299, 308, 314, 316
PUT or GET Individual Records,
    Japanese.Ran File (QBME1104), 314

Q

QB Advisor, 6
QB Express, 5, 6
QB45ENER.HLP file, 5, 6, 18, 20, 52
QB45QCK.HLP file, 5, 6, 16, 19
QB.EXE file, 5, 6, 16, 18
QBME0001, QuickBASIC Made
    Easy Program File Names, 160,
    167
QBME0301 program, 68, 69, 71
QBME0302 program, 76
QBME0401 program, 102
QBME0402 program, 106
QBME0403 program, 107
QBME0404 program, 108
QBME0405 program, 109
QBME0406 program, 110
QBME0407, Sales Tax Program, 111
QBME0408, Value of Stocks, 113
QBME0409, Value of Stocks, 113
QBME0410, Future Value of
    Money—Compound Interest
    Program, 115
QBME0411, Future Value of
    Money—Compound Interest, 116
QBME0412, Future Value of
    Money—Compound Interest, 118
QBME0501, Input String Variables
    Program, 126
QBME0502, Sales Tax Program with
    DO...LOOP, 132
QBME0504, Value of Stocks with
    DO...LOOP, 135

QBME0505, Value of Stocks with DO...LOOP & Graceful Exit, 138

QBME0506, Future Value—Compound Interest with DO...LOOP, 140

QBME0507, COLOR Demonstrator, 148

QBME0508, SOUND Demonstrator, 152

QBME0509, Scale of C with C, D, E, ..., 153

QBME0510, Sound Effects with DO...LOOP & UNTIL, 154

QBME0602, QuickBASIC Made Easy Program File Names, 168

QBME0701, Demonstrate TIMER Numeric Function, 184

QBME0702, Demonstrate FIX and INT Numeric Functions, 188

QBME0703, Demonstrate INPUT$ String Function, 190

QBME0704, Demonstrate LCASE$ and UCASE$ String Functions, 190

QBME0705, Roll Two Six-sided Dice, 193

QBME0706, Roll Three Six-sided Dice, 194

QBME0707, Coin Flipping, 195

QBME0708, Word Maker (CVCVC), 199

QBME0709, Word Maker with Random Character Function, 200

QBME0711, Number of Days in a Month, 204

QBME0712, Number of Days in a Month (SELECT CASE), 207

QBME0713, Number of Days in a Month with Alpha Input, 208

QBME0714, Word Maker with Word Structure Entry, 210

QBME0801, High, Low, and Average Temperature, 220

QBME0802, High, Low, and Average Temperature, 225

QBME0803, Dot Product of Two Arrays, 229

QBME0804, Dot Product with Line Item Printout, 231

QBME0805, Scramble an Array of Numbers, 235

QBME0806, Scramble and Sort an Array of Numbers, 238, 239

QBME0807, Sort a String Array, 244

QBME0901, Create the NotePad.Txt File, 254

QBME0902, Scan the NotePad.Txt File, 262, 265

QBME1001, File Input/Output Experiments, Unstructured Files, 272

QBME1002, File Input/Output Experiments, Structured Files, 278

QBME1003, File Input/Output Experiments, Numeric Fields, 282

QBME1004, File Input/Output Experiments, String and Number, 284

QBME1005, Japanese Words and Phrases, 285

QBME1006, Scan the Japanese.Txt File, 289

QBME1007, Read the Japanese.Txt File into Arrays, 293

QBME1008, Use Japanese.Txt File for Random Drill & Practice, 295

QBME1101, Create Japanese.Ran Random-access File, 303, 306

QBME1102, Create Japanese.Ran, Input from the Keyboard, 309

QBME1103, Scan Japanese.Ran, a Random-access File, 312

QBME1104, PUT or GET Individual
Records, Japanese.Ran File, 314
QBME1105, Create the Camping.Cat
File, 319
QBME1106, Get Individual Records
from Camping.Cat, 324
QBME1201, Sum and Average
Temperatures, 332
QBME1202, Dot Product of Two
Arrays with a FUNCTION, 338
QBME1203, Create Japanese.Txt File
with SUB Procedure, 342
QBME1204, Scan Japanese.Txt File
with SUB Procedure, 347
QBME1205, Create or Scan
Japanese.Txt File, 350
QuickBASIC
    disk sets, 5
    exiting, 43
    help disk, 1, 14, 52
    keywords, 47, 365-367
    loading, from MS-DOS, 24,
        26
    manuals, 4
    master work disk, 18
    master work/help disk, 18
    package, 4
    Program and QB Advisor disk
        (3 1/2-inch), 6
    Program disk (5 1/4-inch), 5
    QB Advisor disk 6
    quitting, 43
    reserved words, 365-367
    Setup and QB Express disk
        (3 1/2-inch), 6
    Setup and QB Express disk
        (5 1/4-inch), 5
    Survival Guide, 26, 27
    Utilities disk (3 1/2-inch), 6
    Utilities 1 disk (5 1/4-inch), 5
    Utilities 2 disk (5 1/4-inch), 5

QuickBASIC, *continued*
    work and help disks, 1, 14
    work disk, 1, 14, 24
QuickBASIC Made Easy Program
    File Names (QBME0601), 160,
    167
QuickBASIC Made Easy Program
    File Names (QBME0602), 168
Quitting QuickBASIC, 43

R

Random numbers, 185
Random-access file
    fields, 300
    numbers in, 302, 303, 321
    record number, 307
    records, 249, 302
    strings in, 302, 309, 321
RANDOMIZE statement, 186
READ statement, 271, 286
Read the Japanese.Txt File into
    Arrays (QBME1007), 293
Records
    fixed-length, 249, 300, 302
    random-access file, 249, 302
    sequential file, 248, 250, 273, 276,
        301
    variable-length, 248, 250, 301
REM
    program, 160
    program, outline of, 135, 138
    statement, 111, 135, 160
RENAME command (MS-DOS),
    269
Reserved words, 365-367
RIGHT ARROW key, 23, 29
Right Mouse command, 328, 329
RND function, 149, 183, 185
Roll Three Six-sided Dice
    (QBME0706), 194

Roll Two Six-sided Dice
(QBME0705), 193
Run (menu bar option), 30
Run menu, 34, 36, 65, 66
    Start command, 34, 36, 65, 66

S

Sales Tax Program (QBME0407), 111
Sales Tax Program with DO...LOOP
(QBME0503), 134
Save As dialog box, 67, 68, 75
Save As... command, 67, 75
Saving a program, 66, 74, 75
Scale of C with C, D, E, ...
(QBME0509), 153
Scan Japanese.Ran, a Random-access
File (QBME1103), 312
Scan Japanese.Txt File with SUB
Procedure, 347
Scan the Japanese.Txt File
(QBME1006), 289
Scan the NotePad.Txt File, 262, 265
ScanFile SUB procedure, 347, 350
Scramble an Array of Numbers
(QBME0805), 235
Scramble and Sort an Array of
Numbers, 238, 239
SCROLL LOCK key, 124, 131
Scrolling, 158
Scrolling keys, 159
Search (menu bar option), 30
Search menu, 34, 35
SELECT CASE statement, 206
SELECT CASE...END CASE
structure, 183, 206
Selecting text, 162
Semicolons, in PRINT statement, 84
Sequential file
    numeric field, 281
    string field, 276, 277, 287, 301
    structured, 249, 250, 271, 276

Sequential file, *continued*
    unstructured, 247, 250
Setting the date, 24, 59
Setting the time, 24, 59
Short integer, 91, 96
Shortcut keys for accessing menus, 39
Simple function, 184
Single-line function, 184
Single precision numbers, 79, 93, 96
Single precision variable, 112
Sort, bubble, 215, 240
Sort a String Array (QBME0807), 244
Sorting a numeric array, 238
Sorting a string array, 244
SOUND Demonstrator (QBME0508),
152
SOUND statement, 124, 150
SPACEBAR, 55, 142
Start command, 34, 36, 65, 66
Status bar, 28
Stepping through a program, 158, 176
Stopping a program, 124, 127
String
    array, 217, 293
    concatenation, 200
    field variable, 306
    function, 184, 187, 192
    variable, 124
STRING$ function, 256
Structured sequential file, 249, 250,
271, 276
SUB procedures (by name)
    MakeFile, 350
    ScanFile, 347, 350
    UseFile, 350
    WriteFile, 342, 350
SUB...END SUB procedure, 327, 341
SUBs dialog box, 336
SUBs... command, 34, 35, 335
Subscript, 215, 216
Substring, 197

Sum and Average Temperatures (QBME1201), 332
Survival Guide, QuickBASIC, 26, 27
SWAP statement, 215, 238
Syntax checking, turning off, 346
Syntax checking command, 328, 329, 346
Syntax error, 53
Syntax Error dialog box, 51
Syntax Error Help dialog box, 53

T

TAB function, 107, 183, 187
TAB key, 23, 52
Tandy 1000, HOLD key, 127, 131
Text
    copying, 164, 166
    cutting, 163
    deleting, 55, 161, 162
    inserting, 161, 162
    pasting, 164, 166
    selecting, 162
THEN (in IF statement), 137, 142
Ticks, in SOUND statement, 150
Time, setting, 24
TIME$ function, 57, 183, 186
TIME$ statement, 60, 186
TIMER function, 183, 184
Title bar, 28
TO keyword, 209, 217
Toggle Breakpoint command, 158, 180
Topics command, 39, 42
Turning off syntax checking, 346
TYPE statement, 306, 320
TYPE...END TYPE structure, 299, 306, 320

U

UBOUND function, 215, 219
UCASE$ function, 144, 183, 190

Unfreezing the screen, 131
Unstructured sequential file, 247, 249, 250
UNTIL keyword, 143
Untitled, 28
UP ARROW key, 23
Use Japanese.Txt File for Random Drill & Practice (QBME1008), 295
User-defined function, 183, 193, 202

V

Value box in Instant Watch dialog box, 179
Value of function, 184
Value of Stocks Program (QBME0408), 113
Value of Stocks Program (QBME0409), 113
Value of Stocks with DO...LOOP (QBME0504), 135
Value of Stocks with DO...LOOP & Graceful Exit (QBME0505), 138
Variable
    array, 216
    double precision, 112
    global, 330, 341
    local, 195, 330, 341
    numeric, 79, 96
    single precision, 112
    string, 124
    string field, 306
Variable-length field, 276, 301
Variable-length record, 248, 250, 301
View (menu bar option), 30
View menu, 34, 35, 335
View menu, SUBs dialog box, 336
View menu, SUBs... command, 34, 35, 335
View port, 259
VIEW PRINT statement, 247, 257, 258

View window, 28, 47, 62
    displaying text file, 262

W

Watch
    expression, 171
    variable, 171
    window, 171, 172
Watchpoint, 158
Welcome dialog box, 26, 27
WHILE keyword, 145
Windows, 23, 27

Word Maker (cvcvc) (QBME0708),
    199
Word Maker with Word Structure
    Entry (QBME0714), 210
Work disk, 1, 14, 24
Work/help disk, 1, 14
Work Maker with Random Character
    Function (QBME0709), 200
WRITE # statement, 247, 251, 253,
    271
Write-protecting a disk, 6, 7
WriteFile SUB procedure, 342, 350

The manuscript for this book was prepared and submitted to Osborne/McGraw-Hill in electronic form. The acquisitions editor for this project was Jeffrey Pepper, the technical reviewer was Bud Aaron, and production was by Peter Hancik and Kevin Shafer.

Text uses Times Roman for text body and Helvetica for display.

Cover art and color separation by Phoenix Color Corp. Screens produced with InSet from Inset Systems, Inc. Book printed and bound by R.R. Donnelley & Sons Company, Crawfordsville, Indiana.